THE MAGIC PATTERN BOOK

Sew 6 Patterns into 36 Different Styles!

Amy Barickman

WORKMAN PUBLISHING · NEW YORK

Library of Congress Cataloging-in-Publication Data is available.

ISBN 978-0-7611-7162-1

Design by Sarah Smith

Photography by Andrew McLeod

Wardrobe Styling by Ellen Silverstein
Assistant Styling by Lisa Metropolis

Jewelry provided by Lee Angel and Supplements NY

Dritz® sewing supplies provided by Prym Consumer USA (dritz.com)

Much appreciation to our models: Ashley Brown, Anelisa Durham, Lauren Nolting, Cheryl Soell, Kara Vedder, Sarah Voigt, Nikolai Janka, and Mabel Rothman

Special thanks to the following neighbors for graciously sharing their locations as backdrops: Angelica Flowers and Events (angelicaflowersandevents.com), Sweetery NYC (sweeterynyc.com), and Sweet Revenge (sweetrevengenyc.com)

Additional photography:
fotolia: p.5 top chamillew, p.5 bottom jgagarin, p.6 left uriy solovyov, p.6 right Coprid, p.7 top lightningboldt, p.7 middle Eireann, p.7 bottom Sergiogen, p.8 top Kuzmick, p.8 middle Petra Nowack, p.8 bottom robcartorres, p.9 left Mark Scott, p.9 top Ilya Akinshin, p.9 bottom right vvoe, p.10 top left pixelrobot, p.10 middle keerati, p.10 right bottom PinkBlue, p.11 bottom left Coprid

Melissa Lucier: p.9 top and middle right, p.10 bottom left, p.10 right top, p.11 top left, middle and right

Workman books are available at special discounts when purchased in bulk for premiums and sales promotions as well as for fund-raising or educational use. Special editions or book excerpts can also be created to specification. For details, contact the Special Sales Director at the address below, or send an email to specialmarkets@workman.com.

Workman Publishing Co., Inc.
225 Varick Street
New York, NY 10014-4381
workman. com

WORKMAN is a registered trademark of Workman Publishing Co., Inc.

Printed in China
First printing August 2014

10 9 8 7 6 5 4 3 2 1

The Magic Pattern Book is dedicated to Mary Brooks Picken (1886–1981), whose life's work was devoted to teaching fashion and dressmaking to millions of women all across the world. The exceptional content she published during her long life has provided the inspiration for this book.

ACKNOWLEDGMENTS

I first want to recognize my mother and her fabulous style and love for sewing. Her enthusiasm and energy to create have always been key to the success of my entrepreneurial endeavors. Thanks, Mom!

A commitment to continuing interest and advancement in the art of sewing is always at the forefront of my work. This is especially true as I look at my daughter, Emma, and consider all the creative and artistic work she will do in the future. I hope that what I accomplish today will inspire her and her generation, as she inspires me.

There are many current designers and sewing teachers who are contributing to the rebuilding of today's popular interest in sewing. Nancy Zeiman and Amy Butler are two such inspiring people.

Thanks, also, to the talented team that made this book a reality:

Sarah Burningham, my agent, whose enthusiasm for the concept inspired me to take it to the next level and submit our proposal to Workman.

Mary Ann Donze, whose design and sewing talent was indispensable throughout the creation and production of our fashions, patterns, instructions, and illustrations. I am forever grateful for your creative contribution.

To other members of my Indygo Junction team who assisted with their knowledge throughout the production process: Cheryl Pinkman, Mary Meyer, Nancy Ornce, and Betsy Blodgett.

Megan Nicolay, you were a perfect match as an editor. Your contribution from fashion to writing has molded and refined *The Magic Pattern Book* to its full potential. Thank you, also, Liz Davis and Amanda Hong, for helping to dot all those i's and cross all those t's.

Ellen Silverstein, your styling of the models from head to toe was truly magical—just the right accents in all the right places. To Lisa Metropolis, Ellen's assistant, thank you for your wonderful energy and keen eye. Andrew McLeod, thank you for capturing those gorgeous images. Anne Kerman, your orchestration of the photo shoot was nothing short of miraculous. What fun it was to work with you all!

Thank you to Sarah Smith, who managed to make the text, photos, and illustrations come together on the page to create a book that is, happily, both easy on the eyes and easy to use. And to James Williamson, who painstakingly prepared every pattern piece to perfection—thank you.

And, lastly, thanks to my family and friends for their support and encouragement through my entrepreneurial journey—it has been quite a ride!

CONTENTS

THE MAGIC PATTERN BOOK

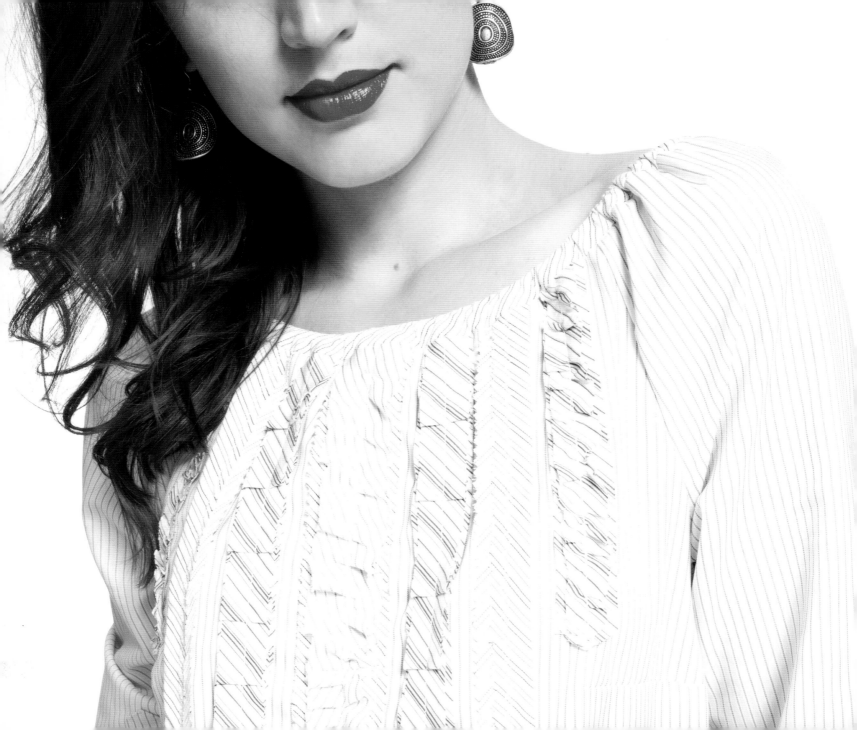

INTRODUCTION

Making Magic

Welcome to *The Magic Pattern Book*! If you sew, you're already familiar with the concepts of sewing books and patterns, so the question you might be asking is really, what's so magical about these? Quite simply, a magic pattern is a single set of pattern pieces that can be transformed and pieced together in different ways to yield an impressive array of finished pieces. And, like most magic, it can actually be explained through simple mathematics: There are 6 patterns included in this book that represent 6 basic wardrobe elements (tank top, skirt, dress, cardigan, coat, accessory); from the 6 patterns you can make 6 different looks each (for example, pocketed A-line skirt, a maxi skirt, pleated skirt, pencil wrap skirt, bias skirt, and miniskirt) for 36 different designs. Multiply that by the 6 fabric suggestions for each of the 36 designs, and you have 216 possible different looks—and that's all before you bring your own hands and your own creativity to the equation.

Those hands of yours are capable of magic. And though sewing is not at all akin to waving a magic wand over some fabric (anyone who's pricked a finger with a needle or sat hunched over a sewing machine for hours on end, or made an errant scissor snip through an amazing piece of silk knows this truth), there is something magical about the process of creating that is rather enchanting despite—or maybe because of—the amount of effort you put into it.

Although your hands (and mine!) may not be able to channel the creative genius of the great fashion designers, the power of

expression is inherent in us all. By making your own clothes, you're not limited when it comes to shapes, fabrics, or silhouettes. And with just a bit of guidance you'll be creating your own one-of-a-kind garments in no time. *The Magic Pattern Book* will allow you to design a personal wardrobe that represents who you are. By selecting and then combining the color and texture of the fabric with the form and line of the design, you will learn how to implement your sewing skills while improving your design expertise. These pages are meant to serve as a handbook to refer to again and again. As fashions evolve, you can

continue to turn to this book for reference and, with just a bit of creative impulse, be able to update the patterns in small but meaningful ways to stay au courant.

MARY'S MAGIC PATTERN
(and Other Inspirations from the
Fairy Godmother of Modern Sewing)
In 1990, while following my own passion for fashion, textiles, and design, I founded Indygo Junction, Inc., a pattern company that offers a range of designs and ideas for sewing enthusiasts. Through the years, I have been encouraged and inspired by so many of you who share the same

> *"And how does one acquire this genius for seeing the hidden possibilities in patterns? Simply by a thoughtful analysis of their lines and details as compared with the lines and details of the dresses you wish to make."*
>
> —Mary Brooks Picken, 1929

passion. I continue to scour the globe for new resources, but I always return to my inspiration, Mary Brooks Picken, an extraordinary woman and teacher who founded the Woman's Institute of Domestic Arts and Sciences in the early 1900s. Her correspondence school attracted more than 300,000 students from around the world—women learning to enrich their lives through dressmaking, millinery, cooking, fashion design, beauty, and homemaking—and reached thousands more through its newsletters and other publications, making it the largest school in the history of the United States for home study of the home arts. Mary became a leading authority on fashion and dressmaking, and she consulted with brands like Singer and Coats & Clark to create educational materials, products, and marketing programs. Her weekly column on sewing was syndicated in 300 newspapers over the course of two decades. She was a founding member of the Fashion Group, the international organization for those engaged in all phases of fashion work, as well as one of the five original directors of the Costume Institute, now part of the Metropolitan Museum of Art in New York City. But perhaps her most significant achievement, in the context of this book, was penning the popular feature "Magic Patterns" in the Woman's Institute's *Inspiration* pamphlets and *Fashion Service* magazines. Her initial Magic Patterns were patterns you drew or cut yourself, or cut directly from the fabric using the measurements and diagrams that were provided in the textbooks. The spirit behind them, of course, was in the malleability of the design— they could become anything! The patterns I've developed for this book are my ode to Mary Brooks Picken's original concept—and though my Magic Patterns have more structure (and they work like traditional patterns), the spirit is the same: Take what's given, and add your own spark to it.

I can only imagine the type of reach Mary's teachings and publications would have today. Poring over my vast collection of her newsletters and books, I've selected some of her timeless style advice and wisdom to share throughout the book in hopes that her words may inspire you as you read, design, and sew. She was one very talented, empowered, smart, and stylish lady, indeed, and I continue to turn to her teachings when I'm in need of guidance from my sewing fairy godmother.

CARE AND HANDLING OF YOUR MAGIC WAND (aka the Book in Your Hands)
Here's how the book works: In the envelope on the inside back cover of the book, there's a CD with downloadable, printable PDF pattern pieces for six basic wardrobe elements: the Tank Top, the Skirt, the Dress, the Cardigan, the Coat, and the Accessory. (They are also available for download at workman.com/magicpattern—if that's more convenient.) Using the base pattern pieces in each group, along with supplemental pattern pieces provided, you have the option of constructing six unique silhouettes. For example, from the Skirt pattern, you can create a pocketed A-line with an inverted pleat (page 86), a tiered maxi (page 91), an A-line trimmed with a kicky pleated band (page 96), a pencil wrap skirt with yoke (page 102), a full and flirty bias-cut skirt (page 111), and a classic denim mini (page 115). You can adapt each pattern to your personal style, drawing out both casual and formal garments from the same pattern with a simple wave of your magic wand (or a simple alteration of fabric, length, closure, or other design element).

At the end of each of the 36 looks, you will discover two more resources: A list of suggestions for construction variations under the heading Make Your Own Magic, and a fabric swatch index of six fabric recommendations to serve as an additional catalyst for creativity.

LET'S GET STARTED!
(Or, *Abracadabra, alakazam!*)
I am so pleased that you've chosen to create your own clothes, and whether you are just embarking on your sewing journey or are an experienced seamster or seamstress, I hope you will enjoy using *The Magic Pattern Book* as an ongoing resource in your personal sewing adventure. And let me know how it's going! I'd love to hear about all the magic you're making. Happy sewing!

CHAPTER 1

Sewing Basics

HOW TO MAKE MAGIC

〰〰〰〰〰〰〰〰〰〰

I n order to enjoy the most success in the sewing room, you need to start with a clean workspace (large or small), a flat surface for cutting and pinning fabrics, the right tools (including a machine that you can operate efficiently), and a familiarity with the techniques necessary to complete your project. Before you begin a project, make sure to read through the materials and notions list as well as all the assembly instructions to see if you need a brief how-to on a required technique or need to gather any additional tools.

"To build a house, one must have first a plot and a plan, then materials and tools, and then patience. To make a dress . . . we must take heed of the little things that make for success in dressmaking."

—Mary Brooks Picken, 1923

Tools You Will Need

The following is a list of tools I find essential for efficient sewing . Some, of course, are obvious, like needles and thread, while others, such as a point turner, may not appear to be life-altering (that is, until you use one and discover for yourself the fleeting joy of a properly turned corner!). But they will all help you create professional-looking results—and if your results look professional, you'll be more likely to tackle additional projects with confidence. There are so many innovative sewing gadgets available today that are worth exploring. Beyond the machines, most of the basic tools listed here, however, are relatively inexpensive and will give you a proper send-off as a successful seamstress.

Sewing machine

Because your machine is your best friend when sewing, it's important to really get to know it. Whether you have a simple one or a modern computerized system, read and follow the machine manual, practice all the stitches that your machine is capable of, and familiarize yourself completely with the straight stitch, which is far and away the primary stitch you'll use to make the projects in this book. Most machines will also have a zigzag

stitch, which I recommend in a few instances for finishing edges or sewing with knits (more on that in a bit). If you're familiar with machine sewing, you know that the number of presser feet you have for your machine will vary. Most of the projects in this book require one standard machine foot, though two require a zipper foot (the Avery tank top, Pattern A2, page 49, and the Abigail tank dress, Pattern A5, page 67), and two require a buttonhole foot (the Chloe tank dress, Pattern C4, page 152, and the Evelyn cape, Pattern E5, page 242). If you're shy about buttonholes, though, rest assured that both patterns C4 and E5 can be made using a hidden snap instead!

Sewing machine needles

The most important thing, when it comes to needles, is that they are the right size and type for the fabric you are planning to sew. Sharps, or sharp-point needles, pass

easily through fine, thin fabrics without breaking the weave. A ballpoint needle (featuring a blunter tip) is best when sewing knits, because it will pass through the knit without snagging or piercing the fibers. If you're ever unsure what needle you should be using, ask an expert at your local quilting or fabric shop, or consult the Internet.

Needle sizes correspond with machine and fabric recommendations. Read the packaging to select the appropriate size for the fabrics you are sewing. A medium-size needle is good for most medium-weight fabrics (like standard cottons, linen, flannel, shirting, and twills). A fine fabric like silk requires a smaller needle, whereas heavier fabrics like men's suiting call for a larger one—and when sewing with denim, it is imperative that you use needles with "denim" printed on the packaging.

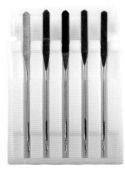

Serger

A serger is a specialty sewing machine with two needles that holds up to seven cone-shaped spools of thread. It includes a hidden blade that can trim away fabric as you sew. The serger can stitch and finish seams simultaneously, a process applied most often to knit fabrics since it allows the fabric to maintain its stretch. After stitching a traditional seam, you can go back and serge the seam allowances together, trimming as you go. But for all of the projects in this book, the serger may simply be used to finish the raw, cut edges of the fabric to prevent fraying, and to lend a professional appearance to your garments. The stitching can be purely functional, reinforcing fibers on interior seams, or decorative, adorning edges on the outer garment.

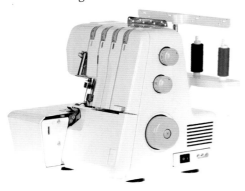

If you have and plan to use a serger, which can accommodate two to seven spools, I recommend using four spools of thread to complete the projects in the book. In the four-spool setup, two spools, threaded through the overlock needles, provide straight stitches parallel to the fabric edge, while two other spools of "looper" thread wrap the edge of the fabric. The palette of serger threads available is not nearly as extensive as regular sewing thread, so sometimes I use two or three colors that visually blend together on the fabric to achieve a complementary effect.

Although I recommend using a serger to finish the raw edges of your fabric in each project, almost every pattern featured in this book can be constructed without one. If you don't have a serger, using a small zigzag setting with your regular stitch length will create a stitch with similar properties. The slight zigzag will give some stretch to the seam, and the stitches should give with the stretch of a knit fabric. Some newer machines even have a stretch stitch option that is appropriate for knits. Only two projects feature serging as a visible design element, and these are the Beatrice skirt (Pattern B2, page 91) and the Eloise coat (Pattern E3, page 229). At the end of both patterns, you will find ideas and instructions for completing them without a serger.

If you sew with any regularity, a serger is a worthwhile investment. Some of the simpler machines are quite affordable now, and spending a little more for additional features and durability can prove to be invaluable. Your garments will last longer through washing and drying cycles and your accessories will be sturdier if enclosed seam allowances are trimmed and finished with serging.

Thread

It is always preferable to buy the best-quality thread available. Good thread will appear tightly twisted and will have fewer loose fibers that can snag and cause breakage. Cotton/polyester thread is suitable for most fabrics, with a few exceptions. Polyester thread should be used for knits, to better accommodate the stretch in the fabric. Use silk thread on silk (if possible). Silk thread is also nice for hand-sewing and hand-basting—if you press a garment that has hand-basting, the fabric is left smooth while thicker threads may leave "dents" in the fabric after the basting stitches have been removed. Other fine thread is available for extra-delicate fabrics. Extra-strong threads should be called upon when

tackling a project made from denim, like in the Bernadette skirt (Pattern B6, page 115), so that they can hold up to the weight of the fabric when holding it together. One is a variegated blue denim color and the other is the heavy gold thread most often used for denim topstitching.

Topstitching thread is somewhat heavier than standard-weight thread and will carry incredible visual impact, but colors are more limited. Determine the look you want before choosing your thread. For more subtle, hidden topstitching, use regular-weight thread in the same color as your fabric or just slightly darker. For more visual impact, try using two strands threaded together through the needle (a needle with a slightly larger eye may be necessary). Use a twin needle and two spools of thread, and you can apply two rows of topstitching at once. When you topstitch, adjust the stitch length on your machine before you start. Longer stitches will lie flatter on the surface of your fabric and be more visible. If there is not a topstitching thread color available that works for your project, try using a triple stitch with standard-weight thread or switch to a decorative stitch.

Thread storage system

Whether you go with a classic wooden spindle thread rack, a clear plastic thread box, or another organizing container, it's good to have a system that keeps your spools of thread neat, tangle-free, and visible. Be creative and repurpose another

system—I use an old wooden tray to store my thread, and I know one sewist who keeps hers in a tackle box!

Bobbins and bobbin box

If you have only a few bobbins, you may find yourself unwinding a bobbin of one color thread so that you can rewind it with the appropriate color for a new project. So it's a good idea to purchase extras to save yourself time—and headaches!. While you're building a supply of bobbins, you may also want to invest in a clear bobbin box. Your threads

will remain clean and untangled, and the colors will be easy to see.

Sewing basket

Keep your tools together so you can always find them when the creative urge hits. Sewing baskets come in various sizes, most with an interior tray to organize small sewing tools, and a pincushion

on the inside lid. The handle, of course, makes it portable—so you can easily move from one location to another.

Scissors

I can't say enough about a good pair of scissors. They are positively indispensable throughout the sewing process. If you can afford only one, get a pair of shears that have straight blades with an offset handle (allowing the lower blade to stay flat on the cutting surface). To keep them sharp, use these shears exclusively on fabric (use your regular, all-purpose scissors for cutting paper for patterns).

- **Embroidery scissors:** If there's room in your sewing toolbox, another pair should be embroidery scissors. They are small, with fine blades that allow you to snip off threads from small or hard-to-reach areas of your work.

- **Appliqué scissors:** Also small, and often with offset blades, these shears are designed specifically for delicate appliqué work. To complete the Fiona Scarf (Pattern F2, page 267), you will need appliqué scissors (or, in a pinch, sharp embroidery scissors will do).

- **Thread snips:** A pair of thread snips or thread nippers (they resemble tweezers) are handy to precisely cut a thread or fine yarn when sewing.

- **Pinking shears:** Pinking shears (those scissors with sharp, zigzag-edged blades) are another important item to have in your sewing kit if you don't already. When finishing a raw edge, pinking the fabric is an option if you don't have a serger or a zigzag feature on your machine—it helps reduce fraying. As

with your standard fabric shears, use the pinking shears only on fabric!

Large, flat surface

Make sure your cutting surface is flat, clean, and large enough to lay out and assemble your fabric and pattern pieces. If you don't have a true cutting table, a protected dining room table works well—as does a hardwood floor. You don't need a dedicated sewing table if you don't have access to one. Just don't try cutting out a pattern on carpeting—it's not a firm enough surface to work on, and it will be difficult to lay out the fabric smoothly.

Iron

Keep an iron (with a steam option) nearby to press your seams as you sew. If your iron doesn't have a steam function, keep a small spritzer bottle of water, or use a dampened press cloth to protect the nap of more delicate fabrics. Always test a sample of fabric first—some will shrink with steam—and be sure to check that you are using the correct temperature setting. Synthetics typically require a lower setting than natural fabrics.

Press cloth

A press cloth is placed between fabric and the iron to help protect the fabric from scorching or crushing. (The nap of fabrics like velveteen or corduroy is particularly susceptible to crushing!) A press cloth also protects the fabric from shine or iron marks and too much direct heat. I use a piece of washed muslin for a press cloth, but you can also use an old T-shirt scrap, a pillowcase, or a store-bought press cloth. Napped fabrics such as corduroy can be pressed from the wrong side if you place a piece of terry cloth under or on top of the fabric to keep from crushing the nap. Velvet and velveteen should be ironed on a needle board, a specially designed tool that protects the pile (texture) from getting crushed.

Sewing pins

The most common straight pin has a blunt head at one end, but I prefer pins with a colored or white glass bead at the head—I can manage them better, and they don't

melt (like the plastic heads do) when I am pressing. Sharp, fine pins are just as important as scissors. Dull or bent pins can damage or snap fabric fibers and should be thrown away.

Pincushion

I love the traditional tomato-shaped pincushion for keeping my needles and pins close at hand, but there are many options available. A good cushion is filled with sawdust and wool roving, which keeps pins sharp and prevents rusting.

A convenient alternative to the traditional pincushion is a magnetic pin caddy. It stores pins, and provides easy pickup for any strays that fall on the floor.

Hand-sewing needles

Needles come in a variety of sizes and styles for different uses. *Sharps* range in size from 1 to 10, determined by the diameter of the needle, with size 1 being the longest and thickest and 10 the smallest and thinnest. Sharps are the most commonly used hand-sewing needle because their sharp point can pass through all types of woven fabrics. *Ballpoint* needles, ranging in size from 5 to 10, are recommended for knits of any kind—their slightly rounded tip allows them to pass through knit fabrics without snagging the fibers.

Embroidery needles, available in a variety of sizes, have larger eyes so that thicker flosses can be threaded through them. *Betweens*, sometimes called *quilting needles*, are shorter than sharps or ballpoint needles and quite thin—and, as you might have guessed, are used mainly for quilting.

You may also come across *tapestry*, *beading*, and *chenille* needles, but they are considered more specialty needles and aren't needed for any of the projects featured in this book.

As with machine needles, the lighter the fabric, the finer the needle you will need to use. If you have difficulty seeing up close, a needle threader is an inexpensive tool that makes threading your needle quick and easy.

Tailor's chalk or fabric-marking pen/pencil

Use these tools to mark darts, hems, and other notations directly on fabric without leaving a stain. Despite their promise of temporary results (chalk can be brushed or washed away, disappearing ink will evaporate), your marking tools should always be tested on a corner of your fabric before use.

Dressmaker's tracing paper and wheel

These items are used together to transfer darts, pocket placement, hems, or any other notes onto fabric. Use them instead of or in conjunction with tailor's chalk or a fabric marker. The tracing paper and wheel work especially well for marking darts.

Flexible tape measure

When measuring your body (or someone else's) to determine the proper pattern size, you will need a tape measure that can be easily manipulated. Though it needs to be flexible, a good, accurate tape measure should never stretch. Most flexible tape measures are 60" long.

Clear ruler

An 18" to 24" clear ruler is very helpful when measuring and marking patterns onto fabric, marking pleats, pocket placement, hems, and button or snap placement. Because the gridded measurements are printed across the width and length of the ruler, you can easily measure and see right angles, and

view your fabric, pattern, and any existing notations through the grid. It's like having X-ray vision! The grid on the ruler will give you an accurate measurement up to $\frac{1}{16}$". It can also be used to check that the grain of the fabric is aligned and straight. To do this, align one grid of the ruler with the selvage of the fabric, while simultaneously aligning another grid with the grainline on the pattern piece.

Seam ripper

As its name suggests, a seam ripper is critical when undoing a seam. It works better than scissors (even tiny embroidery scissors!) for reaching and removing the delicate threads. The curved blade inside the tip will cut threads without doing damage to your fabric. Not only is it great for removing mistakes, but it can also quickly remove basting threads, or the threads securing buttons and snaps. A seam ripper is essential for completing the styles in this book that are comprised of repurposed fabrics, especially those made from denim like the Bernadette skirt (Pattern B6, page 115).

Tailor's ham

A tailor's ham is a rounded, firmly packed cushion that allows you to support the garment as you press in shapes or contours created by curved seams such as princess seams, armholes, darts, lapels, and collars. One side of the ham is covered with wool and the other side with cotton. Use the wool side for wool or softly napped fabrics such as tweed or corduroy, and use the cotton side for most others.

Sleeve board

A sleeve board looks just like a miniature ironing board and will ideally come with a pad and cover. It is generally placed on top of your regular-size ironing board for use. While not essential in most

instances, it is yet another tool to help you produce professional-looking garments. Its main use is to help you press open the seam allowance on a sleeve during sewing construction. This is especially helpful for long, thin sleeves: The small, curved end of a sleeve board is much narrower than the curved end of a tailor's ham, so you can press small areas more accurately.

Seam gauge

This 6" ruler has a sliding marker that's perfect for measurements that need to have a consistent width and must be checked frequently. It is most often used to evenly mark a hem, but it's also great for cuffs, tucks, and pleats. If you're adding a 1" hem, you would slide the gauge to the 1" mark and leave it in place while you press your garment, checking at various intervals to make sure the hem is folded 1" around the lower edge.

Thimble

This lightweight metal tool has a closed end that fits snugly on the middle finger of your sewing hand. It is used to protect your fingertip as you hand-sew.

Point turner

Made of plastic or bamboo, a point turner is a small, inexpensive tool that will quickly become one of your favorites. Its pointed end is used to create professional, crisp corners; the rounded end can be used to press open short seams.

Loop turner

Loop turners are available in several styles (shown) and are relatively inexpensive.

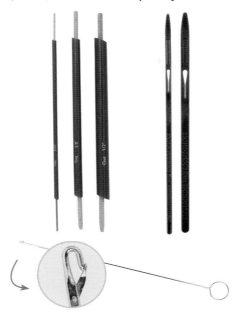

Although they're not called for extensively in this book, they can be a great addition to your sewing basket. Their specific application is to turn long, thin tubes of fabric, such as ties or drawstrings, right side out. For example, when making the Davina cardigan (Pattern D4, page 190), I used a loop turner to complete the front ties.

Bias tape maker

Packaged bias tape can be purchased in a variety of widths, but in a relatively limited number of colors and fabrics (it's usually a cotton/polyester blend). A bias tape maker is a small, inexpensive tool that allows you to make your own bias tape in fabric of any type, color, or print. Each bias tape maker has a designated width, ranging in size from ¼" to 2". Also available in this category are fusible bias tape makers. These tools apply fusible web to the inside of the bias tape as it is folded, so that you can iron on the tape instead of having to pin and stitch it.

Fabric

In many ways, sewing is all about the fabrics that you choose for your garment. Sometimes a wonderful fabric will inspire the design, and other times, a particular design will direct the fabric choice. Just by swapping out different fabrics, you can magically transform almost any pattern, including the ones in this book. So if you find a pattern that flatters and suits you, don't hesitate to try it in a whole spectrum of fabrics. For example, a classic style like the Bridget skirt (Pattern B4, page 102) can be made to suit any occasion. Need a casual summer skirt? Try cotton. Getting ready for a business meeting? Make it out of wool. Going out to dinner? It will look stunning in silk!

TYPES OF FABRIC

There are seemingly limitless fabric options available today, and it can be tricky deciding what fabric to use for your pattern. I have collected textiles for years, and still, I love the thrill of the hunt. Whether I am picking up vintage bark cloth at an antique fair or looking for a luscious silk at my local fabric store, the colors, designs, and textures of fabric fill me with joy. (Warning: This joy can fuel highly addictive behavior and before you know it, your closets will be filled to the brim!)

First, the basics. Fabrics are formed from fibers. There are four different types of fibers: (1) Natural fibers, such as cotton, wool, and silk, are derived from plant or animal sources; (2) artificial fibers, such as rayon, acetate, and viscose, are man-made using natural plant cellulose; (3) synthetic fibers, such as polyester, nylon, or acrylic, are chemical structures usually derived from petroleum; and (4) blended fibers, which, appropriately, combine any number of fibers from the first three categories. These four types of fibers can be made into fabric through a variety of methods—the most common include weaving, knitting, and felting. Since the fiber content of a fabric affects the care instructions, be sure to look for the instructions, which are normally printed at the end of the bolt.

> *"Besides being smart this season, cottons are good for a beginner to use because they can be handled with great ease and generally produce results of which one may be proud."*
>
> —Mary Mahon,
> the Woman's Institute's
> *Fashion Service* magazine, 1927

Before you step into the often overwhelming world of the fabric store, make sure you know what type of fabric you are looking for, if it is suitable for your pattern, and if it is within your sewing skills. I've highlighted some of the fabrics we used in this book so you can see how they differ, and how they work in different garment styles.

Natural Fibers: Plant-Based

Cotton

Cotton is the most versatile of all fabrics and is a great fabric for beginning sewists. It is often used on its own or is blended with other fibers like rayon or polyester because of its durability and strength. Cotton is simple to care for—all it takes is an easy machine-wash and -dry. Ideally, you should launder your cotton yardage before you begin your project, because it will shrink. The amount of shrinkage will vary by fabric, but can be minimized by washing in cold water and drying on low heat. (If you are unsure about the end result, buy a bit of extra fabric.) A hot steam iron will efficiently remove any wrinkles.

Cotton comes in a range of weights and textures. On one end of the spectrum are the lightweight cottons, like batiste and voile, while more substantial fabrics like cotton velvet, cotton velveteen, and denim balance out the other end.

Cotton poplin/Quilting cottons

Poplin is a strong, medium-weight, plain-weave fabric. It's among the most common available and also one of the most versatile, as it can be used in garments, accessories, home decor, and even quilting.

Cotton voile

Voile is a lightweight, soft, semisheer woven fabric that is excellent for layering. It's also ideal, because of its weight, for projects with gathers, pleats, or flounces.

Cotton denim

Denim is woven tightly to make it stronger and more durable. Apart from the traditional blue, there are now many options when it comes to colors, prints, and weight. Sometimes a small percentage of Lycra or spandex is added to denim for ease of movement. Since they're such a wardrobe staple, denim jeans are a great source to keep in mind when you're looking to make a repurposed garment.

Cotton duck

Duck is a sturdy, tightly woven cotton without sizing or chemical finishes. It is available in many colorful solids and prints and often used for upholstery, both indoors and out—even awnings! Although it's too heavy for most clothing, its structure lends itself well to hats and handbags.

Decorator-weight cotton

Decorator-weight cotton can open up a whole new world of choices for your coat, skirt (see the Beatrice, Pattern B2, page 91), handbag, or hat styles (a remnant is a great find for creating a new hat!). Many fabulous prints are available, but be mindful of the scale of the pattern, since it is generally much larger. A decorator fabric is a great option when a two-sided fabric is called for, because the reverse side is woven in the opposite colors of the front side. When you're selecting a piece of decorator-weight cotton, feel the "hand" of the fabric: Does it drape or is it stiff? Smooth or textured? For a pattern that requires gathering or pleating, be certain to select fabric that is flexible enough. Wash and dry your decorator-weight yardage twice to soften the fibers before cutting out your project. I like to use ECOS natural laundry detergent, because it will not fade the colors. You could also add some liquid fabric softener to the wash, to keep the fabric flexible for use.

"Indeed, almost an entire wardrobe can be developed of cotton materials, the coat of velveteen, service dresses of prints and gingham, sports clothes . . . a bewildering array from which to choose."

—The Woman's Institute's
Fashion Service magazine, April 1928

Waxed cotton

This fabric was developed in the mid-nineteenth century in Scotland to use for sails in the Scottish shipping industry. Although the original waxed cotton was very stiff, by the 1920s the process had changed and a more supple version of this wind- and water-resistant fabric was born. Designers began to use the fabric in garments and accessories. Though none of the main projects in this book call for waxed cotton, it's a fun fabric to try for sturdier outerwear—namely the Edith coat (Pattern E4, page 234—see Make Your Own Magic). Waxed cotton products should be dried gently, so as not to reduce their effectiveness. For garments that get a lot of wear, regular rewaxing is recommended.

Cotton knits

Cotton fibers can also be machine-knit into fabric instead of woven, producing the soft and comfortable fabric we all love for T-shirts. Cotton knits will tend to shrink a bit more than woven cotton—as much as 10 to 20 percent. For this reason, use preshrunk material, and exercise caution when laundering cotton knits: Use cold water unless the manufacturer has specified otherwise. Hang the fabric to dry, or tumble dry on low for a short period of time and then hang to let it dry completely.

Linen

Linen is a natural fabric produced from fiber in the flax plant. It is a durable fiber, breathes well, and is often used in summer clothes. It has a beautiful texture and is easy to sew, although it does fray, so cut edges need to be finished. It should be washed to soften the fabric before you begin your project. Unless the manufacturer specifies otherwise, cold water should be used to prevent shrinkage. Wrinkles are an inherent quality of linen and should be considered when you're choosing the look you want. Linen comes in a wide range of weaves and weights, from lightweight handkerchief linen to much thicker suiting weaves. It

A NOTE ABOUT KNITS

Knits can be substituted in any pattern designed for wovens, but a pattern designed *for knits only* cannot be made in a woven fabric and fit as intended. For the most part, the patterns included here have "ease" (the difference between a finished garment's particular measurement and the coordinating body part's measurement) factored into each pattern, since I've designed them to be made from woven fabrics with no stretch. The one exception is the Diana cardigan (Pattern D1, page 174), the long jersey number with an open front, which I initially made from knit fabric (but, as you'll see from the fabric suggestions, may be made from wovens). Though the Davina cardigan (Pattern D4, page 190) is featured in a wool knit, it can also be made from wovens. This is true, too, for the Faith hat (Pattern F3, page 272)—the beret pattern shown in repurposed cashmere. There are stretch wovens on the market now that can be used, but again, the fit of the garment will be slightly different and may need some alterations.

If you decide to choose a knit fabric for any of these garments, there are a few things to take into consideration: Knits are made with moderate stretch to full stretch. With a knit, you gain additional ease from the fabric itself, so a knit with a smaller amount of stretch would be a better choice. (Again, the final fit in a garment made with a knit fabric will not be the same as the fit in a garment made with a woven. Alterations will most likely have to be made.) Remember when you select a pattern to check the suggested fabric information before choosing your fabric. Knit patterns are sized according to the amount of stretch in the knit. The pattern pieces themselves have been drafted to use the fabric's stretch to create the ease needed.

is also an excellent fabric to use if a two-sided fabric is required—the reverse is essentially the same in appearance.

Bamboo

Bamboo is a textile that is considered to be sustainable and relatively eco-friendly. The bamboo plant is heavily pulped until it separates into threads of fiber, which can then be spun and dyed for weaving into cloth. It is often bleached before use, but if it's left unbleached, it is designated "organic." The fabric feels very soft next to the skin and has excellent wicking properties. It can be easily washed and dried, but laundering instructions will vary with different blends. Bamboo knit is approximately 97 percent bamboo and 3 percent spandex. It is also a two-sided fabric, great for use with garments that show the reverse side.

Natural Fibers: Animal-Based

Wool

Wool fabrics are made from animal-fleece fibers (sheep, goats, alpacas, llama, vicuna) that are spun into threads and woven or knit into tweeds, jerseys, and crepe—best for cold weather garments. However, tropical-weight wool—a surprisingly lightweight fabric—is an exception; it can be worn in warm temperatures. Wool can range from

heavy coat materials to soft crepe or gabardine. Napped wool can be itchy to wear, so it's good to include a lining when sewing wool garments.

Two-sided wool

A woven wool is often a two-sided fabric, and it can be used for jackets that you don't want to line. We've employed this technique in the Eloise coat (Pattern E3, page 229), a look finished with serged edges and made from a repurposed wool blanket.

Silk

Silk is woven from the natural fibers of silkworm cocoons. It can be challenging to sew because of the fineness and fluidity of the fabric, but the resulting drape is beautiful. With its natural luster and softness, silk is often used for scarves and delicate garments that are worn close to the skin (lingerie, pajamas).

When two or more silkworms spin their cocoons closely together, they produce a tangled, uneven filament that can be made into *dupioni* (meaning "double"), a slubbed silk with a rough, uneven texture. It is a tight weave, so the fabric is thicker and has less drape, making it easier to sew. Silk of different varieties work well when a two-sided fabric is called for, since the reverse is often attractive enough to be shown. Keep in mind that silk usually needs to be dry-cleaned.

"Gradually have woolens approached silks in weight and weave until they now come in such sheer, featherweight qualities as wool crepe, wool voile, and wool georgette, ideal fabrics for designs formerly reserved for silks."

—The Woman's Institute's *Fashion Service* magazine, 1927

Rayon (viscose)

This fiber is formed from regenerated cellulose of wood pulp. It is comfortable against the skin, absorbs moisture, is breathable, and takes dyes well. It does wrinkle, however, and can be damaged when wet due to the inelasticity of the fibers. Rayon blends well with other fibers, so it's often found in blended fabrics. It can resemble cotton or silk, but is also used to produce a velvet that is more lightweight than cotton velvet. It shrinks more than cotton and does not react well to water, so it needs to be dry-cleaned.

SEWING PROJECTS BY FABRIC

If you'd like to have the fabric guide your decision-making process, here's a quick rundown of the fabrics featured in each garment as they appear in this book. However, as I've mentioned, at the end of each project, there's a recommendation of six different fabric styles that would work well with each pattern, so don't feel as though you have to duplicate the fabrics I've chosen—there is more than one magical transformation to be made with each look!

Cotton Poplin
The Avery (Pattern A2, page 49)
The Alma (Pattern A4, page 61)
The Betsy (Pattern B3, page 96)
The Cecelia (Pattern C1, page 126)
The Charlotte (Pattern C3, page 139)*
The Chloe (Pattern C4, page 152)

Cotton Voile
The Adelaide (Pattern A3, page 55)
The Catherine (Pattern C5, page 159)

Cotton Denim
The Bernadette (Pattern B6, page 115)*
The Farrah (Pattern F5, page 281)

Cotton Duck
The Frida (Pattern F4, page 276)

Decorator-Weight Cotton
The Beatrice (Pattern B2, page 91)

The Emma (Pattern E2, page 222)
The Farrah (Pattern F5, page 281)

Cotton Knit
The Fiona (Pattern F2, page 267)

Linen
The Daisy (Pattern D3, page 184)*
The Evangeline (Pattern E6, page 250)

Bamboo Knit
The Diana (Pattern D1, page 174)

Wool
The Bridget (Pattern B4, page 102)
The Delia (Pattern D2, page 179)
The Evelyn (Pattern E5, page 242)
The Freddie (Pattern F1, page 262)

Wool Knit
The Davina (Pattern D4, page 190)
The Faith (Pattern F3, page 272)*

Two-Sided Wool
The Eloise (Pattern E3, page 229)*

Silk
The Alice (Pattern A1 variation, page 45)*
The Alma (Pattern A4, page 61)
The Camilla (Pattern C2, page 132)
The Candace (Pattern C6, page 164)
The Francesca (Pattern F6, page 290)

Rayon
The Alice (Pattern A1, page 40)
The Anne (Pattern A6, page 73)
The Francesca (Pattern F6, page 290)

Synthetic Fabrics
The Anne (Pattern A6, page 73)
The Daphne (Pattern D5, page 196)
The Estelle (Pattern E1, page 214)

Blended Fabrics
The Abigail (Pattern A5, page 67)
The Billie (Pattern B5, page 111)
The Edith (Pattern E4, page 234)

* Indicates a design made from repurposed fabric. For more, see page 19.

Synthetic Fibers

Polyester

Polyester fabrics are woven or knitted from polyester thread or yarns. They are durable, wrinkle-resistant, dry quickly, wash and dry without requiring ironing, and retain color well. Some disadvantages: Polyester doesn't breathe well and some types require dry cleaning.

Acetate

Acetate is a manufactured fiber with a silky, luxurious finish that dries easily, and usually requires dry cleaning. Acetate's synthetic fibers are often blended with natural fibers, and can be produced to imitate the appearance of natural fabrics such as cotton, wool, silk, or linen.

Nylon

Nylon was introduced as a fabric at the 1939 World's Fair. It was developed to replace silk, and has been used in everything from stockings to bridal gowns to parachutes. It is extremely durable and easy to care for. Be sure to check care instructions, since nylon can melt at high temperatures.

Spandex/Lycra

Spandex is known for its incredible elasticity and easy care. It is used for garments where comfort, fit, and flexibility are needed. Often, a small percentage of spandex is added to other fabrics to add stretch.

Blended Fabrics

Natural fibers can be blended with other materials—natural or synthetic—to improve performance, durability, and ease of care. The addition of polyester will help reduce wrinkles; spandex or Lycra will add stretch to a fabric; and nylon will make a fabric more durable and strong. Blending more than one fabric will likely change the way you care for the garment, so, as always, be sure to check for the proper care instructions before laundering.

CHOOSING YOUR FABRIC

Choosing fabrics is one of the most exciting steps in creating your own wardrobe. It is through your fabric choice that you can bring individuality to your style, completely change the look of a garment, and make the best piece for your coloring, body type, and personal style. And though we'd like to imagine that every design could be made from any type of fabric, that isn't always

the case, so it's important to take into consideration the properties of each fabric (weight, level of stretch, color, design) before you make any cuts. Here are some things to consider when matching the fabric and the pattern.

Is the fabric the right weight for the design?

Most patterns will offer fabric suggestions (a more structured dress pattern, for instance, may take a heavier woven fabric—some of the details would be harder to pull off in a delicate silk), so read the recommendations for the best results. On the flip side, though, don't get discouraged if your dream fabric isn't a match for your pattern—it may work, but it probably shouldn't be your first attempt.

Is the pattern on the fabric the right scale for you?

Unwrap a couple yards from the bolt of fabric and hold it up to you in front of a mirror to get an idea of what it will look like. I am often pleasantly surprised by the results (although there have been a few alarming occasions!). For instance, I am always on the lookout for large-print florals. However, some of these prints are better left aside (you don't want to end up looking like the couch!). Stripes are another favorite, but dominant stripes, while beautiful on the bolt, can overpower. It's always better to find this out at the fabric store before you've invested your time and money in a garment.

Is the scale of the print appropriate for the pattern?

Although the size of the garment does not always correspond to its print size, it is helpful to consider it when selecting fabric. For example, is that large-scale print too dominating for the delicate blouse? Or will the tiny floral print be lost in the coat pattern? Also, remember that you will be trying to match your print at the seams. A smaller print that covers the whole fabric will blend across the seams better than a large-scale print. If you're in love with a fabric with a large print, seek out a project with fewer seams that require matching.

What is the width of the fabric?

Fabrics come in different widths, so make sure you know the width of the fabric you have selected. Many of the cottons used in the book are 45" wide. You will also find apparel fabrics (such as rayon, denim, or linen) that are 54" or 60" wide. Most patterns have fabric-requirement

"In buying for economy, watch closely the width of your fabric."

—The Woman's Institute's *Fashion Service* magazine, 1924

information covering multiple fabric widths, so you know how much to buy. Consider purchasing a little extra to allow for shrinkage or to match a print.

Will I need more fabric if there is a nap or if matching a print (e.g., plaid) is required?

Fabrics with a nap, are textured fabrics that may be brushed two different ways, like corduroy or velvet. With velvet, if you brush it in one direction, the fabric will look matte, but if you brush it in the opposite direction, it appears shiny. Because you don't want your garment to have a shiny sleeve next to a matte bodice, you need to make sure that you cut your pattern pieces with the tops all going in the same direction. This will often require more yardage than is suggested by the pattern. The same thing goes for fabrics that need to be matched, like plaids or one-directional prints. For napped fabrics, here's the general rule: Add an extra 10 percent to the suggested yardage. When trying to match plaids or prints, there's a little more math to consider: First, count the number of main pattern pieces (not accessory pieces such as collars, pockets, or cuffs). Add one to this number for safety. For example, the Billie skirt (Pattern B5, page 111) has two main pattern pieces, the Front and Back,

so you would calculate 2 pattern pieces + 1 for safety = 3 total pieces. Then, find a main horizontal line of your plaid (or a graphic element on your print fabric) that runs from selvage to selvage and mark it with a pin. Move down the selvage of your yardage until you see this line or design element again and mark it with a pin. Measure the distance between the two pins. Multiply that measurement by the number of pieces you calculated. Let's say there are 6 inches before the plaid repeats on the fabric. For the Billie, you would multiply 6 inches × 3 total pieces = 18 extra inches of fabric.

WHERE TO FIND FABRICS

The best resources for fabrics vary, from your local specialty quilt shops or fabric stores—any that carry a variety of fashion fabrics—to your favorite thrift store.

New Fabrics

Large fabric sources such as Jo-Ann and Hancock Fabrics have a broad range of decorator, quilt, and garment fabrics to choose from, too. Most fabric manufacturers offer their fabric online, in case you're not near a brick-and-mortar store, but I recommend shopping in person whenever possible. It can be difficult to see the scale of a pattern online, and you certainly can't get a feel for the fabric's hand. Most retailers will offer swatches for a small fee to ensure you are getting what you want, which can be helpful, particularly if you are trying to match a color.

Repurposed Fabrics

My favorite places for good fabric finds are antique stores, estate sales, garage sales, and thrift stores (and all of their online equivalents). When shopping for vintage fabrics, check for wear on folded edges, small holes from wear or bugs, and make sure you have enough extra fabric to work around such flaws. Be aware that most vintage fabrics are 36" wide (significantly narrower than fabrics available today). Also, when shopping for vintage fabrics, don't always look for fabric yardage. Check out tablecloths and curtains— or already constructed garments that could be deconstructed. There are some beautiful vintage linen tablecloths with detail stitching that works well on skirts and shirts. Antique lingerie and lace are beautiful accents to consider for delicate details. And I love to shop for antique buttons to use on blouses, purses, fabric flowers, and more . . . there are so many possibilities! Even vintage zippers with metal teeth can be removed from thrift store garments and repurposed as a decorative element across the hem of a skirt or the bodice of a top.

If you are purchasing a garment to use as fabric, always, always invest in the largest size possible—the larger the size,

DESIGNS MADE WITH REPURPOSED FABRIC

Recycling a piece of vintage fabric or an old, tired garment languishing in the closet into a fresh, updated design is one of the most magical transformations you can make. One look in each of the Magic Patterns has been fashioned from repurposed fabric. Here's an inventory of

the upcycled looks to get your creative juices flowing.

- **The Alice tank top** (Pattern A1, page 40) is styled from a deconstructed vintage rayon curtain.

- In the **Bernadette skirt** (Pattern B6, page 115), old denim jeans are repurposed into a new miniskirt.

- The **Charlotte dress** (Pattern C3, page 139) features three men's dress shirts refashioned into an embellished ladies' top.

- In the **Daisy cardigan** (Pattern D3, page 184), a large linen tablecloth with handwork gets a new start as a tie-front jacket.

- The **Eloise coat** (Pattern E3, page 229) starts out as functional as you can get: A drab woolen army blanket transforms into a chic wrap jacket edged in fuchsia.

- Any sweaters with holes? In the **Faith accessory** (Pattern F3, page 272), a cashmere sweater is repurposed into a soft beret.

"Surely the making of a comfortable, becoming, and attractive dress from a garment discarded and seemingly useless is cause for rejoicing."

—Mary Brooks Picken's
Inspiration newsletter, 1924

the more fabric there is, and it likely won't cost more!

Each of the six pattern groups has at least one variation featured in a repurposed fabric. The reasons for repurposing, recycling, or upcycling—whatever you care to call it—are diverse. For one, you can save money by not having to purchase new fabric, or at least cut your costs significantly by buying at thrift stores. Plus, vintage fabrics or well-loved denim lend a whimsy to your creations that's not possible with all-new materials. You are sure to produce a unique, one-of-a-kind result, and you can feel good about creating a functional yet artistic statement piece from something that may have been thrown away. Wools, denim, sweater knits, drapery fabrics, table linens, blankets, and more can all be restyled into a new silhouette.

Basic Techniques

You've chosen your fabric and pattern and are ready to jump into sewing. But wait! For a professional-looking garment, a few basic sewing principles should be followed. The first regards sizing and fit: Always make sure you are working with correct measurements. Second, but also important: Prepare your fabric and pattern so you can cut your pattern pieces smoothly. And third, I always recommend making a muslin, a draft of your garment, out of inexpensive fabric to check for proper fit. When you start working on your finished project, be sure to reference the seam- and hem-finishing techniques below to give you a clean, professional garment.

SIZING

In order to help you choose the correct size pattern to work from, I've provided the approximate bust and hip measurements for each of the finished garments at the beginning of the pattern. The height of the model wearing each sample is indicated, too, so you can have a reference for the length of the garments.

Record your own measurements in the chart, on page 21. There are additional measurements that aren't needed for the patterns in this book, but may be handy for future projects (after you've exhausted all 216-plus possibilities included here!). The measurements that will be most

helpful are: bust, waist, hip, back neck to floor, front shoulder to floor, and waist to floor. A wrist measurement is also helpful for garments with cuffs.

Bust: To measure the bust, measure around the fullest part of the bust, making sure the tape is straight across the back.

Waist: To help you determine your natural waistline, tie a piece of ribbon or elastic around your waist. Bend at the waist from side to side until the elastic or ribbon settles. Then, place the tape measure over the elastic or ribbon to measure your waist at the correct location.

Waist to Floor: Hold a piece of ribbon at your natural waistline, letting the end fall to the floor. Insert a pin on the ribbon to mark the place where you are holding it. Then use a tape measure to determine the distance between the mark and the end of the ribbon. If you have a friend to help, just hold the end of the measuring tape at your natural waistline and let your friend measure down the length to the floor.

Hips: Hip measurements are taken 7" to 9" below the natural waist at the fullest part of the hip. The range given is dependent on height; 7" below the waist would probably be where you would measure if you're on the shorter side; 9" works better for the taller sewists among us.

SIZING REFERENCE CHART

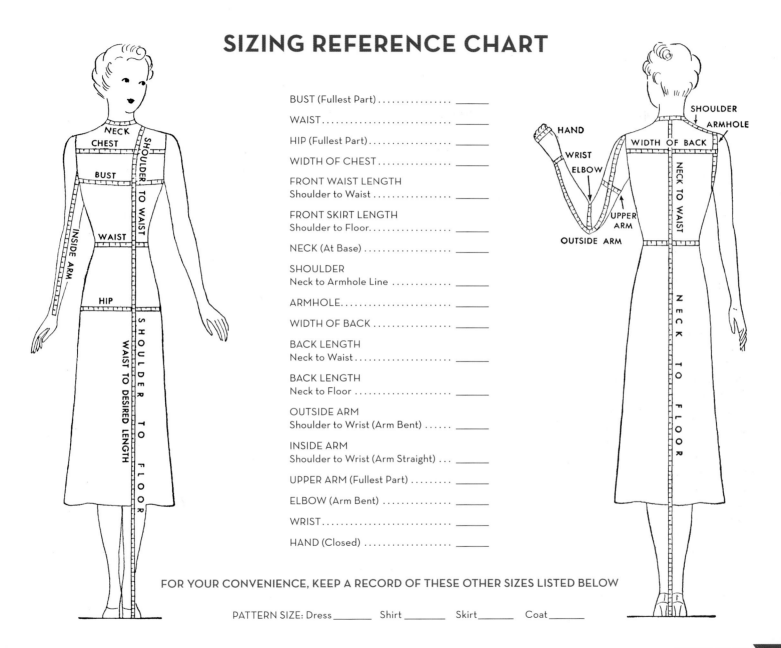

BUST (Fullest Part) . . . . _____

WAIST . . . . _____

HIP (Fullest Part) . . . . _____

WIDTH OF CHEST . . . . _____

FRONT WAIST LENGTH
Shoulder to Waist . . . . _____

FRONT SKIRT LENGTH
Shoulder to Floor . . . . _____

NECK (At Base) . . . . _____

SHOULDER
Neck to Armhole Line . . . . _____

ARMHOLE . . . . _____

WIDTH OF BACK . . . . _____

BACK LENGTH
Neck to Waist . . . . _____

BACK LENGTH
Neck to Floor . . . . _____

OUTSIDE ARM
Shoulder to Wrist (Arm Bent) . . . . . . _____

INSIDE ARM
Shoulder to Wrist (Arm Straight) . . . _____

UPPER ARM (Fullest Part) . . . . _____

ELBOW (Arm Bent) . . . . _____

WRIST . . . . _____

HAND (Closed) . . . . _____

FOR YOUR CONVENIENCE, KEEP A RECORD OF THESE OTHER SIZES LISTED BELOW

PATTERN SIZE: Dress _____   Shirt _____   Skirt _____   Coat _____

Shoulder to Floor: Full-length measurements (see chart) are needed for maxi-length garments. I find it helpful to take these measurements while wearing shoes, so you have an accurate read on the rise of the hem from the floor.

PREPARING YOUR PATTERN (AND FABRIC)

There are a few steps to using your pattern, from downloading to printing, to assembling the pieces and cutting out the pattern you choose to use. Each Magic Pattern is available as a complete pattern (every look included) so that you can see how the patterns interact and overlap (which is great for making DIY sizing adjustments). For your convenience, each of the six designs included within each Magic Pattern has also been separated out from its "family" so that you can print only the pattern you want to make.

How to Print the Patterns in This Book

On the CD found in the envelope at the inside back cover of this book (and online at workman.com /magicpattern), there is an array of downloadable PDF files: 6 complete magic patterns, plus 36 individual patterns representing each design featured in the book (so if you know you just want to make the Alice tank top, page 40, you can click straight through to Pattern A1). Here's how to access, print, and assemble all the patterns so you can make every project in this book! And be patient, some of the larger patterns have a lot of pages, but the payoff, once they're tiled together, is so very worth it.

1 Locate the pattern you'd like to make and double-click on it to open it.

2 Scroll through it to make sure that it has downloaded completely. This is an example of what the first page will look like.

A1. Alice

3 Check that your printer settings are at 100 percent, with scaling turned off. These patterns are designed to print on both U.S.-sized letter paper (8½" × 11") *and* the more global A4 paper.

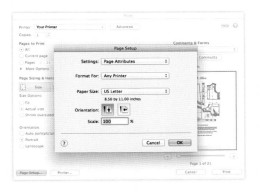

5 The first page of the PDF features a pattern map that will serve as your guide when you piece all the pages together. (It's like the photo on the front of a jigsaw puzzle box.) Measure the test square on the printed test page one more time before you start cutting.

4 Scroll through the PDF to locate the test sheet (labeled "TEST SQUARE") and print that page first. Measure the 4" × 4" (10 cm × 10 cm) square to make sure that it has printed at 100 percent. If it hasn't, check back to make sure your printer settings are at 100 percent and that you have not selected "scale to fit" or cropped the pages. If it *has* printed at 100 percent, don't change a thing. Proceed with printing the entire file.

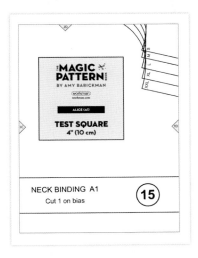

6 Cut along the gray lines on each sheet to remove the borders. (The gray lines are the grid lines; the black lines are the actual pattern piece edges.) Align and tape the pattern together, starting at the bottom-left corner.

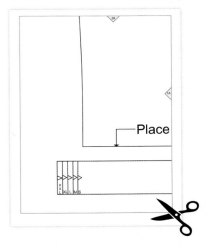

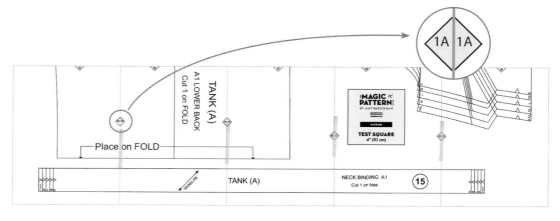

7 Match the pieces using the markings on the page (match 1A on one sheet to 1A on the next, and so on), and keep cross-checking against the pattern map to make sure everything's lining up. Tape an entire row, left to right, then turn it over to reinforce the back with tape. Tape the second row completely before taping it to the first row. Continue taping rows, reinforcing corners and lining up the markings, until the pattern is complete.

8 Select the size you want based on the Approximate Measurement of Finished Garment chart at the beginning of each project in the book, and cut out all the coordinating pattern pieces listed under Pattern Pieces Used. *Note:* The patterns are nested, so if you're between sizes, you can easily get the perfect fit by marking and cutting into the space between the lower and upper sizes. Just make sure that you apply your adjustment to all relevant pattern pieces so they will fit together correctly.

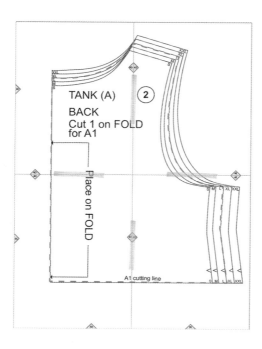

9 Arrange the pattern pieces onto the fabric, following the Cutting Diagram(s) featured at the beginning of each project in the book, and start cutting and stitching!

How to Prepare Your Fabric

Always prewash your fabrics before you sew them to avoid future shrinkage. (Exception: If you are using a fabric that requires dry cleaning only, then you don't need to do anything.)

1 Once you have washed your fabric, iron it flat to ensure it is wrinkle-free before cutting out the pattern.

2 Lay out your fabric on a flat, clean surface as you get ready to pin your pattern and cut out the pieces. Note: If you are using a dining table, you may want to protect it from scratches by using a cutting mat or a large piece of cardboard.

3 Again, make sure the fabric is flat and free of any wrinkles or creases before laying out your pattern and cutting.

How to Cut Your Fabric

Cutting fabric isn't, as they say, brain surgery, but there are things to consider based on the type of fabric you're cutting, its properties, and the effect you're attempting to acheive with the pattern.

Cutting fabric on the grainline

All the pattern pieces provided in this book have a grainline printed on them in the form of a line with an arrow at each end. It is important to pin the pattern pieces on the fabric with the grainline arrows running exactly parallel to the selvages (sides of the fabric).

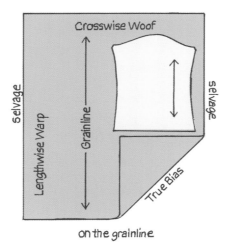

on the grainline

Use a clear ruler with grids (see page 10) to align the printed grainline with the selvage of the yardage.

Cutting fabric cross-grain

Occasionally, you may wish to cut a pattern piece cross-grain to reverse a print on the fabric for visual effect.

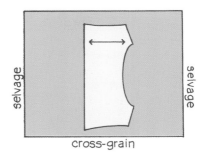

cross-grain

An example of this technique is seen on the back yoke of the Emma coat (Pattern E2, page 222). I don't recommend using this technique for any of the large, main pattern pieces of a garment, since it won't hang properly, but you might try it with a pocket, cuff, yoke, or part of a handbag.

Cutting fabric on the bias

Woven fabrics have a warp thread and a weft thread, perpendicular to each other. The vertical thread running the length of the yardage, parallel to the selvage, is the warp. The horizontal thread, running from selvage to selvage, is the weft. The bias direction of a piece of fabric is at 45 degrees to its warp and its weft.

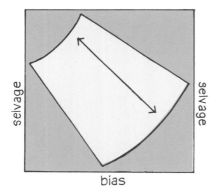

A garment is said to be cut on the bias when the fabric's warp and weft (woof) threads are at 45 degrees to its main seam lines. When cut on the bias, woven fabric will have more stretch and flexibility. As such, we cut the binding on the bias for all of the Tank Top (Pattern A) projects in this book. Bias-cut fabric will also appear to be more fluid and will have more drape, making it ideal for flounces, such as those on the Adelaide tank top (Pattern A3, page 55). When selecting fabrics to cut on the bias, avoid any that are heavy or stiff, like cotton duck or thick denim. Natural fabrics like cotton, linen, wool challis, or silk are easier to work with and give the desired effect. Very slinky fabrics and synthetics may be challenging to handle unless you are a very experienced sewist. And remember: Plaids will appear diagonal when cut on the bias, and if you're using stripes, you will need to allow plenty of extra fabric to align the now diagonal lines at the seams. When trying to match up designs on patterns, cut one layer at a time.

How to Mark Pattern Notations on Fabric

Pattern notations are vital to a successful sewing project. After you have cut out the pattern pieces from your fabric, do not remove the pattern until you have transferred all the necessary notations onto your fabric. Some marks will need to be made on the wrong side of the fabric while others will need to be accessed from the right side.

Marking on the wrong side of the fabric

Dart notations should be applied to the wrong side: Use a ruler and a fabric pen or chalk pencil, a dressmaker's tracing paper and wheel—or alternatively, make clips in the seam allowance at the "legs" of the dart where they meet the outer edge and use a fabric pen or chalk pencil to mark the dart's point.

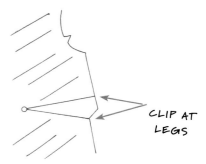

CLIP AT LEGS

Another notation for the wrong side of the fabric is pleat placement (see the Betsy skirt, Pattern B3, page 96). Large dots are also frequently used to denote sleeve placement, inseam pocket placement, or the end of a stitching line. These should be noted on the wrong side of the fabric using a fabric pen or chalk pencil.

A few patterns will require you to transfer stitching lines onto the fabric— use a fabric pen or chalk pencil with a ruler if necessary to mark these on the wrong side of the fabric (where they'll be visible when you're stitching). For the Cecelia and Camilla dresses (Pattern C1, page 126 and Pattern C2, page 132), you will need to draw stitch lines onto the interfacing of the sleeve facing and neck facing, respectively.

MAKING BIAS TAPE, MAGICALLY

Bias tape is used to cover raw edges of cut fabric. Because it's cut on the diagonal, it's flexible and easy to maneuver around curved areas such as armholes or necklines. Packaged bias tape is available in standard widths in solid colors of a cotton/polyester blend. But by creating your own, you can add just the right accent to garments, handbags, or home decorator projects. If you have a favorite remnant of fabric that you can't bear to part with, give it new life as bias tape. Scraps are great.

If you do not have a bias tape maker, follow these simple directions to make a strip of bias tape:

1 If your pattern doesn't tell you exactly how much bias tape you'll need, use your flexible tape measure to get a rough idea of the necessary length. Piece together fabric strips as shown to attain the desired length, and remember to figure in seam allowances.

For double-fold bias tape, cut your bias fabric strips four times as wide as the desired finished tape:

Width of bias fabric strips	Width of finished bias tape
1"	1/4"
1 1/2"	3/8"
2"	1/2"
3"	3/4"
4"	1"

2 Cut the ends of the bias fabric strips on the diagonal and overlap them, right sides together, at a 45-degree angle. Pin the ends as shown.

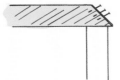

3 Stitch in a 1/4" seam.

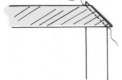

4 Press open the seam allowance, pressing the binding flat.

5 Fold the binding in half lengthwise, with wrong sides together, and press.

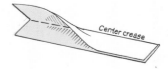

Open, and fold the outer long edges in to meet the center crease and press again.

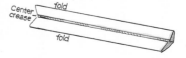

Fold in half once again along the center crease and press.

Marking on the right side of the fabric

Now for the right side: Notations such as closure placement (for buttonholes, buttons, snaps, and loops), placement guidelines for pockets (or faux pocket flaps), and belt loops or carriers should all be made on the right side of the fabric. Several patterns in this book also have pocket placement guidelines, and there are several ways to transfer them. One way is to transfer the markings to the wrong side of your fabric and then use a single strand of thread (preferably silk) to hand-baste along the lines, making the placement visible on the right side. If your fabric is suitable, use a disappearing fabric marker or chalk pencil to transfer guidelines to the right side of the fabric. (You usually don't need to mark anything more than the corners.) Lastly, you can use straight pins, inserted perpendicular to each other at the corners of placement notations. The only potential disadvantage to this method is that the pins may slip out, requiring a repeat of the process!

Be certain to mark the notches, too. The time-honored method is just making a shallow clip in the seam allowance at their location, but you can also use a fabric pen or chalk pencil to mark them in the seam allowance. In standard pattern notation, the front pattern pieces are marked with a single notch on the arm openings, while the back pieces are marked with a double notch. Accordingly, sleeves will have one notch along the front edge and a double notch along the back edge, to correspond with the notches on the main pattern pieces. Remember: Mark one notch for the front and two for the back.

MAKING A MUSLIN

Before you start sewing your garment out of the fabric that you have so carefully chosen, make a muslin: a draft garment from inexpensive fabric, like cotton muslin, or repurposed fabric. With a muslin, you can omit steps like making and adding the facing, finishing cut edges, closures, and hemming. There is also no need to add interfacing or pockets, because fit is really the focus. When you try on the garment, if there are any adjustments to be made, you can mark and pin right on the fabric.

In general, making a muslin is most advisable before stitching a formfitting garment. While none of the styles in this book are truly formfitting, some—like the Abigail tank dress (Pattern A5, page 67)—will skim the body, so you'll want to make sure to leave ample room in the bust and hips. If you are very petite or slender, you may want to make a muslin of the size small to see if you would like to make it smaller still. Only the skirts will require an exact fit at the waist (they also fit fairly close at the hips, so be sure you have enough ease there).

"As sewing experience increases, [so does] the confidence that says of the most intricate or elaborate design, 'I can make that.'"

—Laura McFarlane, the Woman's Institute's *Fashion Service* magazine, 1930

Some shortcuts can be made to save time and effort on your muslin. For example, if you decide to make a muslin for the Beatrice skirt (Pattern B2, page 91), cut just one front and one back piece, instead of stitching all the sections together—it will have the same fit. The Coat (Pattern E, page 211) has a basic swing shape, so the silhouette angles out from the shoulders down. This will most likely eliminate any issues with the waist or the hips being too snug, but you should make sure that the bust measurement is adequate, and that the sleeve length is tailored to your body. Compare your own measurements carefully against the pattern.

When you construct the muslin, try it on as you go. For instance, you should try on the bodice of a dress before you set in the sleeves; try on the skirt before you sew on the waistband.

You will find that you rarely have the exact measurements to match the pattern sizing. Jumping into a new pattern can often lead to ill-fitting garments and heartache—especially if you're using expensive material. Although it takes a bit more time, making a muslin allows you to perfect the pattern for your body.

ALTERATIONS

To alter a pattern is to change its structure so that the end garment will fit your particular body. Most pattern sizing is based on a single bust/waist/hip proportion—but not all bodies conform to that proportion! Before you decide on the size, measure the pattern pieces and compare them to your measurements. Keep in mind that there is a certain amount of ease built into the patterns in this book to allow for freedom of movement. If there aren't any major discrepancies in measurement, go ahead: Choose your size and make a muslin. The patterns in each group are based on the same main pattern pieces, so once you've determined any changes that need to be made, they will apply to any garment you make from that category, saving you from measuring again.

Often, there are small alterations that need to be done, with concerns toward height or sleeve length. These are easy to fix, since many of the pattern pieces already have preprinted lines where you can lengthen or shorten your garment. If the pieces you need to lengthen do not have lengthen/shorten lines, add your own! (In order to maintain the original silhouette of the garment, it's important to adjust the garment from a fairly central location, allowing any pattern pieces that attach to the lower edge of the garment piece to still fit.) The best place to add these lines, generally speaking, is (for a dress, top, vest, cardigan, or coat) about halfway between the bottom of the armhole opening and the hem. For a skirt, add the line about halfway between the crotch and hem, and for a sleeve, add it halfway between the bottom of the armhole opening and the hem.

"In planning and designing your own clothes, you need first to know your type, what to emphasize, and what to subdue. And then you should have a good, reliable style magazine, a full-length mirror, and a determination to persevere until [the] right effects are obtained."

—Mary Brooks Picken, c. 1920s

To Lengthen a Garment

1 Gather all of the pieces you will be altering. Be sure to change the front and back as well as any facings. (It is imperative that they all have the same changes made!)

2 If the pieces you need to lengthen do not have lengthen/shorten lines, add your own. (Remember, add length in the middle, not at the edge, of the pattern piece.) Using a clear ruler with a grid, draw a horizontal line perpendicular to the grainline or fold of the pattern piece all the way across it.

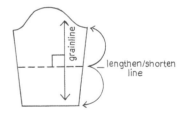

grainline

lengthen/shorten line

3 Cut straight across the pattern piece on the line.

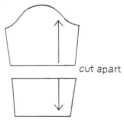

cut apart

4 Tape a piece of lightweight paper underneath the upper piece that is larger (i.e., wider) than the length you need to add. Line a ruler up with the grainline and draw it onto the added paper.

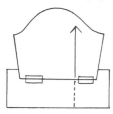

Determine how much length you want to add, and draw a horizontal line marking that length beneath the cut edge of the pattern.

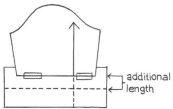

additional length

5 Align this drawn line with the cut edge of the bottom pattern piece and tape.

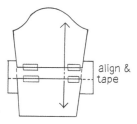

align & tape

6 Now, fill in the side edges with your pen or pencil. If the lines are uneven, just use your eye to connect them smoothly. Cut along these drawn lines to remove extra paper at sides.

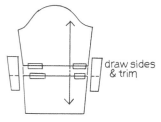

draw sides & trim

To Shorten a Garment

1 Gather all of the pieces you will be altering. Be sure to apply the same alterations to every pattern piece involved: front, back, facings, and so on. If the pattern pieces do not have lengthen/shorten lines, add them as in Step 2, page 29.

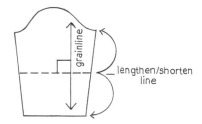

grainline

lengthen/shorten line

Remember, subtract length in the middle, not at either edge, of the pattern piece.

2 Determine how much shorter you want your garment. For example, if you want to shorten the garment 2", draw a horizontal line with your ruler 2" above your lengthen/shorten line.

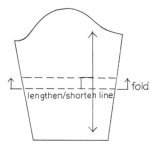

lengthen/shorten line

fold

Fold the pattern back on itself, aligning the grainline, neatly creasing the paper along the new line and lengthen/shorten line.

3 Tape the fold in place, if desired. Use a clear ruler to make sure the fold is even all the way across.

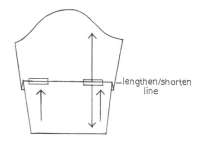

lengthen/shorten line

4 If the outer lines of the pattern are now uneven, use your pen or pencil to draw a new line making a smooth

transition across the fold. Cut the pattern paper along the newly drawn line. You have shortened your garment by 2".

How to Adjust Pocket, Button, Snap Placement, and More . . .

Another thing to consider when lengthening or shortening a garment is pocket placement. A pocket placement guide is marked on the pattern pieces, but if you alter the garment's length, you may wish to move the pocket placement up or down slightly. There may be notations on pattern Front pieces for snaps, buttons, buttonholes, or other closures, and even spacing of these may be affected by altering the length of your garment. If necessary, use your ruler to measure and apply revised placement notations that are equidistant and work with the new length.

If you find that other small alterations are needed on your muslin, try it on, and grab a friend who can pin any area that needs to be taken in, or mark areas that need to be let out. Sometimes, however, more complicated alterations need to be made—often in the shoulders, bust, and waist. For more detailed alterations, I recommend you invest in one of the many good alteration technique books that are on the market (see the Appendix, page 297, for recommendations). They will take you step-by-step through the process to redraft the pattern to fit your body.

When altering your pattern, copy the original pattern piece onto pattern tracing paper, which is available at your local fabric store, or even onto freezer paper, available at a grocery store. (For smaller pieces, even newspaper will suffice.) This way, you will still have the original pattern piece, as well as your altered version. Take notes about the pattern as you sew, which will help you when you go to make it again. Although you are investing a little more time in making a muslin and learning about alterations, in the end it will make future projects sew more smoothly, and your finished projects will look tailored and professional.

"Making and finishing [seams] correctly is very important, for however well you have done your work up to this point, your dress can be a complete success only by the exercise of unerring choice and deft execution in this matter of seams."

—The Woman's Institute's
Fashion Service magazine, 1931

FINISHING TECHNIQUES

Ironing vs. Pressing

When you iron a garment, you use the iron to flatten out a large fabric surface that has been washed. Pressing, however, arguably the most important part of sewing, requires gently lifting the iron and pressing an area of fabric without distorting its grain (no sliding the iron over the fabric, as you might do when ironing). It is best to press seams as you go, so keep your ironing board and iron close at hand. A press cloth (page 8) may be used to help protect the fabric.

Pressing seams

First, press the seam flat along the stitching lines to allow the stitches to blend into the fabric. Then, with the right sides of the fabric facedown, open the seam and gently press it. Turn the piece over and press it again on the right side of the fabric.

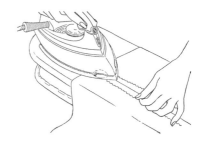

Preparing curved seams (inward and outward)

You might come across a seam that curves inward when you're sewing around an armhole. An outward-curved seam might occur in a pocket with rounded corners. In order for an inward-curved seam to spread evenly (and not bunch up) when turned, you need to clip the seam. This means that, after the seam is complete, you should trim the seam allowance to approximately ⅜", and then make small snips in the fabric approximately ½" apart, extending almost to the stitch line.

Gently press open the seam using a tailor's ham or the curve of the ironing board. Turn and press around the edge, making sure the seam is smooth.

As with an inward-curved seam, you want to trim the seam allowance of an outward-curved seam to about ⅜". Then you'll make snips along the seam allowance about 1" apart on the bias, also just shy of the stitch line. Next, clip in the other direction to meet the points of the first clips, making small notches in the fabric.

Gently press the seam open, turn the fabric, and press the seam flat.

"The finished perfection of any dress depends largely on the perfection of its finishes."

—The Woman's Institute's *Fashion Service* magazine, 1925

Understitching

Understitching is a great way to achieve a professional finish to a garment area (neck, armhole, under collar, or front facing) where you want to keep the fabric underneath, a sewn seam, from peeing out on the right side. After stitching the seam, trim the seam allowance and clip any curved areas.

With the right side of the garment facing up, press the seam allowances toward the under layer of the garment. (If you are sewing a facing to a neckline, for example, you would press the seam allowances toward the facing, which would be the under layer.) Make sure that the seam allowances and facing are lying flat. With one hand on the garment and one on the facing, machine-stitch about 1/16" to 1/8" away from the stitched seam through the under layer of the garment and seam allowances.

Press the under layer to the inside of the garment. The

stitched seam will, as if by magic, roll to the inside and lie flat.

If necessary, you can tack the under layer at the seams to keep it in place.

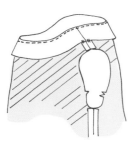

Darts

Darts (and princess or curved seams, opposite) are used to transform a 2-dimensional fabric into a 3-dimensional garment that can conform to contours or curves on a body. Darts are used in the bodice, and on skirts, pants, and sleeves. When you read a pattern, you will see a triangularly shaped line, with a dot at its point, which marks where you will take in the fabric. Using a marking pen or chalk

pencil with a ruler or dressmaker's tracing paper and wheel, transfer these lines to the wrong side of your fabric, bring them together, and pin the fabric.

For a single-point dart, start at the widest end of the dart and stitch to the final point. Stitch off of the edge of the fabric. Do not stop before the end of the dart or

a dimple will be created at the end of your dart, which is not a result you want. Do not backstitch. Instead, leave a long tail of the two threads.

Tie the threads in a double knot to secure the stitching and trim the threads.

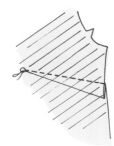

It is preferable but not necessary for darts (and princess or curved seams) to be pressed on a tailor's ham to keep the shape you have created.

Finishing Edges and Seam Allowances

If instructions say to finish the edge or seam allowance, this means to stitch along the raw edge with serging (a), zigzag (b), or any other overcast stitch (c) you have on your machine. This step prevents the fabric from raveling or fraying and provides a more professional appearance. With a serger, you can trim and finish the seam allowance simultaneously (d) or just finish the cut edge by wrapping it with thread (e).

   If your machine does not have a finishing stitch, you may also use pinking shears to finish the fabric edges (f). For hemming, you can press the lower edge under ¼" and then again the desired hem allowance and stitch as directed, by hand or machine (g).

Hem

One of the last steps to finishing a garment is the hem, and it is one of the most important, because the quality of the hem determines how professional the garment looks. Generally, the shape of the bottom edge of the garment determines the width of the hem—the more curve, the smaller the hem—so always refer to the directions suggested on the pattern. For instance, a circle skirt would most likely support a very narrow

7 Ways to Finish an Edge

Refer to text at left for additional information.

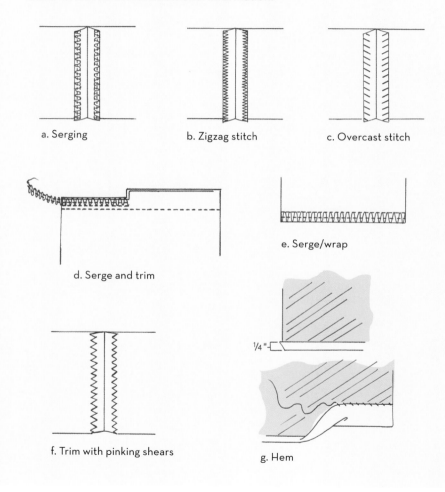

a. Serging

b. Zigzag stitch

c. Overcast stitch

d. Serge and trim

e. Serge/wrap

f. Trim with pinking shears

¼"

g. Hem

hem (like ¼", doubled), whereas a pencil skirt could take on a wider hem (like 1½").

Hems can be hand- or machine-stitched. When you hand-stitch a hem, you can use a blind-stitch technique where you don't see the stitching on the outside of the garment. If your machine has a blind-stitch foot, you can use that as well, or, if you don't mind seeing stitching on the outside of your garment, just use a straight stitch.

If your garment is sewn on the bias, (the Billie skirt, Pattern B5, page 111) be sure to hang it for 24 hours (or more) before hemming, since there will usually be a bit of stretch in the fabric that needs to be coaxed out. Hem lengths should be measured with a yardstick or floor hem marker from the floor to determine the

"An uneven hem will not make a perfect one, no matter how carefully it is pressed and sewed."

—Mary Brooks Picken, 1923

correct hemline. Add the hem allowance to the finished marked hemline, and trim away excess fabric before hemming. After hemming, it's best to lay a bias garment flat—if it is hung in your closet, the hem can still "grow" and become uneven.

CHAPTER 2

The Tank Top

MAGIC PATTERN A

Now that you're refreshed and ready to bring these Magic Patterns to life, it's time to meet a handful of ladies who are here to help you along the enchanted journey. First up is Alice, wearing the anchor piece for this pattern: a classic tunic-length tank top with a flattering A-line silhouette. After you've gotten to know Alice, you'll be introduced to Avery, Adelaide, Alma, Abigail, and Anne in turn—a veritable flock of fashionistas who are all sporting variations on the tank theme.

The characteristic that stays consistent in a tank top, of course, is the lack of sleeves, but beyond that, there are infinite directions to go in—from length to strap width and arrangement, to cut and silhouette. We've narrowed down that infinity to the six designs included here in Pattern A. From a retro mod dress to an edgy racer-back tank with an exposed zipper; from a casual summer cross-back tank to an elegant little black dress, there are surprises at each turn. No two hemlines are alike, with traditional, asymmetric, or variegated hemlines each making appearances. Are you ready? Abracadabra . . .

Meet the Family

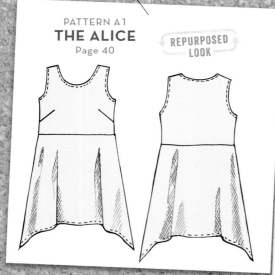

PATTERN A1
THE ALICE
Page 40

REPURPOSED LOOK

PATTERN A2
THE AVERY
Page 49

PATTERN A3
THE ADELAIDE
Page 55

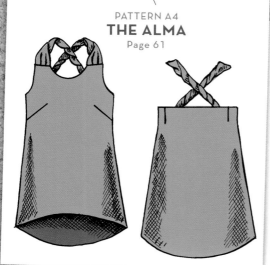

PATTERN A4
THE ALMA
Page 61

PATTERN A5
THE ABIGAIL
Page 67

PATTERN A6
THE ANNE
Page 73

Magic Pattern A Notes

"Though a small item in itself, the blouse is an important aid to any clever woman who will use it as a connecting link between the wardrobe of two seasons."

—Clarice Carpenter, the Woman's Institute's *Inspiration* newsletter, 1926

✂ Please read thoroughly all directions for the pattern before you start cutting or sewing.

✂ All seams in the A patterns are ⅝" unless stated otherwise. There will be variations, so please read carefully.

✂ Refer to page 26 for a detailed explanation of how to cut fabric on the true bias (useful for cutting out the flounces on the Adelaide style, Pattern A3).

✂ Refer to page 27 for the nuances of bias tape (binding) making; this knowledge is essential to constructing Patterns A1, A2, A3, and A6.

✂ For professional results, consult page 32 for the tutorial on preparing curved seams.

✂ All the styles shown have darts for shaping, so refer to page 33 for complete instructions on how to apply them successfully.

✂ Refer to page 32 for instructions on understitching, a technique recommended when constructing Abigail (Pattern A5).

MAGIC PATTERN PIECES A

In the cutting diagrams, each pattern piece is labeled with a number, and the key, with the corresponding number, is listed below. Be sure to refer to this list when laying out the pattern pieces on your fabric.

1. Front
2. Back
3. Pocket
4. A5 Front Neck Facing
5. A5 Back Neck Facing
6. A5 Front Arm Facing
7. A5 Back Arm Facing
8. A4 Front

9. A4 Back
10. A4 Front Facing
11. A4 Back Facing
12. A4 Strap
13. A1 Lower Front
14. A1 Lower Back
15. A1/A6 Neck Binding
16. Arm Binding

17. A2 Upper Back
18. A2 Lower Back
19. A3 Back
20. A3 Flounce
21. A3 Neck Binding
22. A6 Ruffle

Denotes wrong side of fabric

A RELAXED SILHOUETTE WITH CLASSIC APPEAL

Model height: 5'9"

The Alice

REPURPOSED LOOK

Alice, like her literary namesake, is practical and adventurous. She likes a silhouette that matches her personality: comfortable, attractive, with a little bit of flare, but without a lot of fuss. Stylistically, her go-to tank top is classic without being boring (note the extra points of fabric along the bottom edge). Dress it up or down depending on the season or the circumstance: Look sharp paired with leggings or pencil pants and booties or exude a more relaxed elegance with flowy Bohemian beach pants and sandals. In the variation, stitch a silk scarf at the bottom of the bodice for a peek into Alice's daydreams (but without the crazy tea parties).

FABRIC AND NOTIONS

NOTE: Sizes S, M, and L of View 1 can be made from 44"/45" fabric or 60" fabric. Sizes XL and XXL must be made from 60" fabric.

- 1⅞ yards 45" fabric (Sizes S, M), 2¼ yards 45" fabric (Size L); or 1⅞ yards 60" fabric (Sizes S, M), 2 yards 60" fabric (Size L), 2¼ yards 60" fabric (Sizes XL, XXL)
- Thread to match fabric
- Serger thread, if applicable

For optional elastic casing:

- ¼ yard of ¼" elastic
- One package of ½" single-fold bias tape

TOOLS

- Straight pins
- Scissors
- Tailor's chalk or fabric-marking pencil
- Clear ruler or seam gauge
- Medium safety pin (if adding elastic casing)

MACHINE(S)

- Standard sewing machine with needle appropriate to fabric choice
- Serger (optional)

APPROXIMATE MEASUREMENT OF FINISHED GARMENT

	Small	Medium	Large	XL	XXL
Bust measurement	38"	39½"	41½"	43½"	45½"

Approximate length of finished garment (Size M) from center back neckline to lower edge: 27½" with ⅝" hem

> *"We are now in a season of personality clothes. Women are wearing individual things."*
>
> —Mary Mahon, the Woman's Institute's *Fashion Service* magazine, 1929

PATTERN PIECES USED

Front (traced and cut on the A1 cutting line)—1

Back (traced and cut on the A1 cutting line)—2

A1/A6 Neck Binding—15

Arm Binding—16

A1 Lower Front—13

A1 Lower Back—14

CUTTING DIAGRAMS

For 45" fabric, sizes S, M, L:

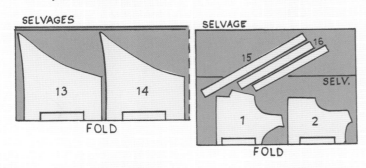

For Lower Front, Lower Back, Arm Binding, for 60" fabric, all sizes:

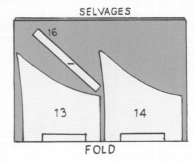

For Front, Back, Neck Binding, for 60" fabric, sizes S, M, L:

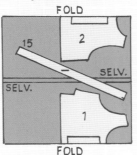

For Front, Back, Neck Binding, for 60" fabric, sizes XL, XXL:

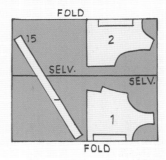

Assembly

NOTE: Optional directions are provided at the end of Step 2 for applying elastic casing to the back of the bodice to cinch the tank for a slightly more fitted look. Proceed to Step 3 if you do not want to add elastic casing.

1 Pin and cut out the pattern pieces using the A1 cutting lines. Using chalk and a clear ruler, mark the dart lines on the Front.

2 Form the darts on the bodice by folding the Front with the right sides together, aligning the solid lines to the large dot. Pin. Begin at the side edge and stitch to the dot, stitching off the edge of the fold at the dot rather than

backstitching. Cut the thread, leaving a few inches to tie off.

Tie and trim the thread. Repeat to form the second dart, then press both darts down.

Optional: To apply an elastic casing, center

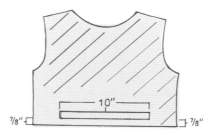

a 10" length of bias tape on the wrong side of the Back bodice with its lower edge ⅞" above the cut edge of the bodice.

Pin along the long edges of the tape. Stitch close to the long folded edges of the bias tape.

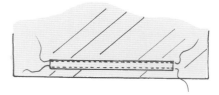

After completing all remaining steps, attach a safety pin to the end of a 5" length of elastic, insert it into the casing, and pull it through until the edges of the elastic are even with the edges of the casing.

Pin and stitch through the short ends of the casing, catching the ends of the elastic between the layers of the fabric and casing.

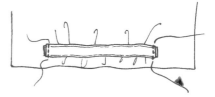

3 With right sides together, pin the Front bodice to the Back bodice at the shoulders. Stitch. Press open the seam allowances.

4 With right sides together, pin the Front bodice to the Back bodice on the sides. Stitch.

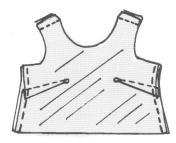

Press open the seam allowances.

5 With right sides together, pin the short ends of the Neck Binding together. Stitch.

Press open the seam allowance. With wrong sides together, press in half lengthwise, aligning the raw edges.

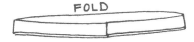

FOLD

6 With right sides together, place the seam of the Neck Binding on the center Back, and pin the raw edge of the binding around the neck edge, adjusting to fit. Stitch a ⅜" seam.

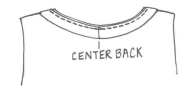

CENTER BACK

Trim the seam allowance and press the binding to the inside along the seam. With the garment wrong side out, pin and stitch close to the outer fold of the binding.

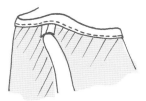

7 With right sides together, pin the short ends of the Arm Binding together. Stitch. Press open the seam allowance. With wrong sides together, press in half lengthwise, aligning the raw edges.

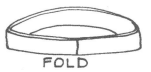

FOLD

8 With right sides together, place the seam of the Arm Binding on the side seam of the bodice and pin the raw edge of the binding around the arm opening. Stitch a ⅜" seam.

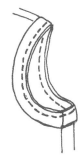

Trim the seam allowance and press the binding to the inside along the seam.

With the garment wrong side out, pin and stitch close to the outer fold of the binding.

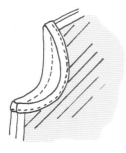

9 Finish the lower edges of the Lower Front and Lower Back. With right sides together, pin the Lower Front to the Lower Back along the sides. Stitch.

Press open the seam allowances. Trim the seam allowance flush with the point.

10 Press up a ⅝" hem, folding it in at the points as shown. Pin. Machine-stitch through the finished edge to secure it.

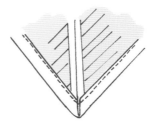

11 With right sides together, pin the completed bodice to the completed lower tank, aligning the fronts and backs, side seams, and raw edges. Stitch a ⅜" seam.

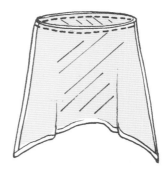

Finish the seam allowance and press it upward.

MAKE YOUR OWN MAGIC

✂ Use a contrasting fabric for the Neck and Arm Bindings. Reverse the application so that it is visible on the right side of the garment. Pin and stitch the binding to the wrong side of the bodice and fold it over to the Front. Pin and stitch close to the outer folded edge of the binding from the right side.

✂ After Step 10, baste one finished end of a rectangular scarf off center to the lower Front. Place the scarf on top of the completed lower tank at the desired location, mark the required length, and cut across the scarf at the mark. Then, with the scarf right side up, pin the cut edge to the raw edge of the lower tank. Gather the top edge of the scarf if desired. Baste the scarf to the tank, and proceed with Step 11.

CONTRAST BINDING CAN BE SUBTLE

Model height: 5'9"

The Alice tank top takes a decidedly flow-y turn when the bottom pieces are replaced by a single wrapped vintage scarf.

FABRIC AND NOTIONS

NOTE: Choose a scarf made of fabric that is fairly substantial in weight, one that drapes nicely and is not considerably lighter than the bodice fabric.

- For bodice: ½ yard 45" fabric (Size S), ⅞ yard 45" fabric (Sizes M, L), 1 yard 45" fabric (Sizes XL, XXL); or ½ yard 60" fabric (All sizes)
- For contrasting Neck and Arm Bindings: ⅝ yard fabric, any width (All sizes)
- For lower tank: large square, or almost square, new or vintage scarf (All sizes)
  NOTE: The circumference of the lower edge of your finished bodice needs to be approximately the same as the measurement of the upper edge of your scarf. Variations within a few inches are fine.
- Thread(s) to match bodice fabric, scarf, and contrasting binding (if desired)
- Serger thread, if applicable

For optional elastic casing:

- ¼ yard of ¼" elastic
- One package of ½" single-fold bias tape

TOOLS

- Straight pins
- Scissors
- Tailor's chalk or fabric-marking pencil
- Clear ruler or seam gauge
- Tape measure
- Hand-stitching needle
- Medium safety pin (if adding elastic casing)

MACHINE(S)

- Standard sewing machine with needle appropriate to fabric choice
- Serger (optional)

"Scarfs [sic] are very important, both separate and attached to garments."

—The Woman's Institute's *Fashion Service* magazine, 1931

PATTERN PIECES USED

- Front (traced and cut on the A1 cutting line)—1
- Back (traced and cut on the A1 cutting line)—2
- A1/A6 Neck Binding—15
- Arm Binding—16

CUTTING DIAGRAMS

For 45" fabric, sizes M, L, XL, XXL:

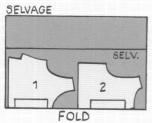

For 45" fabric, size S, and 60" fabric, all sizes:

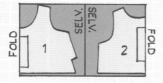

For 45" and 60" fabric, all sizes:

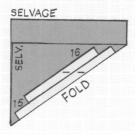

Assembly

1 Pin and cut the required pattern pieces. Using chalk and a clear ruler, mark the dart lines on the Front bodice. On the wrong side of the Front and Back bodice, measure up 1⅝" from the lower edge and draw a line with chalk. Cut off the lower edge of the Front and Back bodice along this line.

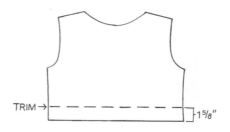

2 Proceed with Steps 2 through 8 of A1, making sure to include the optional elastic casing in back, if desired.

3 Cut the scarf in half horizontally.

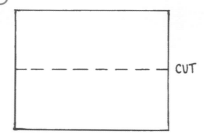

With right sides together, pin and stitch along one short edge of each scarf piece to make one long fabric piece. Be sure to align the cut edges and the finished edges.

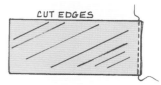

Press open the seam allowance.

4 To determine the placement of the scarf, lay it horizontally on the table, wrong side up. With the completed Front bodice right side up, align its lower edge with the cut edge of the scarf.

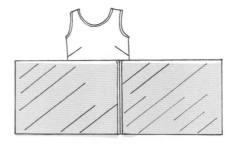

Wrap the left edge of the scarf, keeping it flat against the bodice's lower edge, until it is approximately 3" from the left-side seam. Pin and mark the bodice at this point.

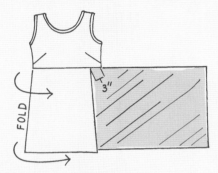

Wrap the right edge of scarf over the lower edge of the bodice until it is approximately 3" from the right-side seam. Pin and mark both the scarf and the bodice at this point.

The remaining scarf length will drape down in front.

NOTE: If the end of the scarf is too long, remove length from the left edge of the scarf by cutting and hemming until the scarf is the length you desire after wrapping. Do not cut the right end of the scarf. Make sure you have made all markings on the bodice and scarf and then remove the scarf from the bodice.

5 Fold and stitch a narrow hem along the cut raw edge, from the mark on the right end of the scarf to the front corner.

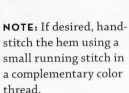

NOTE: If desired, hand-stitch the hem using a small running stitch in a complementary color thread.

6 With right sides together, pin the raw edge of the scarf to the bodice. Begin by placing the right end of scarf (where it begins to drape) on the marking that is 3" from the right side seam. Pin.

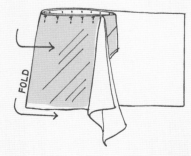

Wrap the scarf around the lower edge of the bodice, aligning the raw edges and pinning. When you reach the front again, place the left end of the scarf over the first layer until the left end lines up with the marking 3" from the left side seam. Stitch a ⅜" seam through all the layers.

Finish the seam allowance and press upward.

← A cool, gray cotton will keep you comfortable on a hot day.

Ikat is a classic, all-over print fabric that adds a vibrant, textured look. →

You'll be pretty as a peacock (or as sassy as a sparrow) wearing a feather-inspired print! →

6 Suggested Fabrics *for the* Alice Tank Top

← Made up in a soft voile, this tank top will have you floating like a butterfly.

A whimsical print adds a strong personality to your tank top. →

A Morrocan-style medallion design perfectly accentuates the simplicity of this tank top style. →

The Avery

S he may be sweet, but Avery's no pushover—her tank's delicate, gathered detailing in the front gives way to exposed hardware in the back for a little rock 'n' roll edge. Likewise, the narrow binding finish around the neck and armholes balance the bold swatch of contrasting fabric on the upper back panel. Wear it tucked in or out, to a coffee shop or concert.

FABRIC AND NOTIONS

- ⅜ yard fabric, any width, for Upper Back (Sizes S, M), ½ yard fabric, any width, for Upper Back (Sizes L, XL, XXL), 1⅓ yards 45" fabric for Front and Lower Back (Sizes S, M), 1½ yards 45" fabric for Front and Lower Back (Sizes L, XL, XXL); or ⅞ yard 60" fabric (Sizes S, M), 1½ yards 60" fabric (Sizes L, XL, XXL)

- Thread(s) to match fabric, exposed zipper, and binding

- Serger thread, if applicable

- 9" fashion zipper with metal teeth (aluminum or brass)

- 4 yards (one package) double-fold ¼" bias tape

TOOLS

- Clear ruler or seam gauge
- Straight pins
- Scissors
- Tailor's chalk or fabric-marking pencil
- Hand-stitching needle

MACHINE(S)

- Standard sewing machine with zipper foot and needle appropriate to fabric choice
- Serger (optional)

Model height: 5'6"

BACK ZIPPER DETAIL!

APPROXIMATE MEASUREMENT OF FINISHED GARMENT

	Small	Medium	Large	XL	XXL
Bust measurement	38"	39½"	41½"	43½"	45½"

Approximate length of finished garment (Size M) from center back neckline to lower edge: 25" with 1½" hem

PATTERN PIECES USED

- Front (traced and cut on the A2 cutting line)—1
- A2 Upper Back—17
- A2 Lower Back—18

CUTTING DIAGRAMS

For 45" fabric, all sizes:

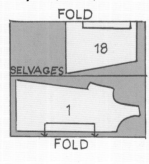

For Upper Back, 45" or 60" fabric, all sizes:

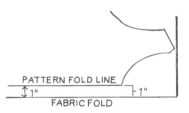

For Front and Lower Back, 60" fabric, sizes S, M:

For Front and Lower Back, 60" fabric, sizes L, XL, XXL:

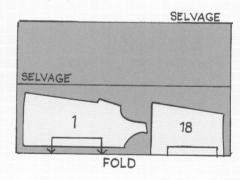

Assembly

1 Place the pattern fold line for the Front 1" from the fold of fabric. Extend the neck and hem cutting lines to the fold, then pin and cut out the Front pattern piece, using the A2 cutting line.

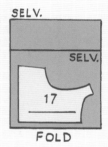

(This allows for extra fabric for the center gather.) Pin and cut out the remaining two A2 pattern pieces. Using chalk and the clear ruler, mark the darts on the Front and the large dot, designating the bottom of the zipper, on the Upper Back.

2 With right sides together, pin the two Upper Back pieces together along the center back edge. Begin at the lower edge and stitch up to the large dot; backstitch, then machine-baste to the neck edge.

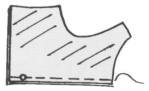

Press open the seam allowance.

3 With the Upper Back right side up, center the zipper, right side up, over the seam. The top of the zipper pull should be aligned ¾" below the neck edge. Pin and hand-baste the zipper in place.

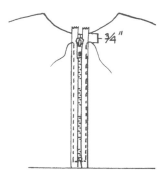

The zipper tape will extend beyond the upper edge. Using a zipper foot, begin stitching ¾" below the neck edge, and stitch close to the teeth; pivot and stitch across the lower edge; then pivot and stitch up the opposite side, stopping ¾" beneath the neck edge. Stitch again very close to the outer edge of the zipper tape on both sides, beginning and stopping ¾" beneath the neck edge. Remove the basting.

4 With right sides together, center and pin the notched edge of the Lower Back to the lower edge of the Upper Back, aligning the raw edges. Stitch a ⅜" seam.

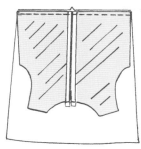

Press the seam allowance down.

5 Trim ⅜" from the Front only around the neck and arms (the seam allowance is unnecessary when using binding, see Step 9). Form the dart by folding the upper Front with right sides together, aligning the solid lines to the large dot. Pin. Begin at the side edge and stitch to the dot, stitching off the edge of the fold at the dot rather than backstitching. Cut the thread, leaving a few inches to tie off.

Tie and trim the thread. Repeat to form the second dart, then press both darts down.

6 Baste a scant ¼" from the neck edge 2" to the left and 2" to the right of the center Front.

Pull up the basting threads to tightly gather the fabric.

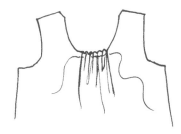

Secure the threads to maintain the gathering.

7 With right sides together, pin the Front to the Back at the shoulder. Stitch. Press open the seam allowance.

STYLE SECRET

Classic men's button-down shirts are always great to use as fabric if you're going for a more tailored look. For example, you could use the front button placket for the back closure of this pattern and use another contrasting men's shirt fabric for the rest of the top. Use the fabric from the first shirt to make the bias trim for the neck edge and armholes. Carefully remove the shirt pocket with a seam ripper and stitch it to your Avery tank on one of the lower front corners.

8 With right sides together, pin the Front to the Back on the sides. Stitch.

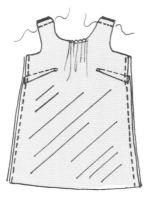

Press open the seam allowances.

9 Remove the bias tape from the package and lightly press out any creases caused by the packaging. Unfold (open up) one long edge of the tape and lightly press it, leaving the original crease faint. Press under one short end of the tape ½".

10 With the pressed long edge up, place the pressed fold at the center back neck and pin, aligning the raw edge of the neck with the unfolded tape edge. Temporarily fold down the tops of the zipper tape (so they're out of the way), and pin around the neck.

When you reach the center Back again, extend the tape ½" beyond the center and cut it. Fold the cut edge under ½" and pin. Stitch in the lightly pressed crease of tape around the neck.

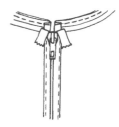

11 Fold the tape over the edge of the neck to the wrong side, and pin. Using thread to match the tape, hand-stitch the tape to the seam allowance of the neck.

12 To finish the arm openings, press under one short end of the tape ½". With the pressed long edge up, place this fold at the underarm seam of the arm opening and pin, aligning the raw edge of the arm opening with unfolded edge of the tape. Continue pinning around the

arm opening. When you reach the fold at the underarm seam again, extend the tape ½" beyond the fold and cut the tape. Pin. Stitch in the lightly pressed crease of tape around the arm opening.

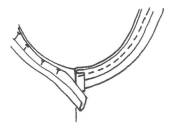

13 Fold the tape over the edge of the arm opening to the wrong side and pin. Using thread to match the tape, hand-stitch the tape to the seam allowance of the arm opening. Repeat on the opposite side.

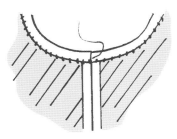

14 Align the upper ends of the zipper tape with the center back edge of the tank, letting the tape extend beyond the neck, as shown.

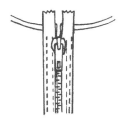

Pin. From the wrong side, hand-tack the zipper tape to the bias tape at the neck. Fold the top of the zipper tape to the wrong side, and hand-stitch to secure.

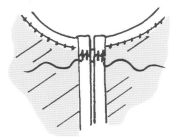

15 To hem, press the lower edge of the tank under ¼". Press under again 1¼" and pin. Hand-stitch to hem.

MAKE YOUR OWN MAGIC

✂ Instead of the folded hem, cut the tank to your desired length and apply ¼" bias tape to the lower edge in the same manner as you did the neck and arm openings.

✂ Apply the zipper to the upper back in the traditional manner rather than having it exposed.

✂ Trade in the zipper for some fun, decorative buttons as the closure at the back of the tank top. Tiny pearl or antique buttons will add a softness, or try three large flat buttons for drama and a bolder effect. Or skip the buttons altogether—add loops to both sides of the back and lace up the opening.

← Mix multiple and mismatched prints in one garment for a bold, clever look.

Bright colors are perfect for breezing through spring and summer days. →

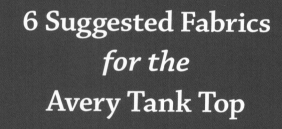

A traditionally summertime top can work year-round when made with neutral colors and prints. →

6 Suggested Fabrics *for the* Avery Tank Top

← Classic chambray never goes out of style.

Use classic men's shirting prints in your garments. →

Linen lends this tank top rich texture and beautiful drape. →

AS PRETTY AS A LAYER CAKE!

Model height: 5'9"

PATTERN A3

The Adelaide

Feminine and flirty, Adelaide's fluttery profile is perfect to wear to a bridal shower, happy hour, or just for a stroll in the downtown shopping district. The wide, raw-edged bias-cut flounces are stitched across the front to create the light and airy silhouette—it's like wearing a layer cake. The gal who wears this tank values practicality with her flair: The front of the neckline arcs tastefully above the playful ruffles; the back dips slightly lower, but not so much as to require any special undergarments.

FABRIC AND NOTIONS

- For tank: 1⅔ yards 45" fabric (Sizes S, M), 1¾ yards 45" fabric (Size L), 1⅞ yards 45" fabric (Sizes XL, XXL); or 1⅔ yards 60" fabric (Sizes S, M, L), 1¾ yards 60" fabric (Sizes XL, XXL)
- For bias flounces: 1 yard fabric, any width (Sizes S, M, L, XL), 1¼ yards fabric, any width (Size XXL)
- Thread to match fabrics
- Serger thread, if applicable

TOOLS

- Straight pins
- Scissors
- Tailor's chalk or fabric-marking pencil
- Clear ruler or seam gauge

MACHINE(S)

- Standard sewing machine
- Serger (optional)

APPROXIMATE MEASUREMENT OF FINISHED GARMENT

	Small	Medium	Large	XL	XXL
Bust measurement	38"	39½"	41½"	43½"	45½"

Approximate length of finished garment (Size M) from center back neckline to lower edge: 18¾" with ⅞" hem (Note: The center back begins 6" to 7" below base of neck on this style.)

PATTERN PIECES USED

- Front (traced and cut on the A3 cutting line)—1
- A3 Back—19
- A3 Flounce—20
- A3 Neck Binding—21
- Arm Binding—16

CUTTING DIAGRAMS

For 45" or 60" fabric, sizes S, M:

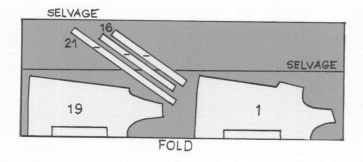

For bias Flounces, for 45" or 60" fabric, all sizes:

For 45" or 60" fabric, sizes L, XL, XXL:

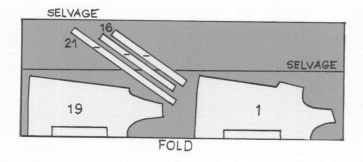

Assembly

1 Pin and cut the pattern pieces, using the A3 cutting line on the Front pattern piece. Using chalk and the clear ruler, mark the darts on the Front.

2 Form the darts by folding the upper Front with right sides together, aligning the solid lines to the large dot. Pin. Begin at the side edge and stitch to the dot, stitching off the edge of the fold at the dot rather than backstitching. Cut the thread, leaving a few inches to tie off.

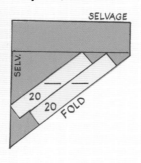

Tie and trim the thread. Repeat to form the second dart, then press both darts down.

3 Press a light crease down the center front of the tank. Ease-stitch the top of each Flounce by basting ¼" beneath the long edge. Do not pull up the ease stitching to gather; it should just add some fullness to the Flounce. Leave the edges of the Flounces unfinished.

4 Fold each Flounce in half, aligning the short ends, and press a light crease to mark the center.

5 The Flounces are numbered 1 through 4, counting from top to bottom. With the Tank Front right side up, mark the placement/stitching lines as follows: Using chalk, place a ruler across the fabric aligned with the lower point of the dart seam on both sides. Draw a line straight across, edge to edge. This is the placement line for Flounce 2. With the ruler, draw a line straight across fabric exactly 4½" below this line, edge to edge, to create the placement line for Flounce 3. Exactly 4½" below this line, draw a line straight across the fabric, edge to edge, to mark the placement line for Flounce 4.

Finally, measure up 4½" from the Flounce 2 line and draw a line straight across the fabric, edge to edge, to mark the placement line for Flounce 1.

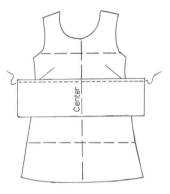

6 With right sides up, using the lightly pressed creases for guidance, center a Flounce along each of the four placement lines. Align the ease-stitch of the Flounce with the drawn line, and pin to the tank Front, centering pins under the ease-stitch.

Trim the sides of all the Flounces so they are flush with the tank sides.

7 Stitch across each Flounce on top of the original ease-stitching.

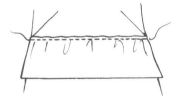

8 Arrange the lower edge of Flounce 1 over the top of Flounce 2. Place the lower edge of Flounce 2 over the upper edge of Flounce 3 and place the lower edge of Flounce 3 over the upper edge of Flounce 4. Pin the sides of the Flounces to the sides of the tank and baste them together. Optional: Finish the edges of the sides.

9 With right sides together, pin the Front to the Back at the shoulder. Stitch. Press open the seam allowance.

10 With right sides together, pin the Front to the Back at the sides. Stitch.

Press open the seam allowances.

11 With right sides together, pin and stitch the notched short ends of the Neck Binding.

Press open the seam allowance. With wrong sides together, fold the binding in half lengthwise and press, aligning the long edges.

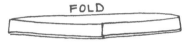
FOLD

12 With right sides together and raw edges even, pin the Neck Binding to the tank with the seam at the center back. Stitch a ⅜" seam.

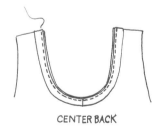
CENTER BACK

Trim the seam allowance and carefully clip the curves. Then turn the binding to the inside along the seam, press, and pin. With the tank wrong side out, stitch close to the outer fold of the binding.

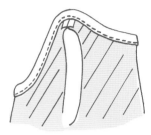

13 With right sides together, pin and stitch the short ends of the Arm Binding. Press open the seam allowance. With wrong sides together, fold the binding in half lengthwise and press, aligning the long edges.

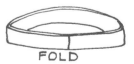
FOLD

With right sides together, and raw edges even, pin the Arm Binding to the arm opening of the tank, aligning the binding seam with the underarm seam. Stitch a ⅜" seam.

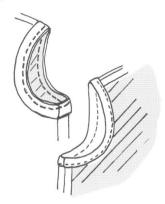

Trim the seam allowance and carefully clip the curves. Turn the binding to the inside along the seam, press, and pin. With the tank wrong side out, stitch close to the outer fold of the binding.

14 Finish the lower edge of the tank. Press under a ⅞" hem and pin. Hand-stitch to secure.

"In ornamenting our dresses, we should work for beauty and smartness."

—Mary Brooks Picken, c. 1920s

MAKE YOUR OWN MAGIC

✂ Press up the hem so that the lower edge of the tank is even with the bottom Flounce and stitch.

✂ Add narrow bias binding to the bottom edges of the Flounces to give them more structure.

✂ Alternate different fabrics to create the Flounces or use a sheer fabric for them to create a soft, airy, fairy-tale-inspired look.

✂ If you prefer a finished edge to your Flounces, draw a line ¾" beyond one long edge of your Flounce pattern piece on the fabric for each of the four flounces. Cut out the Flounces on this drawn line. This will allow you enough extra fabric to make a ⅜" hem on both long edges.

```
- - - - - - - - CUT HERE - - - - - - ⌐ 3/4"
┌────────────────────────────┐
│  FLOUNCE PATTERN PIECE      │
└────────────────────────────┘
```

Press under both long edges of each Flounce ⅜", and machine-stitch to hem.

Then proceed with the instructions as written.

← A bright paisley channels the retro.

Small, pretty florals accentuate this inherently feminine top. →

Lawn cotton is as soft as voile, but lends a little more heft to the tank top. →

6 Suggested Fabrics *for the* Adelaide Tank Top

← Sport an update to the classic preppy look with a wide gingham.

A tank top in classic blue floral says "beach vacation!" →

Animal prints never go out of style! →

The Alma

F rom the graceful twist of the straps (fashioned from an upcycled vintage scarf) to the sweeping back hemline (a hint of asymmetry), the Alma tank is relaxed—and practical, too. If you have a crossback bra, try the tank on before marking the strap placement so you can make adjustments to keep bra straps hidden—or wear a strapless one.

CROSSBACK STRAPS STAY SECURELY ON THE SHOULDERS

FABRIC AND NOTIONS

- For tank: 1⅝ yards 45" fabric (All sizes); or 1⅓ yards 60" fabric (Sizes S, M), 1½ yards 60" fabric (Sizes L, XL, XXL) **NOTE:** This yardage allows for matching straps if desired.

- For contrasting straps: ⅝ yard fabric, any width (Size S), ⅔ yard fabric, any width (Sizes M, L, XL), ¾ yard fabric, any width (Size XXL) **NOTE:** Choose a soft fabric that can be twisted easily or one large scarf, new or vintage.

- Thread to match fabric

- Serger thread if applicable

- ½ yard fusible interfacing in a weight suitable to the fabric used

TOOLS

- Straight pins
- Scissors
- Tailor's chalk or fabric-marking pencil
- Seam gauge or ruler
- Point turner (optional)

MACHINE(S)

- Standard sewing machine with needle appropriate to fabric choice
- Serger (optional)

Model height: 5'8"

APPROXIMATE MEASUREMENT OF FINISHED GARMENT

	Small	Medium	Large	XL	XXL
Bust measurement	38"	39½"	41½"	43½"	45½"

Approximate length of finished garment (Size M) from center back to lower edge: 19⅜" with a 1" hem (Note: The center back begins at the shoulder blades for this halter style.)

PATTERN PIECES USED

- A4 Front—8
- A4 Back—9
- A4 Front Facing—10
- A4 Back Facing—11
- A4 Strap (optional)—12

CUTTING DIAGRAMS

For 45" fabric, all sizes:

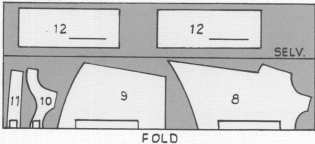

For 60" fabric, all sizes:

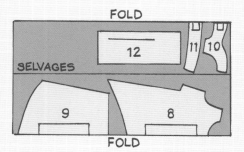

Assembly

1 Pin and cut the A4 Front and Back pattern pieces. Pin and cut the A4 Front and Back Facing pattern pieces. Pin and cut the A4 Strap pattern piece if you're using fabric yardage that is medium-weight.

NOTE: If you're using a scarf or lightweight fabric, cut them 10½" to 12" wide and the same length as the pattern piece.

Using chalk and a clear ruler, mark the darts on the Back. Mark the strap placements on the upper Back. Mark the darts on the Front.

2 Form the back darts by folding the Back piece with right sides together, and aligning the solid lines to the large dot. Pin. Beginning at the upper edge, stitch to the large dot, stitching off of the fold at the dot rather than backstitching. Cut the thread, leaving a few inches to tie off.

Tie and trim the thread. Repeat to form the second dart, then press both darts toward the center back.

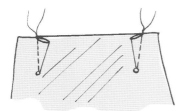

3 Form the front darts by folding the Front piece with right sides together, aligning the solid lines to the large dot. Pin. Begin at the side edge and stitch to the dot, stitching off the edge of the fold at the dot rather than backstitching. Cut the thread, leaving a few inches to tie off.

Tie and trim the thread. Repeat to form the second dart, then press both darts down.

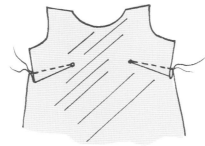

4 With right sides together, pin the Front to the Back on the sides. Stitch. Press open the seam allowances.

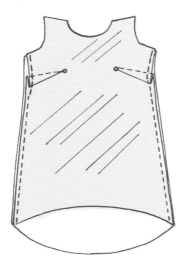

Turn right side out.

5 Following the manufacturer's directions, apply fusible interfacing to the wrong side of the Front and Back Facing pieces. With right sides together, pin the Front Facing to the Back Facing on the side edges. Stitch.

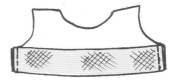

Press open the seam allowances. Finish the lower (outer) edge of the Facing.

6 With right sides together, pin the long edges of the Strap fabric together. Stitch a ¼" seam to form a tube.

Center the seam allowance and press it open. Turn right side out.

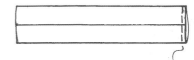

Baste the raw edges of one end together close to the end. With the seam facing up, center this end of the Strap on the Front, leaving the ¼" seam allowance on each side, as shown. Pleat the fabric as necessary to fit. Pleats should be folded toward the center of the tank. Pin and baste in place.

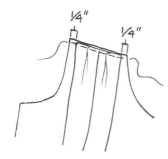

7 With right sides together, pin the Facing to the upper edge of the tank, over the Straps, aligning the side seams and raw edges. Stitch a ¼" seam, pivoting at the points.

On the Back, when you reach the Strap

placement marks, baste across the marks and resume regular stitching after crossing them.

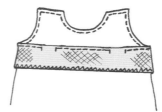

8 Clip the points of the seam allowance. Remove the basting on the Back in the Strap placement areas. Turn the Facing to the inside. Press, gently pushing out the points (use your point turner!) and pulling up the Straps.

9 Gently twist both Straps toward the center.

When you have completed twisting, baste across the open end of each Strap to secure each twist. Cross the Straps in back and slide the ends into the open Strap placement areas of the Back seam. Pin.

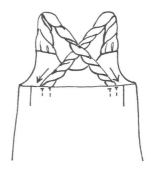

Try on the tank and adjust the Strap length as needed. When you reach the desired fit, pin again along the seam line with right sides together, and stitch across the Strap, backstitching to secure the seam. Trim any excess strap in the seam allowance if necessary.

10 Finish the lower edge of the tank. Press up a 1" hem and pin. Hand- or machine-stitch to secure. If desired, topstitch across the upper Back from side seam to side seam, ¼" beneath the upper edge, through all thicknesses.

STYLE SECRET
Cutting the fabric on the bias will give a dressier, draped feel as well as a more dramatic solution.

MAKE YOUR OWN MAGIC

✂ Use handkerchief linen cut on the bias for the entire piece for a soft, elegant look.

✂ Add button details to the Front bodice just below where the Straps attach.

✂ Make this in a loud, splashy print for a swimsuit cover-up.

✂ Extend the top to make it tunic-length, and wear it over leggings.

"The age of romance appears to have returned. And with it the dressmaker, the milliner, the woman who can produce clothes that are a pleasure to wear."

—Laura McFarlane,
the Woman's Institute's
Fashion Service magazine, 1928

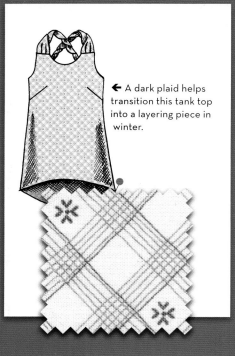

← A dark plaid helps transition this tank top into a layering piece in winter.

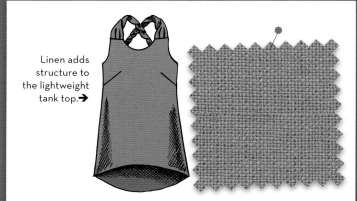

Linen adds structure to the lightweight tank top.→

An all-over pattern brings a visual complexity to this simple style. →

6 Suggested Fabrics *for the* Alma Tank Top

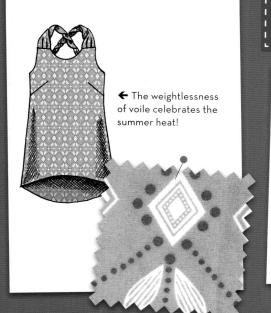

← The weightlessness of voile celebrates the summer heat!

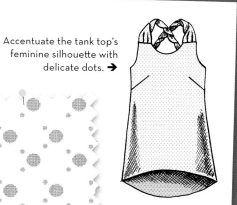

Accentuate the tank top's feminine silhouette with delicate dots. →

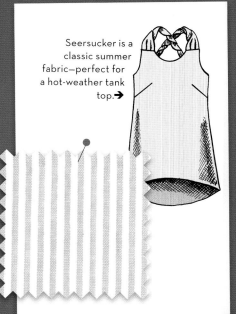

Seersucker is a classic summer fabric—perfect for a hot-weather tank top.→

The Abigail

A DRESS FOR PLAYTIME!

The Abigail dress is for the smart, confident big sisterly type (you know, the one with the best advice—and the best clothes). Her closet is *made* for stealing from, and this Mod variation proves it. You can warm up the look by wearing it over long sleeves and tights in the colder seasons—and while the clean silhouette is well suited to a spirited pattern, there's no reason you couldn't channel another fabulous A-teamer (Audrey!) and make the dress in a smart black, lightweight wool.

FABRIC AND NOTIONS

- 2¼ yards 45" fabric (All sizes); or 1½ yards 60" fabric (Sizes S, M, L), 2 yards 60" fabric (Sizes XL, XXL)
- ½ yard fusible interfacing suitable to fabric used
- Thread to match fabric
- Serger thread, if applicable
- 9" zipper
- Hook and eye closure (optional)
- Fusible web (optional)

TOOLS

- Straight pins
- Scissors
- Tailor's chalk or fabric-marking pencil
- Clear ruler or seam gauge
- Hand-stitching needle

MACHINE(S)

- Standard sewing machine with zipper foot and needle appropriate to fabric choice
- Serger (optional)

APPROXIMATE MEASUREMENT OF FINISHED GARMENT

	Small	Medium	Large	XL	XXL
Bust measurement	38"	39½"	41½"	43½"	45½"

Approximate length of finished garment (Size M) from center back neckline to lower edge: 30¾" with 4" hem

Model height: 5'8"

PATTERN PIECES USED

- Front (traced and cut on the A5 cutting line)—1
- Back (traced and cut on the A5 cutting line)—2
- Pocket—3
- A5 Front Neck Facing—4
- A5 Back Neck Facing—5
- A5 Front Arm Facing—6
- A5 Back Arm Facing—7

CUTTING DIAGRAMS

For 45" fabric, all sizes:

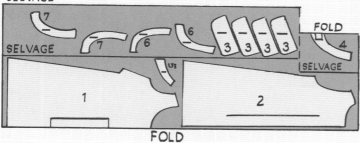

For 60" fabric, sizes S, M, L:

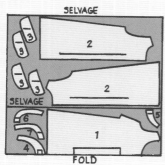

For 60" fabric, sizes XL, XXL:

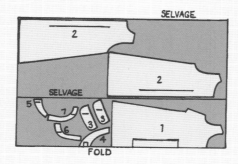

Assembly

1 Pin and cut the pattern pieces using the A5 cutting lines for the Front and Back pattern pieces. Using chalk and a clear ruler, mark the dart lines and Pocket placement on the Front. Mark the large dot on the Back pieces.

2 Form the darts by folding the Front with right sides together, aligning the solid lines to the large dot. Pin. Begin at the side edge and stitch to the dot, stitching off the edge of the fold at the dot rather than backstitching. Cut the thread, leaving a few inches to tie off.

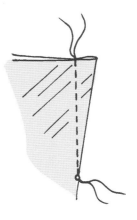

Tie and trim the thread. Repeat to form the second dart, then press both darts down.

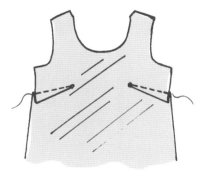

3 With right sides together, pin the two Pocket sections together along the unnotched edges. Stitch a ¼" seam, leaving the notched edge open.

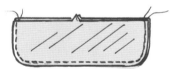

Clip the curves. Turn right side out. Press. Baste the open edges together and finish this edge with serging or zigzag stitch. Topstitch ¼" from the unnotched edge of the Pocket.

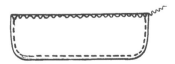

4 With right sides together, align the finished notched edge of the Pocket flap along the placement line on the Front.

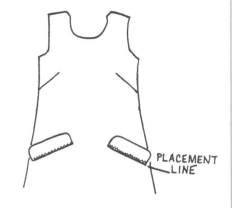

Pin. Stitch ⅜" above the finished edge of the Pocket along the stitch and fold line.

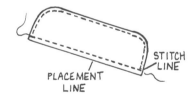

Fold the Pocket down along the stitching. Press.

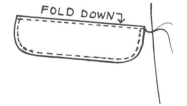

If desired, topstitch ¼" below the fold across the Pocket.

5 Repeat Steps 3 and 4 with the remaining two Pocket pieces.

6 With right sides together, pin the two Backs together along the center back, aligning the long edges. Begin at the lower edge and stitch to the large dot. Backstitch, then machine-baste from the large dot to the neck edge.

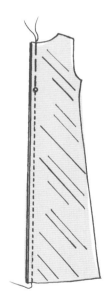

Press open the seam allowance.

7 On the wrong side of the dress Back, center the zipper facedown over the seam with the upper edge of the zipper pull ¾" below the neck edge. Pin. Hand-baste in place if desired. Using the zipper foot, stitch down one side of the zipper tape, pivot, stitch across the lower edge of the zipper, pivot, and stitch up the opposite side of the zipper. Remove basting stitches.

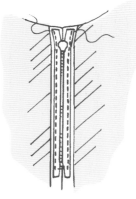

8 With right sides together, pin the Front to the Back at the shoulders. Stitch. Press open the seam allowances.

9 With right sides together, pin the front to the back along the sides. Stitch.

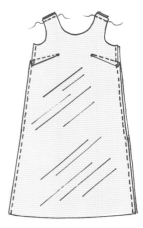

Press open the seam allowances.

10 Following the manufacturer's directions, apply fusible interfacing to the wrong side of all facing pieces. With right sides together, pin the Front Neck Facing to the Back Neck Facing pieces, aligning them on the notched shoulder edges. Stitch. Press open the seam allowances. Finish the outer edge of the completed Neck Facing.

11 With right sides together, pin the Neck Facing to the neck of the dress, aligning shoulder seams and raw edges. Fold the ends of the back facing to the wrong side so that the folds align with the zipper teeth. Stitch a ¼" seam.

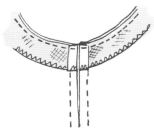

Carefully clip the curves. Turn the facing to the inside. Press. To prevent the facing from rolling to the outside, understitch (see page 32) through the facing and seam allowance, ⅛" from the seam, as far as possible.

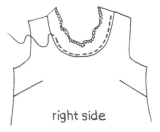

right side

NOTE: Alternatively, following the manufacturer's directions, apply a small piece of fusible web to the wrong side of the front facing at center front to keep it secure on the dress front.) Hand-tack the facing to the shoulder seam allowance. Press under the back facing to keep the facing out of the way of the zipper. Hand-tack the back facing to the zipper tape.

12 With right sides together, pin one Front Arm Facing to one Back Arm Facing, aligning them on the notched shoulder edge and the underarm edge. Stitch.

Press open the seam allowances. Repeat with the remaining Arm Facing pieces. Finish the outer edges of the completed facings.

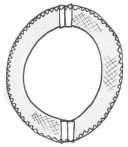

13 With right sides together, pin the Arm Facing to the arm opening of the dress, aligning Fronts and Backs,

shoulder seams, underarm seams, and raw edges. Stitch a ⅜" seam.

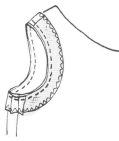

Trim and clip the curves of the seam allowance. Turn the facing to the inside and press. Hand-tack the facing to the side seam allowance and shoulder seam allowance. If desired, apply a small piece of fusible web, following the

MAKE YOUR OWN MAGIC

✂ Substitute antique handkerchiefs as the faux Pocket flaps using the pattern piece provided (cut and line them for best results).

✂ Use an exposed metal zipper with a contrasting tape color.

manufacturer's directions, to the wrong side of the Arm Facing to prevent rolling. Repeat with the second Arm Facing.

14 Press the lower edge of the dress to the wrong side ½". Press under again 3½" and pin. Hand-stitch in place to hem. If desired, sew on a hook and eye to the upper back neck edge above the zipper.

"All garments are characterized by 'dressmaker details.' Make these as perfectly as possible, but at the same time be careful not to oversew the garment, remembering that a soft effect is an important part of the mode, and very essential if you would avoid a home-made look."

—Mary Brooks Picken, 1924

← Rayon offers the drape of silk, without the price tag!

Classic gingham is sweet and feminine. →

An all-over ikat print is for making a bold statement. →

6 Suggested Fabrics *for the* Abigail Tank Dress

← Transform a summer style for winter by making it out of wool.

A denim dress is a neutral you can wear year-round—it goes with *everything!* →

Go with corduroy to add a touch of texture to a simple style. →

The Anne

This pullover tank dress, with its flapper-inspired drop-waist silhouette, is impossible to resist. Wear it with a Gatsby-inspired cloche hat and fishnets to turn on the speakeasy charm, or belt it for a more structured, modern look. Stitch it up in black, as shown, and it's fit for a date night or art opening; switch that out for a flowing paisley, and you're ready to frolic at an outdoor music festival. Repurpose a vintage slip for the wide lower ruffle for a touch of flirt and flounce.

THE LBD: A CLASSIC

FABRIC AND NOTIONS

- For Upper Dress (Front, Back, Neck Binding, Arm Binding): 1¾ yards 45" fabric (Sizes S, M), 1⅞ yards 45" fabric (Sizes L, XL, XXL); or 1½ yards 60" fabric (Sizes S, M), 1¾ yards 60" fabric (Sizes L, XL, XXL)
- For Ruffle: ⅝ yard fabric, any width (All sizes) **NOTE:** constructed from all one fabric, any width: 2¼ yards (All sizes)
- Thread to match fabrics
- Serger thread, if applicable

TOOLS

- Straight pins
- Scissors
- Tailor's chalk or fabric-marking pencil
- Clear ruler or seam gauge
- Hand-stitching needle (optional)

MACHINE(S)

- Standard sewing machine with needle appropriate to fabric choice
- Serger (optional)

APPROXIMATE MEASUREMENT OF FINISHED GARMENT

	Small	Medium	Large	XL	XXL
Bust measurement	38"	39½"	41½"	43½"	45½"

Approximate length of finished garment (Size M) from center back neckline to lower edge: 33⅞" with 2" hem

Model height: 5'10"

PATTERN PIECES USED

- Front (traced and cut on the A6 cutting line)—1
- Back (traced and cut on the A6 cutting line)—2
- A1/A6 Neck Binding—15
- Arm Binding—16
- A6 Ruffle—22

CUTTING DIAGRAMS

For 60" fabric, sizes S, M:

For 45" fabric, all sizes; for 60" fabric, sizes L, XL, XXL:

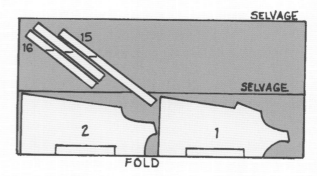

For Ruffle, for 45" or 60" fabric, all sizes:

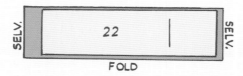

Assembly

1 Pin and cut the pattern pieces using the A6 cutting lines on the Front and Back. Using chalk and a clear ruler, mark the darts on the Front.

2 Form the darts by folding the upper Front with right sides together, aligning the solid lines to the large dot. Pin. Begin at the side edge and stitch to the dot, stitching off the edge of the fold rather than backstitching. Cut the thread, leaving a few inches to tie off. Tie and trim the thread. Repeat to form the second dart, then press both darts down.

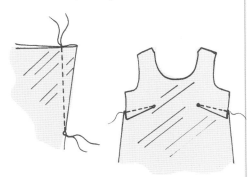

3 With right sides together, pin the Front to the Back at the shoulder. Stitch. Press open the seam allowance.

4 With right sides together, pin the Front to the Back on the sides. Stitch.

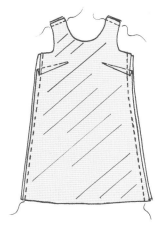

Press open the seam allowances.

5 With right sides together, pin and stitch the short ends of the Neck Binding.

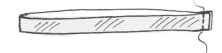

Press open the seam allowance. With wrong sides together, fold the binding in half lengthwise and press, aligning the long edges.

FOLD

"When working with soft fabrics, it is essential that they lie flat and even during cutting."

—The Woman's Institute's *Fashion Service* magazine, 1928

6 With right sides together, and the raw edges even, pin the Neck Binding to the garment, aligning the binding seam with the center back. Stitch a ⅜" seam.

CENTER BACK

Trim the seam allowance and carefully clip the curves. Turn the binding to the inside along the seam, press, and pin. With the garment wrong side out, stitch close to the outer fold of the binding.

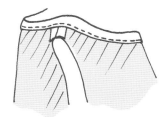

7 With right sides together, pin and stitch the short ends of the Arm Binding. Press open the seam allowance. With wrong sides together, fold the binding in half lengthwise and press, aligning the long edges.

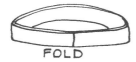

FOLD

With right sides together and raw edges even, pin the Arm Binding to the arm opening of the garment, aligning the binding seam with the underarm seam. Stitch a ⅜" seam.

 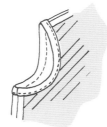

Trim the seam allowance and carefully clip the curves. Turn the binding to the inside along the seam, press, and pin. With the garment wrong side out, stitch close to the outer fold of the binding.

8 With right sides together, pin the short ends of the Ruffle, aligning the raw edges. Stitch.

Press open the seam allowances. Finish the unnotched hem edge. Turn the finished lower edge of the Ruffle to the wrong side 2" and pin. Hand- or machine-stitch the hem, depending on the fabric used.

9 Beginning at one side seam of the Ruffle, baste ⅝" beneath the upper edge to the opposite side seam. Baste again ¼" inside the first stitching. Repeat on the opposite side of the Ruffle.

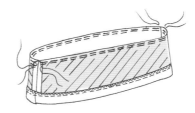

Pull up the basting threads to gather.

10 With right sides together, pin the gathered edge of the Ruffle to the lower edge of the tank, aligning the side seams and distributing the fullness of the gathers evenly. Stitch.

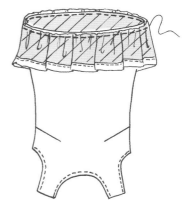

Finish the seam allowance and press upward.

"Watching always what you see in your mirror, your fashion books, on the streets, and in the shops, you will find that which is appropriate, becoming, and wholly lovely for you."

—Mary Brooks Picken, c. 1920s

THE RUFFLE CAN CONTRAST WITH THE REST OF THE DRESS IN COLOR, TONE, OR TEXTURE.

MAKE YOUR OWN MAGIC

✂ Use a vintage slip for the lower Ruffle. Evenly cut off the bottom of a vintage slip in desired length. Baste around the upper edge of the slip section. Align the side seams of the slip and dress if applicable and, with right sides together, pin the cut edge of the slip to the lower edge of the dress, pulling up the basting thread to fit. Stitch. Finish the seam allowance.

✂ Pair brightly colored contrasting fabrics for the dress and Ruffle for a fun summer dress. Go with a straight color block, or push even further and use a floral print for the top and a contrasting plaid or stripe for the Ruffle.

✂ Add a second Ruffle, shorter than the bottom one, at the same seam, in a sheer fabric.

✂ Make a fabric flower using scraps and stitch it to one side along the Ruffle seam line—or, if adding trim, pin an oversized vintage brooch to one side centered on the trim.

✂ Pin a wide trim around the dress with the lower edge of the trim flush with the connecting seam of the dress and Ruffle (you'll need about 2 yards). Begin at the side seam and pin. When you come back to the original side seam, extend the trim 1" and cut. Fold and press under the cut end of the trim ½", place it over the beginning of the trim, and hand-stitch it to secure. Hand- or machine-stitch around the upper and lower edges of the trim to secure it to the garment.

← Dress up a simple shape with raw silk—jewel tones always win.

Keep garments light and silky with voile. →

Velvet both dresses up and winterizes the '20s-style silhouette. →

6 Suggested Fabrics *for the* Anne Tank Dress

Dress down the silhouette for everyday wear by making it in denim. →

← Invoke office attire by using classic men's suiting.

Go with a bright linen if you're in need of a summer garden party dress. →

CHAPTER 3
The Skirt

〰〰〰〰〰〰〰

MAGIC PATTERN B

Meet the Queen Bs: Blythe, Beatrice, Betsy, Bridget, Billie, and Bernadette are the six different styles in the skirt pattern. The silhouettes range from flared to fitted, maxi to mini, Bohemian to buttoned-up. Mind you, there are no actual buttons (or zippers, either!) to manage, because they're all pull-on. The secret? There's a hidden elastic casing in the back. You get all the benefits and comfort of an elastic waist—easy to slip on and a snug fit—with a smooth, flat front that casts out any fleeting thoughts of frumpy sweatpants.

Though the definition of a skirt (a garment fastened around the waist that extends down around the legs) doesn't initially seem like it would allow much room for variation, the elements of length, volume, and silhouette are where you can stretch your creativity and make the magic swirl from this pattern. Each skirt comes with a suggested length, but with DIY, you're ultimately in charge of how you want it to look. Construct a skirt with darts, and it will sit at your natural waist; omit them, and the skirt will take on a more relaxed fit, sitting slightly below the natural waist. Pick out brand-new fabric or reclaim material from something already in your closet.

Meet the Family

Magic Pattern B Notes

✂ Please read thoroughly all directions for the pattern before you start cutting or sewing.

✂ All seams in the B patterns are ½" unless stated otherwise. There will be variations, so read carefully.

✂ Before cutting out your skirt, decide if you want the natural waist fit with two front darts or if you want to omit them, adding 2" and having the skirt sit slightly below the natural waist. Cut your Front Waistband accordingly. Cut out Front Waistband A for a skirt with darts and Front Waistband B for a skirt without darts. The Back Waistband is the same for all the skirts. If you're not adding darts, cut straight across the top of the skirt's Front pattern piece, omitting the small points in the center of the darts.

INSTRUCTIONS FOR ADDING FRONT DARTS

Follow these directions to form darts for any skirt in this chapter. The darts will not be shown in assembly instruction illustrations.

1 Mark the dart lines on the wrong side of the fabric.

2 Fold the fabric with right sides together, aligning the solid dart lines to the large dot. Pin.

3 Beginning at the upper edge, stitch to the dot and continue stitching off the fold. Do not backstitch. Cut the thread, leaving a few inches to tie off. Tie and trim threads.

4 Repeat to form the second dart, then press both darts toward the center of the skirt.

MAGIC PATTERN PIECES B

In the cutting diagrams, each pattern piece is labeled with a number, and the key, with the corresponding number, is listed below. Be sure to refer to this list when laying out the pattern pieces on your fabric.

1. B1/B3/B5 Front
2. B1/B3/B5 Back
3. Pocket
4. Front Waistband A (with darts) and B (without darts)
5. Back Waistband

6. B6 Front
7. B6 Side Front
8. B6 Back
9. B6 Side Back
10. B4 Front Yoke
11. B4 Back Yoke

12. B4 Front
13. B4 Back
14. B3 Front Pleat
15. B3 Back Pleat
16. B2 Front
17. B2 Back

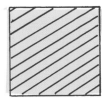

Indicates wrong side of fabric

INSTRUCTIONS FOR APPLYING FRONT AND BACK WAISTBANDS

1 If the fabric is light- to medium-weight, you may add fusible interfacing to the Front Waistband if desired. Cut a strip of interfacing that is 1" wide by the length of your Front Waistband. Trim the seam allowance from the short ends. Following the manufacturer's directions, apply the interfacing to the wrong side of the Front Waistband, placing the long edge of interfacing ⅝" above the long notched edge of the waistband, centered on the band.

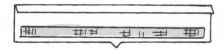

2 Press ⅝" of the long unnotched edge of the Front and Back Waistbands to the wrong side.

3 With right sides together, center the long notched edge of the Front Waistband on the skirt Front and pin, aligning the raw edges. (**NOTE:** The notch only designates the long edge to be centered on the skirt. The notch itself is not necessarily centered and there is no corresponding notch on the upper edge of the skirt.) Stitch.

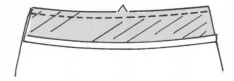

Trim the seam allowance and press it upward. Trim any excess fabric on the ends of the waistband so that the sides of the waistband are flush with the side edges of the skirt.

4 With right sides together, pin the long notched edge of the Back Waistband to the upper edge of the skirt Back, centering and aligning the raw edges. Stitch.

Trim the seam allowance and press upward. Trim any excess fabric on the ends of the waistband so that the sides of the waistband are flush with the side edges of the skirt.

5 To form the casing for the elastic in the Back Waistband, fold back the band to the wrong side so that the folded edge of the waistband extends beyond the seam line a scant ⅛".

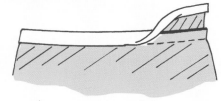

Pin the band to the skirt on the right side. Center the pins under the seam line.

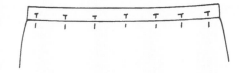

Stitch in the ditch of the seam line, catching in the band beneath.

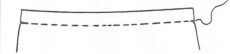

If you are not familiar with this term, it means to stitch in the exact center of an existing seam line so that the stitching is invisible. Now you have a casing for your elastic.

6 Cut a length of ¾" elastic that is 5" shorter than the width of your Back Waistband.

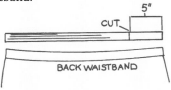

Attach a large safety pin to one end of the elastic and use it to pull the elastic through the Back Waistband casing until the unpinned end is flush with the end of the casing. Pin the elastic to the waistband casing to secure it.

Continue pulling the safety pin until the elastic is flush with the opposite side of the casing and the fabric is gathered. Pin the elastic to the casing on this side and remove the safety pin. Baste the ends of the elastic to the waistband casing fabric ½" from the sides.

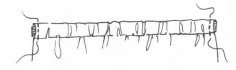

7 With right sides together, align the waistband seams of the Front and the Back. The top of the Back Waistband casing will just meet the fold line of the Front Waistband. Pin them together on the sides. Baste the Front to the Back through the back casing as shown.

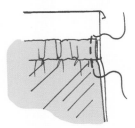

8 Fold the Front Waistband over the Back Waistband casing so that the Front Waistband's pressed fold is even with the Back Waistband's casing seam. Pin down the entire side. Stitch a ½" or ⅝" seam, depending on the skirt.

Clip the back seam allowance to the stitching beneath the casing seam as shown.

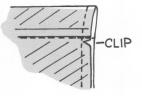

Press open the seam allowance beneath the waistband.

9 Turn the skirt right side out. Press the Front Waistband so that the pressed-under edge is even with the connecting seam.

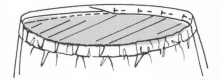

Pin and hand-stitch the Front Waistband to the seam allowance to secure it.

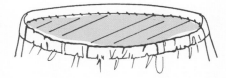

POCKETS +
PLEATS =
PERFECTION

Model
height:
5'10"

The Blythe

Playful, yet work appropriate, Blythe—a simple A-line skirt—is full of sexy retro librarian charm. The skirt's inverted center front pleat offers a smart, pulled-together look that allows for plenty of movement, and the patch pockets offer a place to stash your no. 2 pencils. Pick your season: Make it in wool crepe for the cooler months or a cotton print for spring.

FABRIC AND NOTIONS

- 1¾ yards 45" fabric (Sizes S, M), 1⅞ yards 45" fabric (Sizes L, XL, XXL); or 1⅝ yards 60" fabric (All sizes)
- Thread to match fabric
- Serger thread, if applicable
- ⅔ yard of ¾" elastic
- 1" strip of fusible interfacing for Front Waistband (optional)

TOOLS

- Scissors
- Clear ruler or tape measure
- Straight pins
- Tailor's chalk or fabric-marking pencil
- Seam gauge
- Hand-stitching needle
- Large safety pin

MACHINE(S)

- Standard sewing machine with needle appropriate to fabric choice
- Serger (optional)

APPROXIMATE MEASUREMENTS OF FINISHED GARMENT

	Small	Medium	Large	XL	XXL
Hip measurement	42½"	44"	45½"	47½"	49½"
Waist measurement (without being stretched, with darts)	26½"	28"	29½"	31½"	33½"
Waist measurement (without being stretched, without darts)	28½"	30"	31½"	33½"	35½"

Approximate finished length of skirt: 21⅝" with a 4½" hem

PATTERN PIECES USED

- B1/B3/B5 Front (traced and cut on the B1 cutting line)—1
- B1/B3/B5 Back (traced and cut on the B1 cutting line)—2
- Pocket—3
- Front Waistband A or B—4
- Back Waistband—5

CUTTING DIAGRAMS

For 45" fabric, sizes S, M:

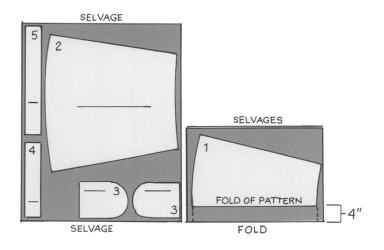

For 45" fabric, sizes L, XL, XXL:

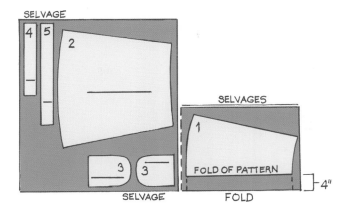

For 60" fabric, all sizes:

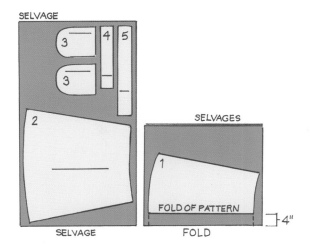

Assembly

NOTE: Step 1 instructions are for the B1 individual pattern. If you use Magic Pattern B to make B1, cut out and carefully fold the B1/B3/B5 Front piece along the fold line.

1 Cut out the B1/B3/B5 Front pattern piece and with the fabric folded right sides together, place the fold line of the pattern exactly 4" from the fold of the fabric. Use a clear ruler to make sure it is straight. Pin and cut straight across from the fabric fold to the upper and lower edge of the pattern piece. Continue to cut along the nonfolded pattern edges.

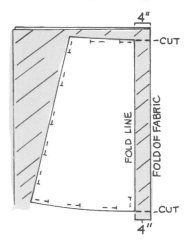

Using chalk and the clear ruler, draw a line on the wrong side of the fabric extending 8" down from the upper edge along the fold of the pattern.

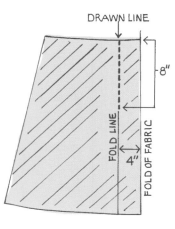

This drawn line will be the stitching line to form the center pleat. Pin and cut out Front Waistband A if adding darts or Front Waistband B if not adding darts. Pin and cut out the B1/B3/B5 Back and Pocket pattern pieces. Mark the pocket placement guideline and the darts, if applicable, on the wrong side of the skirt Front fabric.

2 If desired, stitch the front darts following the instructions on page 83.

3 Finish the outer edges of the Pockets. To form the facing, fold the upper edge of the Pocket to the right side on the fold line and pin on the sides.

Stitch ⅝" from the edge around the entire Pocket.

Clip the upper corner, turn the facing to the wrong side, and press, pressing the Pocket under below the facing along the stitching.

Topstitch across the Pocket 1⅜" below the upper edge. Topstitch again ¼" above the first stitching.

STYLE SECRET

Because this pull-on skirt design has a flat-front waistband without zippers or buttons to add bulk, it is perfect for wearing with fitted sweaters, tanks, or T-shirts.

4 Pin the Pockets to the skirt Front using the guideline. (**NOTE:** The guideline is for Size small, so move the Pocket slightly closer to the side edge for each larger size, keeping the upper edge of the Pocket aligned with the guideline.) Stitch close to the outer edge of the Pocket, backstitching at the beginning and end to secure it. Topstitch again, ¼" inside the first stitching.

5 With right sides together, fold the skirt in half, carefully aligning the raw edges. Pin along the 8" stitching line you drew earlier.

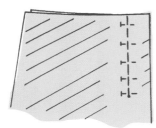

Stitch along the line, beginning at the upper edge. Backstitch to secure at the bottom of the line.

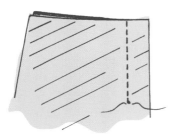

Open out the skirt Front and press the pleat fabric flat, centering the stitching line beneath it.

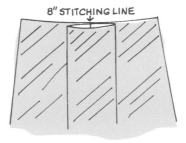

Continue to press the skirt to the lower edge, forming a pleat. Pin and baste across the pleat ½" from the upper edge.

6 Follow the instructions on pages 84 and 85 to apply the Front and Back Waistbands.

7 Stitch ½" side seams.

8 Press the lower edge of the skirt under ⅝". Press under again 3⅞" and pin. Hand-stitch to secure the hem.

MAKE YOUR OWN MAGIC

✂ It's hip to be square: To give this skirt a new twist, change the pocket to a square corner pocket, and add a tab and a button on the top edges.

✂ For another great look, leave off the pockets entirely!

← An A-line skirt in cotton is a must-have for summer.

Add structure to your skirt by using heavier home decor fabric. →

Update a classic fabric, like railroad denim, by pairing it with this modern style. →

6 Suggested Fabrics *for the* Blythe Skirt

← Make your skirt fall-weather appropriate in a neutral brown cord.

Stripes fall into the categories of prints that play well with others! →

The perfect fabric for a season-less, year-round skirt? Denim. →

The Beatrice

Beatrice loves literature; she's the type to quote Shakespeare verbatim and works as the events coordinator at the local independent bookstore. Though she believes that all the world's a stage (of course), she does make an effort to channel her stage presence at open-mike nights, honing her spoken-word poetry. The exposed stitching connecting her maxi skirt's four horizontal panels is just one telltale sign of how Beatrice loves to live the Bohemian dream. Shown with front darts omitted to allow more ease and a below-the-waist fit, the skirt is presented here in a cotton decorator fabric and a 100 percent polyester linen-look fabric. Give your creative side free rein with the fabric choices—Bea would be proud.

FABRIC AND NOTIONS

- 2⅞ yards 45" fabric (All sizes); or 2⅓ yards 60" fabric (All sizes)
- Thread to match fabric
- Serger thread in matching or contrasting color
- ⅔ yard of ¾" elastic
- 1" strip fusible interfacing for Front Waistband (optional)
- Contrasting thread for topstitching (optional)

TOOLS

- Straight pins
- Scissors
- Clear ruler or seam gauge
- Tailor's chalk or fabric-marking pencil
- Large safety pin
- Hand-stitching needle

MACHINE(S)

- Standard sewing machine with needle appropriate to fabric choice
- Serger

TRY THE MAXI SKIRT FOR THE MAXIMUM STATEMENT

Model height: 5'8"

APPROXIMATE MEASUREMENTS OF FINISHED GARMENT

	Small	Medium	Large	XL	XXL
Hip measurement	42½"	44"	45½"	47½"	49½"
Waist measurement (without being stretched, with darts)	26½"	28"	29½"	31½"	33½"
Waist measurement (without being stretched, without darts)	28½"	30"	31½"	33½"	35½"

Approximate finished length of skirt: 41" with a 2" hem

> *"We have had for a time the extreme in short skirts, but they are passing with the 'flappers.' All Paris is talking slightly longer skirts."*
>
> —Mary Brooks Picken, 1922

PATTERN PIECES USED

- B2 Front (sections 1 through 4)—16
- B2 Back (sections 1 through 4)—17
- Front Waistband A or B—4
- Back Waistband—5

CUTTING DIAGRAMS

For Front, for 45" fabric, all sizes:

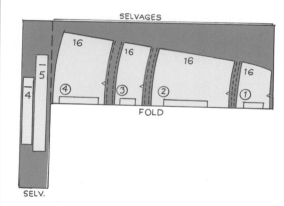

For Back, for 45" fabric, all sizes:

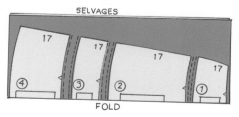

For 60" fabric, all sizes:

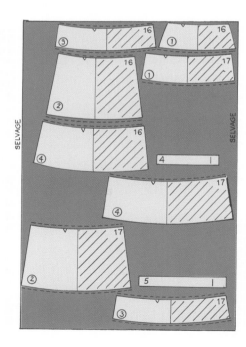

Assembly

1 Cut apart the B2 Front and B2 Back pattern pieces along the cutting lines between sections 1 through 4. Pin and cut out Front Waistband A if adding darts or Front Waistband B if not adding darts. Pin and cut out the Back Waistband. Fold the fabric with right sides together. Pin the Front B2 and Back B2 pattern pieces on the fold and use chalk and a clear ruler or seam gauge to add the necessary seam allowances by drawing on the wrong side of the fabric. Mark notches on each section just to designate that it is the upper edge.

2 Add ⅝" to the lower edge of section 1. Add ⅝" to the upper and lower edges of section 2. Add ⅝" to the upper and lower edges of section 3. Add ⅝" to the upper edge of section 4.

3 If you choose to apply darts, mark the darts on the wrong side of Front section 1. Following the instructions on page 83, stitch the darts.

4 Follow the instructions on pages 84 and 85 to apply the Front Waistband to Front section 1 and apply the Back Waistband to Back section 1. Stitch ⅝" side seams to connect Front section 1 and Back section 1.

5 With right sides together, pin and stitch ⅝" side seams to connect Front section 2 and Back section 2.

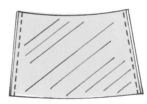

Press open seam allowances. With right sides together, pin and stitch ⅝" side seams to connect Front section 3 and Back section 3.

If desired, reverse the fabric for section 3 so that the wrong side of the fabric is visible. To do this, pin and stitch the Front to the Back with wrong sides together. Press open the seam allowances. With right sides together, pin and stitch ⅝" side seams to connect Front section 4 and Back section 4.

Press open the seam allowances.

6 Serge the upper and lower edges of sections 2, 3, and 4. Serge the lower edge of section 1.

7 With wrong sides together, pin the lower edge of section 1 to the upper edge of section 2. Stitch.

Press open the seam allowance.

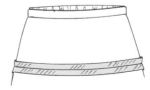

With wrong sides together, pin the lower edge of section 2 to the upper edge of section 3. Stitch. Press open the seam allowance. With wrong sides together, pin the lower edge of section 3 to the upper edge of section 4. Stitch. Press open the seam allowance.

8 Press under the desired hem, pin, and hand- or machine-stitch to secure it.

9 Place a few pins around each exposed seam allowance to keep them aligned. Machine-stitch around each seam allowance, through the center or through the serger thread. If desired, use a contrasting color thread as an accent.

"Compose is a word on every tongue. It means a skilled combining of two, three, or even four tones of the same color, or contrasting colors."

—The Woman's Institute's *Fashion Service* magazine, 1927

MAKE YOUR OWN MAGIC

✂ Stitch together all sections with right sides together, so the seam allowances are enclosed.

✂ If your machine has decorative stitches, use them to stitch around the exposed seam allowances.

✂ For a midcalf-length skirt, stitch together just sections 1 through 3, and hem.

✂ Mix-and-match fabrics: Most cottons are designed in collections, so choose a group of fabrics that will work well together when combined for this skirt. Use an entirely different fabric for each section, or go for a more minimal (and perhaps more dramatic) look using a solid for three sections and a print for one.

✂ Do not cut apart the Front and Back pattern pieces into sections, but rather cut the fabric using the whole pattern piece. If you make a sectioned skirt and wish to make a solid skirt later, simply tape the pattern sections together into the original pattern piece.

✂ Using an exposed serged seam is not your only construction option for the Beatrice maxi skirt. If you don't own a serger, use your machine's overcast stitch or zigzag stitch to finish the cut edges.

✂ Sometimes the wrong side of a piece of fabric has a more interesting color or design than the right side; don't hesitate to try the side you like best—or try them both!

← A thick corduroy adds structure to the traditionally breezy maxi style.

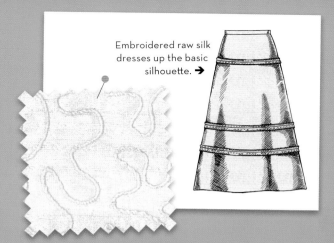

Embroidered raw silk dresses up the basic silhouette. →

Linen has the perfect drape for this flowing skirt. →

6 Suggested Fabrics *for the* Beatrice Skirt

← For everyday comfort, you can't beat a knit skirt!

Go bold and use an all-over print for the ultimate statement skirt. →

A floral cotton fabric initiates a retro Bohemian look. →

PRETTY IN PLEATS!

Model
height:
5'9"

The Betsy

The Betsy, a just-skimming-the-knee skirt finished with a kicky pleated flourish, is key to the outfit that welcomes spring—or, channeling your favorite schoolteacher, welcomes you back to school in the fall when paired with a sweater and tights. Shown in 100 percent cotton with a voile bias trim and front darts, it's a no-nonsense silhouette with a touch of playfulness. Try a contrasting fabric for the pleats to kick it up a notch!

FABRIC AND NOTIONS

NOTE: If you choose to make the Betsy skirt from just one piece of fabric, you'll need 2⅛ yards any width (All sizes).

- 1¼ yards fabric (All sizes), any width, for upper skirt (includes Front, Back, Front Waistband, and Back Waistband)
- ¾ yard fabric, any width (All sizes), for Pleats
- ⅔ yard fabric, any width, for Bias trim
- Thread to match fabric(s)
- Serger thread if applicable
- ⅔ yard of ¾" elastic
- 1" strip of fusible interfacing for Front Waistband (optional)

TOOLS

- Straight pins
- Scissors
- Tailor's chalk or fabric-marking pencil
- Clear ruler
- Tape measure
- Hand-stitching needle
- Large safety pin

MACHINE(S)

- Standard sewing machine with needle appropriate to fabric choice
- Serger (optional)

APPROXIMATE MEASUREMENTS OF FINISHED GARMENT

	Small	Medium	Large	XL	XXL
Hip measurement	42½"	44"	45½"	47½"	49½"
Waist measurement (without being stretched, with darts)	26½"	28"	29½"	31½"	33½"
Waist measurement (without being stretched, without darts)	28½"	30"	31½"	33½"	35½"

Approximate finished length of skirt: 20¼" with 1" hem

"[Pleated] skirts, in spite of the favorable season they have had, are still maintaining popularity over other types."

—Mary Brooks Picken's
Inspiration newsletter, 1921

PATTERN PIECES USED

- B1/B3/B5 Front (traced and cut on the B3 cutting line)—1
- B1/B3/B5 Back (traced and cut on the B3 cutting line)—2
- Front Waistband A or B—4
- Back Waistband—5
- B3 Front Pleat—14
- B3 Back Pleat—15

For Pleats, for 45" fabric, all sizes:

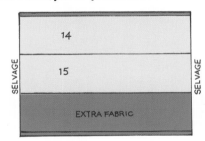

For Upper Skirt, for 45" or 60" fabric, all sizes:

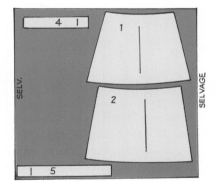

CUTTING DIAGRAMS

For Pleats, for 60" fabric, all sizes:

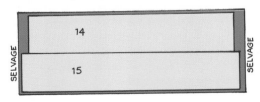

For Pleats, for 54"/55" fabric, all sizes:

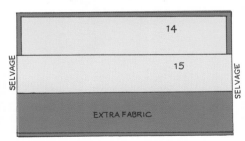

Assembly

1 Pin and cut out the Front and Back on the B3 cutting lines. Pin and cut out Front Waistband A if adding darts or Front Waistband B if not adding darts. Pin and cut out the Back Waistband. If applying darts, mark the darts on the wrong side of the Front.

2 If you choose to add darts, stitch them following the instructions on page 83.

3 Follow the instructions on pages 84 and 85 to apply the Front and Back Waistbands.

4 Stitch ½" side seams.

5 On the bias, cut out 2¼"-wide fabric strips. The total finished length needs to be the circumference of the lower skirt plus 2". If necessary, stitch together pieces to obtain the correct length. Cut the ends of the strips at a 45-degree angle. With right sides together, pin and stitch ¼" seams as shown.

Press open the ¼" seam allowances. When you have the needed length, with wrong sides together, fold the strip in half lengthwise, aligning the raw edges, and press it.

6 Press under one short end of the bias trim ½". Place the folded edge at one side seam and align the raw edges with the lower edge of the skirt. Pin around the entire skirt.

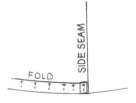

When you reach the pressed-under short end again, extend the trim ½" beyond it and cut the excess. Stitch ⅝" from the raw edge of the lower skirt.

Do not trim the lower edge of the skirt at this point.

7 If you are using a 60" fabric, you will be able to cut out the Front and Back Pleat pieces across the width of the fabric without seaming. Skip to Step 9. For 54"/55" fabric you will be able to cut out all the sizes of the Front Pleat without seaming. You may need to add additional fabric to the width for the Back Pleat. If using 44"/45" fabric, you will need to obtain the necessary length of Front and Back Pleat pattern pieces by stitching two pieces of fabric together.

8 To create a long-enough Pleat from 44"/45" or 54"/55" fabric, press the fabric flat and place it wrong side up on a table. Pin the Pleat pattern piece across it, aligning the edge of the pattern piece with the selvage. Cut across the upper and lower edges of the pattern piece. Measure the fabric piece you have cut and determine how many more inches you need to reach the length of the pattern piece. Add 1" to this number. Below the first cutting, pin the pattern piece again for a guide and cut an additional piece the length you need. With right sides together, pin one of the short ends of the long piece to one of the short ends of the smaller piece. If you have a one-way print on your fabric, be sure both pieces are pinned together with the print going in the same direction. Stitch a ½" seam. Press open the seam allowance. Proceed with the given directions.

9 If necessary, repin the Front Pleat pattern piece to the wrong side of the fabric. Using chalk and the clear ruler, carefully transfer the pleat markings to the fabric, or else cut small notches along the top edge of the Pleat at the markings.

10 Fold the Pleat in the direction of the arrows, aligning the solid lines.

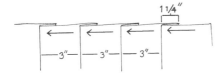

Pin. Baste across the top of all nine pleats.

Press lightly.

11 If necessary, repin the Back Pleat pattern piece to the wrong side of the fabric. Using chalk and the clear ruler, carefully transfer the pleat markings to the fabric or else cut small notches along the top edge of the Pleat at the markings.

12 Fold the Pleat in the direction of the arrows, aligning the solid lines. Pin. Baste across the top of all nine pleats. Press lightly.

13 With right sides together, pin the completed Front Pleat band to the completed Back Pleat band. Stitch a ½" seam allowance.

Press open the seam allowance.

14 Finish the lower edge of the pleated band. Press under a 1" hem. Machine- or hand-stitch to secure it.

15 With right sides together, pin the raw edge of the pleated band to the lower edge of the upper skirt over the bias trim, aligning the side seams. Be certain to place the Front Pleats on the skirt Front and the Back Pleats on the skirt Back—they are different widths. If you need to make a slight adjustment for fit, take out the basting on a pleat or two and make said pleats smaller or larger as necessary. Stitch a ⅝" seam.

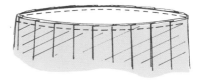

Trim and finish the seam allowance. Press the seam allowance upward and the bias trim down. Press the pleats from top to bottom.

16 With a needle and a single thread, tack the bias trim together on the side seam where the ends meet.

STYLE SECRET

Pleats add so much fun to a skirt. Even more fun? Find a fabric pattern that includes a border design along the selvage, and then cut the pattern piece out along the selvage so that you can incorporate the border design along the hem of the pleat.

"Personality, individuality, distinctiveness, name it what you will, is recognized today as the virtue of virtues in dress, and may always be had at a price. But the woman whose dress allowance is limited, may also wear distinctive clothes."

—Laura McFarlane, the Woman's Institute's *Fashion Service* magazine, 1930

MAKE YOUR OWN MAGIC

✂ All in the details: Use plaid yardage for the trim—when cut on the bias, it will add a whimsical diagonal graphic to the skirt.

✂ For a breezy summer look, use a semisheer fabric for the pleat panel to infuse the skirt with a touch of ethereality.

✂ Fashion the Betsy in black with a dreamy diaphanous pleat of silk chiffon for an enchanting evening design.

✂ Omit Steps 5 and 6 to construct the skirt without the bias trim for uninterrupted visual lines.

✂ Play with proportions. Create a high-spirited skirt with a plucky shortened pleat beneath a petite wisp of a bias trim in an eye-popping color like raspberry or eggplant.

✂ Nail that job interview in a skirt fashioned in tweed, with a slightly longer pleat, and a wider bias trim of the same fabric.

✂ Select a fabric like cotton eyelet or reembroidered cotton lace that incorporates both design and texture to fashion the skirt.

← Channel your inner librarian by using a print corduroy.

Metallic fabrics are sleek, sophisticated, and make a bold statement. →

A slubbed linen adds visual interest and texture beyond the pleated hem. →

6 Suggested Fabrics *for the* Betsy Skirt

← The pleat gets particular attention when you add a sheen with satin!

A skirt made with a neutral winter wool works with *everything*. →

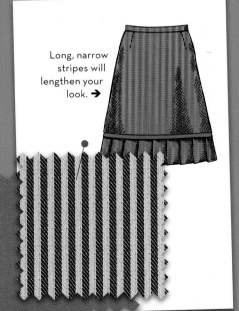

Long, narrow stripes will lengthen your look. →

FTW:
WEEKEND-
WORTHY
AND WORK
APPROPRIATE

Model
height:
5'9"

The Bridget

With the combination of the pencil and wrap skirt details, the Bridget is a classic silhouette for the classic girl. Any cotton print makes the simple silhouette a statement piece, and the pattern can easily transition into basic woven wools, too, for a polished business-casual look. For a bit of a handmade feel, sew a simple running stitch in contrasting embroidery floss down the front panel.

FABRIC AND NOTIONS

- 1¼ yards 45" fabric (Sizes S, M), 1¾ yards 45" fabric (Size L), 1⅞ yards 45" fabric (Sizes XL, XXL); or 1¼ yards 60" fabric (All sizes)
- Thread to match fabric
- Serger thread if applicable
- ⅔ yard of ¾" elastic
- 1" strip of fusible interfacing for Front Waistband (optional)

TOOLS

- Straight pins
- Scissors
- Tailor's chalk or fabric-marking pencil
- Clear ruler
- Large safety pin
- Hand-stitching needle

MACHINE(S)

- Standard sewing machine with needle appropriate to fabric choice
- Serger (optional)

APPROXIMATE MEASUREMENTS OF FINISHED GARMENT

	Small	Medium	Large	XL	XXL
Hip measurement	42½"	44"	45½"	47½"	49½"
Waist measurement (without being stretched, with darts)	26½"	28"	29½"	31½"	33½"
Waist measurement (without being stretched, without darts)	28½"	30"	31½"	33½"	35½"

Approximate finished length of skirt: 23½" with 2¼" hem

"A skirt that is to serve many purposes and is worn with a variety of blouses or sweaters must of necessity, be of a design, fabric, and trimming that will harmonize with each."

—Mary Brooks Picken, 1923

PATTERN PIECES USED

- B4 Front Yoke—10
- B4 Back Yoke—11
- B4 Front—12
- B4 Back—13
- Front Waistband A or B—4
- Back Waistband—5

CUTTING DIAGRAMS

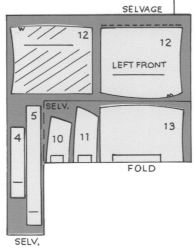

For 45" fabric, sizes S, M:

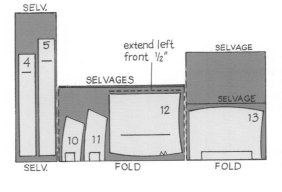

For 45" fabric, sizes L, XL, XXL:

(Continued on next page)

For 60" fabric, all sizes:

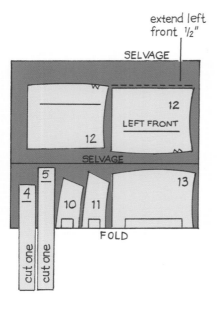

extend left front ½"

SELVAGE

LEFT FRONT

12

12

SELVAGE

5

4

13

10   11

cut one   cut one

FOLD

Assembly

1 Pin and cut out the Right B4 Front and B4 Back. Pin and cut out the B4 Front Yoke, B4 Back Yoke, Front Waistband, and Back Waistband. Cut out Front Waistband A if adding darts and Front Waistband B if not adding darts. Pin the left B4 Front and, using chalk and the clear ruler, draw a vertical line ½" beyond the unnotched front edge of the pattern piece, as shown.

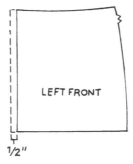

LEFT FRONT

½"

Cut the Left B4 Front on this drawn line.

2 If applying darts to the Front Yoke, mark the darts on the wrong side of the fabric and stitch, following the instructions on page 83.

3 Follow the instructions on pages 84 and 85 to apply the Front and Back Waistbands to the Front and Back Yokes.

4 Stitch ½" side seams.

5 With right sides together, pin the Right and Left Fronts to the Back on the notched side edges. Stitch a ½" seam.

Press open the seam allowances. Finish the lower edge of the skirt.

6 To form the facing, turn the lower edge of the Left Front to the right side 2". Stitch straight across the facing 2¼" above the lower edge.

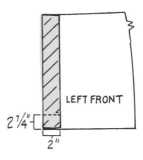

LEFT FRONT

2¼"

2"

Trim as shown.

Turn the facing to the wrong side. Press and baste together the upper edge of the facing and the Left Front.

7 Then turn the lower edge of the Right Front to the right side 1¼".

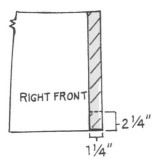

Stitch straight across the facing 2¼" above the lower edge. Trim as shown.

Turn the facing to the wrong side. Press and baste together the upper edge of the facing and the Right Front.

8 Press under a 2¼" hem around the skirt and pin. Hand-stitch to secure it.

9 With right sides together, pin the skirt to the lower edge of the completed Yoke, aligning the side seams and the raw edges. Pin the Left Front onto the Front Yoke first,

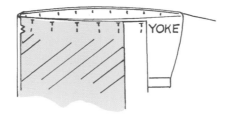

and then wrap the Right Front over it and pin again.

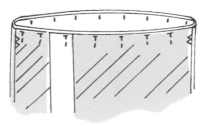

Stitch.

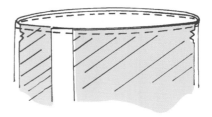

Press open the seam allowance.

"And so, if midwinter finds your wardrobe somewhat depleted, perhaps a separate skirt will prove just what is needed to provide the variety you desire."

—Mary Brooks Picken's *Inspiration* newsletter, 1921

SIMPLE SEAMS SO YOUR LOOK IS SEAMLESS.

Model height: 5'9"

B4 VARIATION

Salvage a couple of pairs of men's trousers from the local thrift store (or closet!) for this skirt. The subtle craftsmanship inherent in men's suiting material will come across as polished and professional.

FABRIC AND NOTIONS

- For Yoke, Front Waistband, and Back Waistband: 1 pair men's trousers (All sizes)
- For Right Front: 1 pair men's trousers (All sizes)
- For Left Front and skirt Back: ⅔ yard 45" fabric (Sizes S, M), 1⅓ yards 45" fabric (Sizes L, XL, XXL); or ⅔ yard 60" fabric (All sizes)
- Thread to match fabric
- Serger thread if applicable
- ⅔ yard ¾" elastic
- 1" strip of fusible interfacing for Front Waistband (optional)

TOOLS

- Scissors
- Seam ripper
- Straight pins
- Tailor's chalk or fabric-marking pencil
- Clear ruler
- Large safety pin
- Hand-stitching needle

MACHINE(S)

- Standard sewing machine with needle appropriate to fabric choice
- Serger (optional)

APPROXIMATE MEASUREMENTS OF FINISHED GARMENT

	Small	Medium	Large	XL	XXL
Hip measurement	42½"	44"	45½"	47½"	49½"
Waist measurement (without being stretched, with darts)	26½"	28"	29½"	31½"	33½"
Waist measurement (without being stretched, without darts)	28½"	30"	31½"	33½"	35½"

Approximate finished length of skirt: 23½" with 2¼" hem

PATTERN PIECES USED

- B4 Front Yoke—10
- B4 Back Yoke—11
- B4 Front—12
- B4 Back—13
- Front Waistband A or B—4
- Back Waistband—5

CUTTING DIAGRAMS

For 45" fabric, sizes S, M:

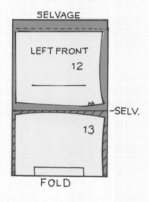

For deconstructed men's trousers, all sizes:

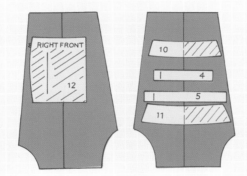

For 45" fabric, sizes L, XL, XXL:

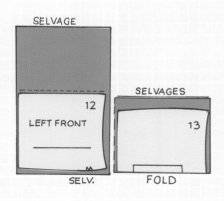

For 60" fabric, all sizes:

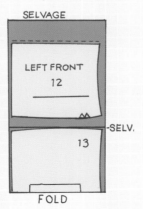

Trouser Deconstruction

1 Cut off the waistband of the trousers.

2 Cut next to the center seam from front to back, around the zipper, separating the trousers into two sections.

3 Remove the hems of the trousers with the seam ripper. Cut close to the interior leg seam or use the seam ripper to remove the stitching of the inner leg. Leave the side seam intact.

4 Press the leg as flat as possible. It is sometimes helpful to make an approximately 6" cut down from the upper edge in the center.

STYLE SECRET

Accessories are the final pieces of the design puzzle. Add a traditional, vintage, or funky necklace; tailored or soft blouse; boots, sandals, or heels; or a unique belt, and a simple skirt can take on a whole new look.

Assembly

1 From a leg of the first pair of trousers, pin and cut out the Right B4 Front, placing the pattern piece over the seam in the leg. If your pattern piece does not fit on one opened out trouser leg, cut fabric from the second leg and piece as necessary to achieve the required width.

2 From a leg (or more) of a second pair of trousers, pin and cut out the B4 Front Yoke, B4 Back Yoke, Front Waistband, and Back Waistband. Pin and cut out Front Waistband A if adding darts and Front Waistband B if not adding darts. Center the Front and Back Waistbands over the side seam of a trouser leg if possible. Center the Front and Back Yokes over the side seam of a trouser leg.

"Would I do better to hold to plain colors or to tan or gray, which are at present evidencing so much smartness even though they are conservative by nature?"

—Alwida Fellows, in Mary Brooks Picken's *Inspiration* newsletter, 1923

3 From the fabric yardage pin and cut out the B4 Back. From the fabric yardage, pin the Left B4 Front and, using chalk and the clear ruler, draw a vertical line ½" beyond the unnotched front edge of the pattern piece as shown.

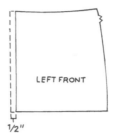

LEFT FRONT

½"

Cut the Left B4 Front on this drawn line.

4 If applying darts, mark the darts on the wrong side of the Front Yoke fabric and stitch, following the instructions on page 83.

5 Follow the instructions on pages 84 and 85 to apply the Front and Back Waistbands to the Front and Back Yokes.

6 Stitch ½" side seams.

7 With right sides together, pin the Right and Left Fronts to the Back on the notched side edges. Stitch a ½" seam.

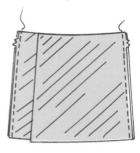

Press open the seam allowances. Finish the lower edge of the skirt.

8 To form the facing, turn the lower edge of the Left Front to the right side 2". Stitch straight across the facing 2¼" above the lower edge.

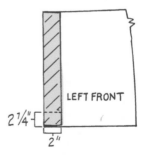

LEFT FRONT

2¼"

2"

Trim as shown.

Turn the facing to the wrong side. Press and baste together the upper edge of the facing and the Left Front.

9 Then turn the lower edge of the Right Front to the right side 1¼".

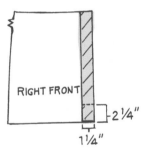

RIGHT FRONT

2¼"

1¼"

Stitch straight across the facing 2¼" above the lower edge. Trim as shown.

Turn the facing to the wrong side. Press and baste together the upper edge of the facing and the Right Front.

10 Press under a 2¼" hem around the skirt and pin. Hand-stitch to secure it.

11 With right sides together, pin the skirt to the lower edge of the completed Yoke, aligning the side seams and the raw edges. Pin the Left Front onto the Front Yoke first,

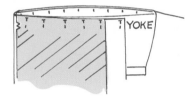

YOKE

and then wrap the Right Front over it and pin again.

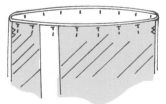

Stitch, then press open the seam allowance.

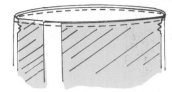

MAKE YOUR OWN MAGIC

✂ Use contrasting embroidery floss to add a running stitch to the front edge of the Left Front of the skirt.

✂ Construct in bright cottons for a spring and summer look.

✂ A pencil skirt is the perfect tailored skirt. Made in solid black it may seem simple, but it's a classic and will go with everything. Or, for a creative twist, cut just the Right Front panel from a coordinating print.

← An Asian print silk complements the structured silhouette of the skirt.

A plaid wool skirt and boots are the perfect fall uniform. →

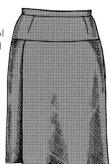

The richness of a neutral velvet adds a dressy vibe. →

6 Suggested Fabrics *for the* Bridget Skirt

← All dressed up in brocade, this skirt could be perfect for a wedding or a night on the town!

A classic denim skirt offers *tons* of coordinating options. →

A ticking stripe cotton lends a casual element to the basic skirt. →

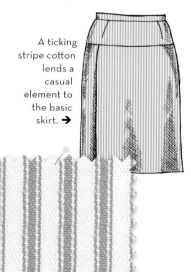

The Billie

The girl wearing the Billie skirt is the girl you wish were your own personal stylist—no detail ever escapes her. The easiest way to grant that wish? Make the skirt yourself and be that girl! This knee-length bias-cut number is featured with front darts for a slimming silhouette, while the charm of the bright linen/cotton blend shown here is unmistakable.

LIGHT AND SWINGY FOR ALL OCCASIONS!

Model height 5'8"

FABRIC AND NOTIONS

- 1⅞ yards fabric, any width (Sizes S, M, L), 2 yards fabric any width (Sizes XL, XXL)
- Thread to match fabric
- Serger thread if applicable
- ⅔ yard ¾" elastic
- 1" strip of fusible interfacing for Front Waistband (optional)

TOOLS

- Straight pins
- Scissors
- Tailor's chalk or fabric-marking pencil
- Clear ruler
- Yardstick
- Large safety pin
- Hand-stitching needle

MACHINE(S)

- Standard sewing machine with needle appropriate to fabric choice
- Serger (optional)

APPROXIMATE MEASUREMENTS OF FINISHED GARMENT

	Small	Medium	Large	XL	XXL
Hip measurement	44½"	46"	47½"	49½"	51½"
Waist measurement (without being stretched, with darts)	26½"	28"	29½"	31½"	33½"
Waist measurement (without being stretched, without darts)	28½"	30"	31½"	33½"	35½"

Approximate finished length of skirt: 21⅛" with 1¼" hem

PATTERN PIECES USED

- B1/B3/B5 Front (traced and cut on the B5 cutting line)—1
- B1/B3/B5 Back (traced and cut on the B5 cutting line)—2
- Front Waistband A or B—4
- Back Waistband—5

CUTTING DIAGRAMS

For 45" or 60" fabric, all sizes:

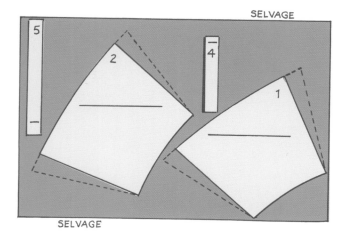

Assembly

1 Lay the B1/B3/B5 Front and Back pattern pieces on the wrong side of the fabric, aligning the diagonal grainlines so they are parallel with the selvages of the fabric. Pin.

2 Pin and cut out Front Waistband A if adding darts or Front Waistband B if not adding darts. Pin and cut out the Back Waistband.

3 Using chalk and a clear ruler, make a small mark on both sides of the Front and Back pieces that is ⅝" below the upper corners.

4 Align the long edge of the ruler with the lower edge of the skirt and one of the lines of the ruler with the side edge of the skirt. Using chalk, draw a line 4" long out from the lower corners of the Front and Back. From this point, use the yardstick to draw a line straight up to the mark you made beneath the upper corners.

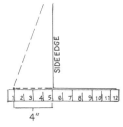

Cut out the fabric on these drawn lines.

5 Finish the side edges of the Front and Back.

6 If desired, mark the darts on the wrong side of the Front and stitch following the instructions on page 83.

7 Follow the instructions on pages 84 and 85 to apply the Front and Back Waistbands.

8 Stitch ½" side seams.

9 Finish the lower edge of the skirt. Press under a 1¼" hem and pin. Hand-stitch to secure it.

"It is always well to remember, too, that materials with glossy, brilliant surface or finish, no matter what the color of the fabric may be, are difficult to wear and not generally becoming . . . whereas materials of a soft finish or dull colors will make the figure appear smaller and attract less attention."

—Mary Brooks Picken, c. 1920s

MAKE YOUR OWN MAGIC

✂ This simple skirt will be a favorite and should be made in multiple colors! The bias cut makes it hang beautifully and fabrics like Tencel or wool crepe would be great options.

✂ The fluidity of this bias skirt can be enhanced if cut longer and sewn from sheer fabric with an attached bias lining.

← A summer skirt in blue and white cotton has you ready for a Fourth of July barbecue.

A bold velvet print lends drama and weight to the simple swing of the skirt. →

Colored denim is modern and playful. →

6 Suggested Fabrics *for the* Billie Skirt

← A brown corduroy skirt is a fashion must-have for back to school.

Use flannel, a material traditionally reserved for pajamas, to keep cozy in the cold. →

Any linen—solid or printed—drapes beautifully in this skirt pattern. →

REPURPOSED LOOK

The Bernadette

This is no boring pair of cutoffs, nor is this your classic jean skirt—with a raw-edged asymmetric ruffle, this repurposed denim mini is a piece to be envied. It's a hardworking skirt (after all, it's already served a lifetime as a pair of jeans!) to wear on your next adventure, whether you're hiking a waterfall or hitting up a backyard barbecue. It strikes the right balance of relaxed (the deconstructed ruffle that's playful while saying no frills) and structure for the classic work-hard, play-hard woman who finds joy in switching up her routine.

THE DENIM SKIRT IS TIMELESS.

Model height: 5'6"

FABRIC AND NOTIONS

NOTE: Larger sizes of jeans will be easier to work with and give you more workable fabric.

To construct from jeans:
- 2 pairs of denim jeans (cotton, with little or no added spandex)
- Thread to match denim

To construct from fabric yardage:
- 1 yard 45" fabric (Sizes S, M), 1¼ yards 45" fabric (Sizes L, XL, XXL); or 1 yard 60" fabric (All sizes). This will allow enough fabric to add hem allowances if desired.
- Thread to match fabric
- Serger thread (optional)
- ⅔ yard of ¾" elastic

TOOLS

- Scissors
- Seam ripper (not necessary if using fabric yardage)
- Straight pins
- Tailor's chalk or fabric-marking pencil
- Clear ruler or seam gauge
- Large safety pin
- Hand-stitching needle

MACHINE(S)

- Standard sewing machine with denim needle or needle appropriate to fabric choice
- Serger (optional)

APPROXIMATE MEASUREMENTS OF FINISHED GARMENT

	Small	Medium	Large	XL	XXL
Hip measurement	42½"	44"	45½"	47½"	49½"
Waist measurement (without being stretched, without darts)	28½"	30"	31½"	33½"	35½"

Approximate finished length of skirt: 13"

PATTERN PIECES USED

• B6 Front—6

• B6 Side Front—7

• B6 Back—8

• B6 Side Back—9

• Front Waistband B—4

• Back Waistband—5

CUTTING DIAGRAMS

For deconstructed denim jeans, all sizes:

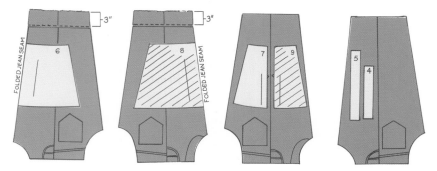

For 45" fabric, sizes S, M:

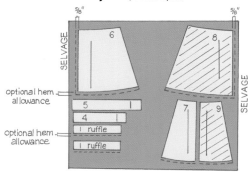

For 45" fabric, sizes L, XL, XXL:

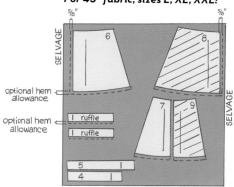

For 60" fabric, all sizes:

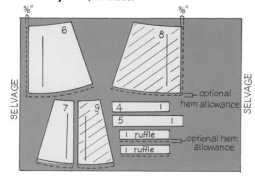

Jean Deconstruction

1 Cut off the waistband of the jeans beneath the belt loops.

2 Cut next to the center seam from front to back, around the zipper, separating the jeans into two sections.

3 Using the seam ripper, remove the stitching from the double seam of both legs. On some jeans this is the inner leg seam and on some it is the side seam. Leave the single seam intact. Remove the hem stitching from both jean legs using the seam ripper. Press the folded hemmed fabric flat. Using a clear ruler, measure up 3" from the lower edge of the jean leg after you have removed the hem and mark it with chalk. Then draw a line across the leg at the marking. Cut straight across the line on both legs and set aside these hem pieces for use as a ruffle.

4 Press the legs as flat as possible but leave the fold of the double seam.

5 Repeat the process on the second pair of jeans to obtain the needed fabric for the skirt. There's no need to cut the hems from the second pair.

Cutting Out Pattern Pieces

If using fabric yardage to construct Bernadette, draw a line ⅝" beyond the front edge of B6 Front and B6 Back on the wrong side of the fabric. Press under this edge ⅝" to mimic the folded edge of the jean legs used in the instructions. Add extra length to the Front, Side Front, Back, and Side Back pattern pieces for the hem allowance if you wish to hem your skirt instead of leaving a raw edge. For the ruffle, cut out two strips of fabric measuring 3" × 15" for a raw edged look. To add a ⅜" hem to the visible edge of ruffle, cut your strips 3⅜" × 15". After stitching the short ends of the two ruffle sections together in Step 2, press under a ⅜" hem on one long edge and machine stitch to secure. Proceed with the remainder of the instructions as written.

1 Place your jean legs from the first pair of jeans on a table with the hem edge up. The leg with the folded double seam on the left will be used for the skirt Front. The leg with the folded double seam on the right will be used for the skirt Back.

2 Position the B6 Front pattern piece with the marked edge on the fold of the leg as shown. Straighten the leg as much as possible to align it with the pattern piece. Pin it and cut it out. Set aside.

3 Position the B6 Back pattern piece (facedown) with the marked edge on the fold of the leg as shown. Straighten the leg as much as possible to align it with the pattern piece. Pin it and cut it out. Set aside.

4 Place a leg from the second pair of jeans on the table with the hem side up. Pin the B6 Side Front piece to one side of the seam on the leg. Cut it out. Pin the B6 Side Back piece (facedown) to the opposite side of the seam on the leg. Cut it out. Mark the notches on both pieces.

5 Use the remaining leg from the second pair of jeans to pin and cut out the Back Waistband and Front Waistband B.

STYLE SECRET

If you are using denim to make a skirt and are leaving the edges unhemmed, wash and dry it to give it a more natural-looking edge.

Assembly

NOTE: Do not add front darts to this skirt.

1 On the wrong side of the large Front piece, using chalk and the clear ruler, draw a vertical line 1" from the folded edge.

On the wrong side of the large Back piece, draw a vertical line 1" from the folded edge.

2 With right sides together, pin the short ends of the two 3"-wide hem sections together, being sure that the cut ends are on one side and the frayed hem ends are on the other. Stitch a ¼" seam.

Press open the seam allowance. Machine-baste a scant 1" from the cut edge, ceasing basting at the seams and renewing basting just beyond the seams. Baste again ¼" inside the first stitching in the same manner.

Pull up the basting threads to gather and to fit exactly the length of the folded edge of the Front. Trim excess length from the ruffle if necessary so that it is flush with the lower edge of the skirt Front. Tie off the basting threads to secure. Press the ruffle to flatten it somewhat.

3 With the right side up, slide the basted edge of the ruffle under the folded edge of the large Front piece, aligning the cut, basted edge of the ruffle with the drawn line. (Turn the pieces wrong side up to check for correct alignment.)

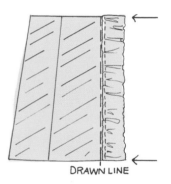

Pin the ruffle to the front on the right side through the folded edge. There should be two parallel stitching lines visible on the fold where the original stitching was removed. Stitch through the inner of these two lines to attach the ruffle.

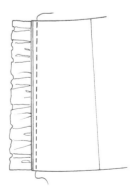

Trim the seam allowance of the ruffle close to the stitching. With the right side up, slide the single notched edge of the Side Front piece under the fold of the large Front piece and align the notched edge with the drawn line. (Turn the pieces wrong side up to check for correct alignment.)

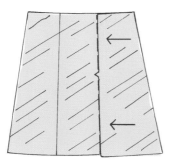

Pin on the right side of the Front through the folded edge. Stitch through the outer stitching line on the folded edge. Baste the upper edge of the ruffle to the skirt, aligning the raw edges.

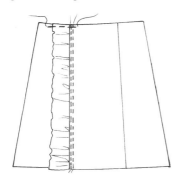

4 With the right side up, slide the single notched edge of the Side Back piece under the folded edge of the large Back piece, aligning the notched edge with the drawn line. (Turn pieces wrong side up to check for correct alignment.)

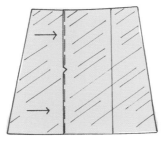

Pin on the right side of the Back through the folded edge. Stitch through the inner and outer stitching lines of the folded edge.

5 Follow the instructions on pages 84 and 85 to apply the Front and Back Waistbands.

6 Stitch ½" side seams.

7 Leave the lower edge of the skirt unfinished or, if desired, press under and hem it.

"Do not remodel a dress simply for the sake of using the material; rather, consider how well satisfied you will be with the result and whether you will get sufficient wear and enjoyment from the dress."

—Alwida Fellowes,
Mary Brooks Picken's
Inspiration newsletter, 1923

MAKE YOUR OWN MAGIC

✂ Use embroidery floss or pearl cotton to embellish the ruffle with a line or more of running stitches in a contrasting color.

✂ If you would like a longer skirt, follow the directions provided on page 29 for lengthening a garment. Be certain to add the identical length to all of the pieces and add the length at the same location, in the approximate center of the pattern piece. If you only want to add a hem allowance, you can add it to the lower edge of the pattern pieces.

✂ There are all colors of denim so for a change in color, punch it up with a selection from the rainbow—or go sleeker and more refined by using black denim.

✂ Give this skirt a new look by using recycled khakis. Tear strips from the pant legs for the asymmetric ruffle.

← A homespun woven fabric adds a textural element to the classic mini.

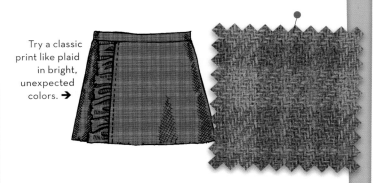
Try a classic print like plaid in bright, unexpected colors. →

↑ For fall fun, look for printed corduroys to wear over basic tights.

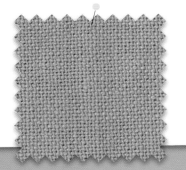

6 Suggested Fabrics *for the* Bernadette Skirt

↑ Don't restrict yourself to blue when it comes to denim—there's a whole rainbow (try teal)—and prints, too!

Don't overlook the home decor fabrics that add necessary structure to a garment. →

A seersucker skirt is made for backyard barbecues and summer picnics. →

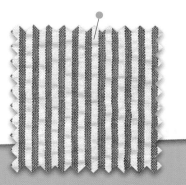

CHAPTER 4

The Dress

〰〰〰〰〰〰〰〰〰

MAGIC PATTERN C

C is for Cecelia, Camilla, Charlotte, Chloe, Catherine, Candace—and cute! This versatile pattern for a pullover garment goes from maxi to mini with a chop in the length. You can mix and match the details to make a one-of-a-kind number not even shown here! The neckline is gently gathered by elastic, self-fabric drawstring tie, or a buttoned fabric band that is pulled through a narrow casing. Depending on the dress, the casing is constructed by folding over the top edge of the garment to the inside and stitching, or by adding a separate bias-cut casing in the same or a contrasting fabric. Four styles include a short halter dress with a contrasting front panel as well as three others with a variety of raglan sleeves. All have an elegant A-line silhouette and range in length from maxi to mini. Each offers unique distinctive details. The two shirt styles fall to midhip. The first is a unique three-quarter-sleeve style constructed from repurposed men's dress shirts, accented with raw-edged fabric strips that have been folded, pinked, pleated, ruffled, and stitched to add texture and interest. The second is a lightweight, easy-to-wear shape with cap sleeves.

Meet the Family

Magic Pattern C Notes

✂ Please read thoroughly all directions for the pattern before you start cutting or sewing.

✂ All seams in the C patterns are ⅝" unless stated otherwise. There will be variations, so read carefully.

✂ The Magic Patterns are meant to be played with: If you prefer a sleeve from one look over the sleeve from another, or like the side vents on the Camilla dress but prefer the look of the Cecelia dress or the Catherine top, feel free to do some Frankenstein-style adaptations and create the garment that suits you. For example, try the Cecelia (Pattern C1), using the ruffled sleeve from Candace (Pattern C6); or try the Camilla (Pattern C2), using the cap sleeve from Catherine (Pattern C5); the gathered sleeve from the Camilla would also work well on the Candace dress.

✂ Lengthen the Catherine top to dress length and use fabric scraps to make a flower pin, using directions from the Candace dress. Very British!

"You'll be proud of your accomplishment. You've always wanted to make a dress all by yourself, haven't you? But you've been timid. Banish your fears."

—The Woman's Institute's *Fashion Service* magazine, 1929

MAGIC PATTERN PIECES C

In the cutting diagrams, each pattern piece is labeled with a number, and the key, with the corresponding number, is listed below. Be sure to refer to this list when laying out the pattern pieces on your fabric.

1. Front
2. Back
3. Sleeve
4. Belt
5. Pocket
6. Sleeve Facing
7. Cap Sleeve
8. Front Facing
9. Sleeve Band
10. C4 Front Panel
11. C3/C5 Front
12. C3/C5 Back
13. Ruffle
14. Denotes fabric for cutting bias strips as needed

Indicates wrong side of fabric

A DRESS WITH A POCKET EQUALS WARDROBE GOLD.

Model height: 5'8"

The Cecelia

This dress is the epitome of a perfectly composed outfit. It's the all-in-one—just slip it on and go. The curved hem on the three-quarter sleeves offers a special detail without being over the top, the side pocket is perfect for stashing your phone when you need to be hands-free, and the fabric belt pulls it all together.

FABRIC AND NOTIONS

- 3¼ yards 45" fabric (Sizes S, M), 3½ yards 45" fabric (Sizes L, XL, XXL); or 2¼ yards 60" fabric (Sizes S, M), 2½ yards 60" fabric (Sizes L, XL, XXL)
- Thread to match fabric
- Serger thread if applicable
- 1½ yards of ¼" elastic
- ¼ yard lightweight fusible interfacing for Sleeve Facing (optional)

TOOLS

- Straight pins
- Scissors
- Tailor's chalk or fabric-marking pencil
- Clear ruler or seam gauge
- Medium safety pin

MACHINE(S)

- Standard sewing machine with needle appropriate to fabric choice
- Serger (optional)

APPROXIMATE MEASUREMENTS OF FINISHED GARMENT

	Small	Medium	Large	XL	XXL
Bust measurement	39½"	42"	46"	50"	54"
Hip measurement	45¼"	48"	52"	56"	60"

Approximate length of finished garment (Size M) from center back neckline to lower edge: 33⅜" with 2¼" hem (Note: Neckline rests several inches below the base of the neck.)

PATTERN PIECES USED

- Front (traced and cut on the C1 cutting lines)—1
- Back (traced and cut on the C1 cutting lines)—2
- Sleeve (traced and cut on the C1 cutting lines)—3
- Sleeve Facing—6
- Pocket—5
- Belt—4

CUTTING DIAGRAMS

For 45" fabric, sizes S, M:

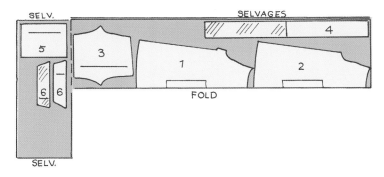

For 45" fabric, sizes L, XL, XXL:

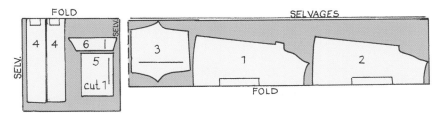

For 60" fabric, sizes S, M:

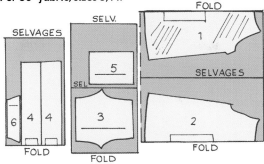

For 60" fabric, sizes L, XL, XXL:

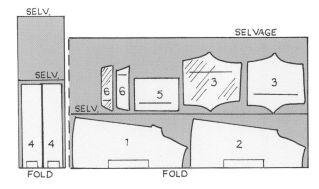

"Frocks-frocks-frocks. What woman doesn't want just that many pretty dresses for summer? Cool ginghams, colorful linens, filmy silks. A different dress for every day."

—The Woman's Institute's *Fashion Service* magazine, 1929

Assembly

1 Pin and cut out the Front, Back, Sleeve, Sleeve Facing, Pocket, and Belt. Mark the darts on the wrong side of the Front fabric. If desired, apply lightweight fusible interfacing to the wrong side of the Sleeve Facing fabric. Transfer the stitching lines of the Sleeve Facing pattern piece to the wrong side of the Sleeve Facing fabric. Using the guideline, mark the pocket placement on either the Right or Left Front.

2 Form the darts by folding the Front with right sides together, aligning the solid lines to the large dot. Pin. Begin at the side edge and stitch to the dot, stitching off the edge of the fold at the dot rather than backstitching.

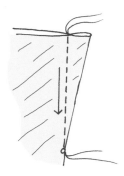

Cut the thread, leaving a few inches to tie off. Tie and trim the thread. Repeat to

form the second dart and press both darts down.

3 Finish all the edges of the Pocket. To form the facing, fold the upper edge of the pocket to the right side along the fold line and pin on the sides. Stitch ⅝" from the edge around the entire pocket, pivoting at the lower corners.

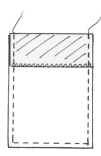

Trim the seam allowance of the facing only.

4 Turn the facing to the wrong side, gently pushing out the upper corners. Press the pocket edges under along the stitching below the facing.

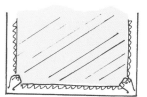

Fold the corners as shown. Topstitch across the pocket, 1½" below the upper edge. Topstitch again ¼" above the first stitching.

5 Place the pocket on the Right or Left Front, using the placement guide, and pin. (**NOTE:** The placement guide is for size small. For larger sizes, keep the lower edge of the Pocket on the guideline but move it so that the side of the Pocket is 1½" from the side edge of the Front.) Stitch close to the outer edge of the Pocket, pivoting at the corners and backstitching at the upper corners to secure it.

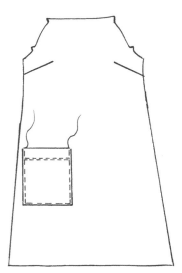

Topstitch again ¼" inside the first stitching.

6 With right sides together, pin the Front to the Back along the sides, aligning the notches and the raw edges. Stitch.

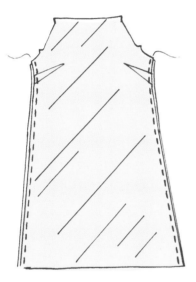

Press open the seam allowances.

7 With right sides together, pin and stitch the underarm seam of both Sleeves. Press the seam allowances open.

8 With right sides together, pin together and stitch the short edges of both Sleeve Facings. Press open the seam allowances. Finish the upper notched edge.

without interfacing

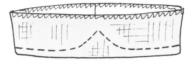

with interfacing

With right sides together and the Sleeve right side out, pin the unnotched edge of a Sleeve Facing to the lower edge of the Sleeve, aligning the seams and the raw edges. Stitch, following the stitching lines transferred to the wrong side of the Sleeve Facing. Trim the seam allowance to ¼", cutting around the curve. Clip the seam allowance to the point where the curves meet.

9 Turn the Sleeve Facing to the wrong side of the Sleeve (wrong sides facing) and press it. Align the seams and pin the finished edge of the facing around the sleeve. Machine-stitch through the finished edge of the facing.

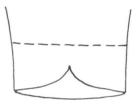

Repeat Steps 8 and 9 with the second Sleeve Facing and Sleeve.

10 With right sides together, matching the front and back notches and the underarm and side seams, pin and stitch the Sleeves to the dress. Clip the curves. Press the seam allowances toward the Sleeve.

STYLE SECRET

Batik cotton fabrics would work well for any of these dress patterns and they are available in wonderful colors and textures.

11 To form the elastic casing around the neck opening, press under ½" twice to the wrong side and pin. Stitch close to the inside folded edge, leaving a small opening at the center back for pulling through the elastic.

12 Attach a safety pin to one end of the elastic and pull it through the neckline casing. Adjust the length of the elastic to attain your desired fit. Overlap the elastic approximately 1" and cut off any remaining length. Stitch the ends of the elastic securely together.

Machine- or hand-stitch the opening in the casing to close it.

13 Finish the lower edge of the dress. Press under the desired hem and pin. Machine-stitch through the finished edge. Topstitch ¼" beneath the first stitching.

14 With right sides together, pin the notched ends of the two Belt pieces together. Stitch a ⅜" seam.

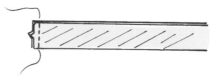

Press open the seam allowance. With right sides together, fold the Belt in half lengthwise, aligning the raw edges. Pin the long edges together. Stitch a ¼" seam, leaving an approximately 3" opening in the center.

Center the seam and press open the seam allowance.

Stitch across the short ends ¼" from edge.

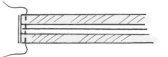

15 Turn the Belt right side out through the opening and press, gently pushing out the corners. Slipstitch the opening to close. Tie it around the waist of the dress.

MAKE YOUR OWN MAGIC

- Instead of tying your belt, shorten it and attach a new or vintage belt buckle.

- Remove length from the dress and wear it without a belt as a tunic.

- Use one cotton print for the main dress and a coordinating cotton print for the raglan sleeves, belt, and pocket.

← Thin cotton corduroy is a great fabric for seasonal transitions.

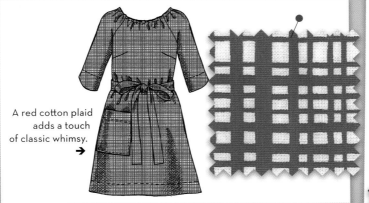

A red cotton plaid adds a touch of classic whimsy. →

A bold, Asian-inspired print is festive and light. →

6 Suggested Fabrics *for the* Cecelia Dress

← A sweet all-over floral is flirty and fun.

Satin sheen cotton dresses up your look while staying casual and comfortable—and easy to care for. →

Look for a midcentury-style cotton print to summon a retro vibe. →

THE EASY, BREEZY MAXI DRESS →

Model height: 5'10"

PATTERN C2

The Camilla

This maxi dress's graceful silhouette supports an active lifestyle (the side vent makes for easy mobility!), while its open drawstring neckline encourages unhurried comfort and relaxation. Belt the flowing fabric and pile on the wrist cuffs for a night of dining alfresco, or simply let a wavy, tousled mane be your only accessory for a day spent in the sun.

FABRIC AND NOTIONS

- 4⅓ yards 45" fabric (Sizes S, M), 4½ yards 45" fabric (Sizes L, XL, XXL); or 3¼ yards 60" fabric (Sizes S, M), 3⅓ yards 60" fabric (Sizes L, XL, XXL)
- Thread to match fabric
- Serger thread if applicable
- ¼ yard interfacing suitable for your fabric

TOOLS

- Straight pins
- Scissors
- Tailor's chalk or fabric-marking pencil
- Clear ruler or seam gauge
- Medium safety pin
- Hand-stitching needle

MACHINE(S)

- Standard sewing machine with needle appropriate to fabric choice
- Serger (optional)

APPROXIMATE MEASUREMENTS OF FINISHED GARMENT

	Small	Medium	Large	XL	XXL
Bust measurement	39½"	42"	46"	50"	54"
Hip measurement	45¼"	48"	52"	56"	60"

Approximate length of finished garment (Size M) from center back neckline to lower edge: 53¾" with 2" hem (Note: The neckline rests several inches below the base of the neck.)

PATTERN PIECES USED

- Front (traced and cut on the C2 cutting lines)—1
- Back (traced and cut on the C2 cutting lines)—2
- Sleeve (traced and cut on the C2 cutting lines)—3
- Sleeve Band—9
- Front Facing—8
- Fabric for cutting bias strips—14

CUTTING DIAGRAMS

For 45" fabric, all sizes:

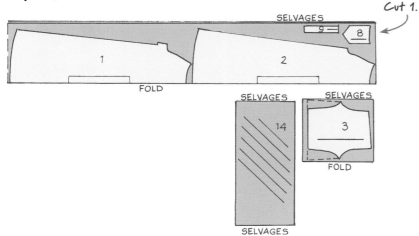

For 60" fabric, all sizes:

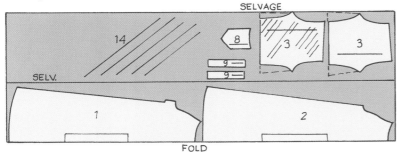

Assembly

NOTE: Step 1 instructions are for the C2 individual pattern. If you use Magic Pattern C to make C2, cut away 1" from the upper edge of the Front, the upper edge of the Back, and the upper edge of the Sleeves.

1 Pin and cut out the Front and Back. Mark the darts on the wrong side of the Front. To cut the Sleeves, pin the pattern piece on the wrong side of the fabric. Measure out 2" from both lower corners and mark them. Draw a line straight down from the lower point of the arm opening to these marks as shown. Cut out the Sleeves along these newly drawn lines.

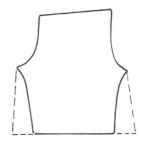

2 Form the darts by folding the Front with right sides together, aligning the solid lines to the large dot. Pin. Begin at the side edge and stitch to the dot, stitching off the edge of the fold at the dot rather than backstitching.

Cut the thread, leaving a few inches to tie off. Tie and trim the thread. Repeat to form the second dart, then press both darts down.

3 Fold the Front in half lengthwise to find the center. Press a light crease along the center beginning at the neck and ending just below the darts.

4 Transfer the stitching lines to the nonfusible side of the Front Facing interfacing piece. Trim ½" from the neck edge of the interfacing. Carefully cut away the interfacing along the dashed stitching lines as shown.

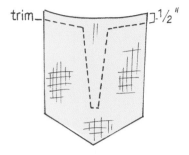

With lower edges aligned, fuse the interfacing to the wrong side of the Front Facing, following the manufacturer's directions. Transfer the solid, center line to the wrong side of the Front Facing fabric. Finish the outer edges of the facing, excluding the neck edge.

5 With right sides together, pin the neck edge of the Front Facing to the Front, aligning the centers and the neck edges. Beginning at the neck edge, stitch down and along the stitching lines just next to where the interfacing was cut away. Along the lower point of the V, make three stitches across, pivot, and stitch up the opposite side. After

stitching, cut straight down on the solid line, stopping just short of the stitching.

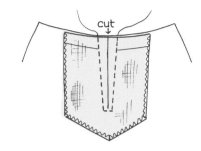

Trim the interior seam allowance to ⅛". Turn the Front Facing to the wrong side of the garment (wrong sides together). Press. Align the upper edges of the Front and the Front Facing, then pin and baste them together.

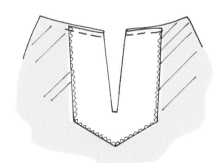

6 Finish side edges of the Front and Back with serging or zigzag stitching. With right sides together, pin the Front to the Back along the sides from the underarm to the large dot, aligning the notches and the raw edges. Stitch, leaving open below the large dot to form the vents. Backstitch at the large dot to secure.

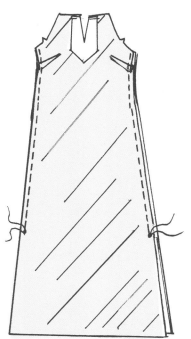

Press open the seam allowances, continuing to press under the seam allowance below the large dots.

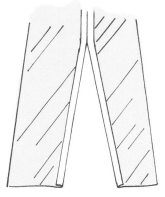

7 Fold the lower edge of the seam allowance to the right side and pin. Stitch across the seam allowance 2" above the lower edge.

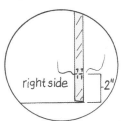

right side   2"

Repeat on remaining lower edges. Then turn the seam allowance to the wrong side and gently push out the corner. Press under a 2" hem even with the stitching. Pin the hem and seam allowance beneath the dots. Hand-stitch with invisible stitch to secure.

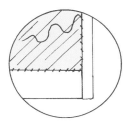

"Frocks this season are so pleasingly individual that, by such means as the placement and the type of fullness or the use of a single trimming detail, they express dignity, youth, simplicity, or ultra chic."

—The Woman's Institute's *Fashion Service* magazine, 1929

8 With right sides together, pin and stitch the underarm seam of both Sleeves. Press the seam allowances open. Turn the Sleeve right side out. Beginning at the underarm seam, machine-baste ½" from the lower edge of the Sleeve. Machine-baste again ¼" inside the first stitching.

Pull up the threads to gather. Set aside.

9 With right sides together, pin together the short ends of the Sleeve Band. Stitch. Press open the seam allowance. Press under the unnotched edge to the wrong side ¼". With right sides together and aligning the seams, pin the notched edge of the Sleeve Band to the lower edge of the Sleeve, pulling up the gathering threads to fit. Stitch.

Turn the Sleeve wrong side out. Fold the Sleeve Band to the inside so that the pressed-under edge of the Sleeve Band aligns with the connecting seam and press. Hand-stitch the pressed-under edge of the Sleeve Band to the seam allowance.

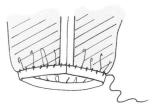

"So then, let us think for a while about dresses for a whole day—simple ones, for they are smartest, and stylish ones, for we must admit the importance of style."

—Clarice Carpenter,
the Woman's Institute's
Fashion Service magazine, 1925

10 With right sides together, matching the Front and Back notches and the underarm and side seams, pin and stitch the Sleeves to the dress. Clip the curves. Press the seam allowance toward the Sleeve.

11 Stay stitch the neck edge of the dress ⅜" from the edge.

12 To make the drawstring tie, cut a strip of fabric on the bias 1½" × 50". Piece the sections together if necessary to obtain the needed length (see page 27). With wrong sides together, fold the strip in half lengthwise and press a center crease. Fold the long edges in to meet the

center crease and press again. Fold them in half on the center crease again and pin the folded edges together. Stitch close to the folds. Set aside.

13 For the neck casing, cut a 2¼" × 50" strip of fabric on the bias. Piece as necessary to obtain the needed length (see page 27). Press under one long edge ¼" to the wrong side. Press under one short end ½". With right sides together, align this short end with the front edge of the dress V. The straight, unfolded edge of the casing should be aligned with the raw edge of the neck. Pin.

When you reach the opposite side, extend the casing ½" beyond the front edge and cut. Press under to the wrong side ½" and pin. Stitch a ½" seam.

Press upward, pressing the seam allowance toward the casing. Fold it up and over the neck edge of the dress. Place the fold just beyond the stitching line. Pin. Hand-stitch the casing to the seam allowance beneath.

14 Attach a safety pin to one end of the drawstring and pull it through the neckline casing. Tie a knot on both ends of the drawstring approximately 1" above the cut edge. Pull up the drawstring to gather the neckline to the desired fit and tie.

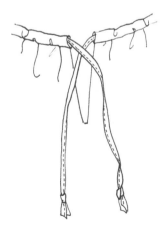

MAKE YOUR OWN MAGIC

✂ Forgo the Sleeve Band for a three-quarter-length bell Sleeve. Just add a narrow hem to the lower edge of the Sleeve.

✂ Construct the dress from cotton and use a contrasting cotton for the Front Facing, reversing the application so that the facing is on the outside. Stitch close to the outer edge of the facing to secure it to the Front.

✂ After pulling the drawstring through the casing, slide a bead onto each end of the drawstring and then tie knots to secure the beads.

← A maxi dress in chambray will quickly become a wardrobe staple.

A casual maxi dress goes elegant in an Asian-inspired cotton print fabric. →

Bright hues and fun prints will make this a stunning summer style. →

6 Suggested Fabrics *for the* Camilla Dress

←Take your maxi to the beach using feather-light voile.

Use a slightly heavier fabric, like light denim, for fall, perfect for pairing with cardigans and boots. →

A flowery voile is a well-suited companion to this soft, shapely silhouette. →

The Charlotte

The gal who wears the Charlotte shirt is practical with a hardworking, down-to-earth attitude. The crisp top is an excellent example of the combination of sweet and girlish (those ruffles!) and tomboyish—it's made from repurposed men's dress shirts. Just throwing on this casual but refined piece can make you feel calm and collected—perfect for a weekend evening spent lounging on the porch with a glass of iced tea.

A MEN'S DRESS SHIRT GETS A MAKEOVER!

FABRIC AND NOTIONS

- 3 or more men's cotton dress shirts (1 large enough to cut the Front, Back, and Sleeves; 1 for the neck casing, Sleeve Binding, and accents; 1 for contrasting accents). **NOTE:** The larger the shirt, the easier it is to cut the required pattern pieces. You may need to use more than one shirt for the main body of the XXL top—look for men's shirts of similar appearance and color that complement each other.

- Thread to match fabrics

- Serger thread, if applicable

- 1½ yards of ¼" elastic

TOOLS

- Scissors
- Seam ripper
- Straight pins
- Tailor's chalk or fabric-marking pencil
- Clear ruler
- Medium safety pin
- Pinking shears (optional)

MACHINE(S)

- Standard sewing machine with needle appropriate to fabric choice
- Serger (optional)

Model height: 5'8"

APPROXIMATE MEASUREMENTS OF FINISHED GARMENT

	Small	Medium	Large	XL	XXL
Bust measurement	39½"	42"	46"	50"	54"
Hip measurement	45¼"	48"	52"	56"	60"

Approximate length of finished garment (Size M) from center back neckline to lower edge: 23" with ¾" hem (Note: The neckline rests several inches below the base of the neck.)

"And finally, remember that very often the well-planned, made-over garment can have better style and smarter lines than it had when new."

—Mary Brooks Picken's *Inspiration* newsletter, 1924

PATTERN PIECES USED

- C3/C5 Front (traced and cut on the C3 cutting lines)—11
- C3/C5 Back (traced and cut on the C3 cutting lines)—12
- Sleeve (traced and cut on the C3 cutting lines)—3

CUTTING DIAGRAMS

For 45" fabric, all sizes:

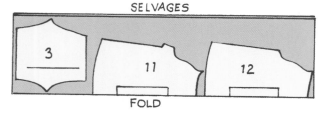

For 60" fabric, sizes S, M:

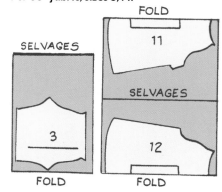

For 60" fabric, sizes L, XL, XXL:

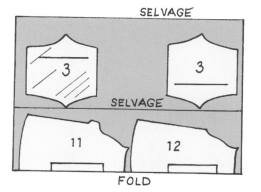

Indicates pattern piece facedown

Deconstruct Men's Dress Shirts

1 Use scissors to cut off the collar just beneath the collar band. Cut along the side seam to the sleeve and then cut around the sleeve next to the seam. Cut off the upper yoke next to the seam, separating the front and the back of the shirt.

2 Remove the cuffs on both sleeves, cutting just next to the seam.

3 With the seam ripper, remove the stitching of the underarm seam on both sleeves. With the seam ripper, carefully remove the pocket from the shirt front. It may be necessary to remove the stitching of the front button placket in order to cut out the front pieces with the added seam allowance. Tip: It is helpful to machine-wash and -dry the pieces at this point to remove any creases and the appearance of the holes left from removed stitching. Press all the pieces. Set aside two buttons from the shirt to stitch to the sleeves later.

Assembly

NOTES: The Front pattern piece is made to cut on the fold, but for this version from repurposed shirts, the two Front pieces will be cut from the shirt fronts and stitched together down the center. You must allow at least ¼" (preferably ⅜" or ½") beyond the center fold line of the pattern piece for a seam allowance. Also, the length you can make your shirt will vary depending on the men's shirt used. Adjust the length as needed.

If you use Magic Pattern C to make C3, remove 1" from the upper edge of the Sleeve pattern piece before cutting out the Sleeves or remove 1" from the upper edge of the Sleeves after cutting from the fabric. If you use the C3 individual pattern, use the Sleeve pattern piece as is. Contrasting binding will be cut and stitched to the shirt, serving as the elastic casing for the neckline.

1 From the first shirt, with right sides together, fold the shirt back fabric and pin and cut out the Back.

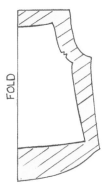

Cut out one Sleeve from the fabric of one shirt sleeve with the Sleeve pattern piece facing up.

Repeat on the remaining sleeve, placing the Sleeve pattern piece facedown on the fabric. Part of the shirt sleeve tab will be included on the lower part of the sleeve you cut. Cut out the one Front with the Front pattern piece facing up, from a shirt front. Cut at least ¼" beyond the fold line of the pattern piece to create a seam allowance.

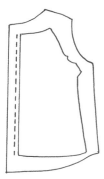

Repeat on the remaining shirt front, placing the Front pattern piece facedown on the fabric. Mark the darts on the wrong side of the Front pieces.

2 From the back fabric of shirt 2, cut out a bias strip 2¼" × 50" for the neck casing. If necessary, piece together shorter strips to achieve the required length.

Cut the ends of the bias strips diagonally at a 45-degree angle. Place the ends right sides together as shown, pin, and stitch a ¼" seam.

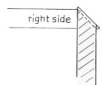

Press open the seam allowance. From the back fabric of shirt 2, cut two 2" × 16" bias strips to finish the lower sleeves.

3 Cut all accent strips on the bias as directed: From shirt 1, cut one strip that is approximately 20" × 1¼". You may piece it to attain this length but be sure both pieces are cut on the bias. From shirt 2, cut one strip that is 13⅝" × 1⅝" and two strips that are 10¼" × 1¾". From shirt 3, cut two strips that are 11½" × 1", two strips that are 22" × ¾", two strips that are 7½" × 1" and two strips that are 12" × ¾".

4 With right sides together, align the center front edges of the two Front pieces. Pin and stitch the seam allowance you added (½", ⅜", and so on).

Finish the seam allowance and either press to one side or press open.

5 Form the darts by folding the Front with right sides together, aligning the solid lines to the large dot. Pin. Begin at the side edge and stitch to the dot, stitching off the edge of the fold at the dot rather than backstitching. Cut the thread, leaving a few inches to tie off.

Tie and trim the thread. Repeat to form the second dart, then press both darts down.

6 Take the 13⅝" × 1⅝" strip from shirt 2 and fold it in half lengthwise. On one end, cut diagonally up from the fold to form a point. Open out the strip and pink the long edges and short diagonal edges if desired. Center this strip on the shirt front over the seam, aligning the straight short end with the neck edge. Pin and stitch ¼" in along both long edges.

7 Take the strip cut from shirt 1 and fold it in half lengthwise. On one end cut diagonally up from the fold to form a point. Open out the strip and machine-baste it down the center of the strip. Pull up the thread to gather slightly. Center this over the pinked strip with the point of the ruffle slightly above the point of the pinked strip. Align the short end with the neck edge. Adjust the gathers to fit. Pin down the center and stitch over the

basting stitches. Press the ruffle flat if desired.

8 Measure ⅜" over from the center strip on both sides and place the two strips from shirt 3 that are 11½" × 1". Align one short end with the neck edge and pin down the center. Stitch down the center of both. Take the two strips that are 22" × ¾" and beginning at the upper edge, measure down 1¼" and mark on the wrong side of the fabric. Continue making marks 1¼" apart. Fold the first mark down to meet the second and press. Fold the third mark down to meet the fourth and press. Continue until no more folds can be made. If desired, vary the depth of the folds for interest. With the folds downward and fabric right side up, align the short end of the strip with the neck edge of the garment, centered over the 11½" flat strips. Pin the folds in place and stitch down the center.

9 Take the two strips from shirt 2 that are 10¼" × 1¾" and pink both long edges. With wrong sides together, fold one long side of the strip over ¾" and press a crease. Position these strips ⅜" from the previously stitched strips and pin with the fold on the outside. Use a wide zigzag to stitch vertically through the folded strip.

"Not only does a successful make-over bring satisfaction to a woman's creative ability, and the joy of conquest to her keen intelligence, but it has a most pleasing reaction upon her sense of economy, for it is gratifying for any woman to be able to dress attractively at moderate cost."

—Mary Brooks Picken's *Inspiration* newsletter, 1924

10 Take the two strips from shirt 3 that are 7½" × 1" and fold them in half lengthwise. On one end cut diagonally up from the fold to form a point. Open out the strips. Position the strips ⅜" beyond the previously stitched strips. Align the flat short end with the neck edge of the garment. Pin down the center and stitch through the center of both strips. Take the remaining two strips from shirt 3 that are 12" × ¾" and fold them in half lengthwise. On one end, cut diagonally up from the fold to form a

point. Open out the strip and machine-baste down the center of the strips. Pull up the thread to gather slightly. Center this over the flat strip with the point slightly above. Align the short flat end with the neck edge. Adjust the gathers to fit. Pin down the center and stitch over the basting stitches. Press the ruffle flat if desired.

View of first layer of strips:

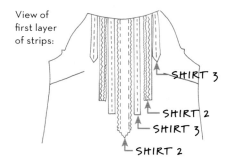

View with second layer of strips:

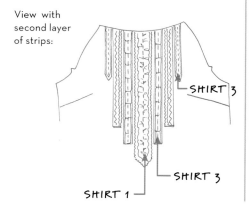

11 With right sides together, pin the Front to the Back along the sides, aligning the notches and the raw edges. Stitch. Press open the seam allowances.

12 With right sides together, pin and stitch the underarm seam of both Sleeves.

Press the seam allowances open.

13 Depending on the sleeve length of the shirt used, you may or may not have a portion of the sleeve cuff tab visible.

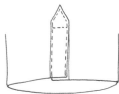

If you do not have any cuff tab visible, simply finish the lower edge, press under the desired hem, and machine-stitch to secure or finish with the bias tape as instructed below. If the cuff tab is visible on the front of the Sleeves (as displayed on the sample), finish it in the following manner: Make ½" double fold bias tape from the 2" × 16" strips of fabric cut from shirt 2, by folding each strip in half lengthwise with wrong sides together and pressing lightly. Press the outer edges in to meet the center crease and press again.

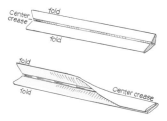

Fold it in half once again along the center crease and press. Alternatively, use a ½" bias tape maker to make the strips. Then open out one long edge of the tape and with right sides together, pin it to the raw edge of the Sleeve on the underside of the tab.

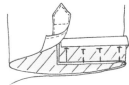

Pin around the Sleeve until you reach the edge of the Sleeve on top of the cuff tab. Extend the tape ½" beyond and cut. Press under this cut end ½" and pin to the edge of the Sleeve. Stitch ½" from the edge of the Sleeve.

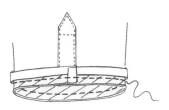

Trim the seam allowance slightly and press toward the tape. Fold the tape to the wrong side so that the fold extends slightly beyond the stitching line. Pin on the right side of the sleeve with the pins centered under the seam. Stitch in the ditch (see page 84, Step 5) to secure it.

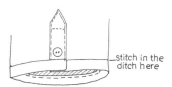

If desired, connect the upper and lower tab by centering and stitching one of the shirt buttons through both layers.

14 With right sides together, matching the Front and Back notches and the underarm and side seams, pin and stitch the Sleeves to the shirt. Clip the curves. Press the seam allowance toward the Sleeve.

15 For the neck casing, make bias tape from the 2¼" × 50" strip of fabric cut from shirt 2. Fold the strip in half lengthwise with wrong sides together and press lightly. Press the outer edges in to meet the center crease and press again. Fold it in half once again along the center crease and press.

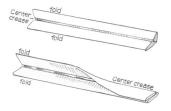

Open out one long edge of the tape and press under one short end ½". Place this pressed-under end at the center back, aligning the raw edge of the tape and the neck and pin. When you reach the beginning of the tape, extend beyond 1" and cut. Stitch ½" from the raw edge.

Trim the seam allowance slightly and press it toward the casing. Fold the casing up and over the neckline's raw edge and position the fold just beyond the stitching line. Pin on the right side of the garment, with the pins centered under the seam.

Stitch in the ditch (see page 84, Step 5) to secure it, leaving a small opening to insert the elastic.

16 Turn the garment inside out. Attach a safety pin to one end of the elastic and pull it through the opening in the neckline casing. Adjust the length of the elastic to attain the desired fit. Overlap the elastic approximately 1" and cut off any remaining length. Stitch the ends of the elastic securely together.

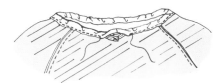

Machine- or hand-stitch the opening in the casing to close.

17 Finish the lower edge of the garment. Press under the desired hem and machine-stitch to secure it. The sample shown has a ¾" hem.

SHORTER SLEEVES= SUMMERTIME!

C3 VARIATION

Combine the cap sleeve of the Catherine (Pattern C5) with the bias strip detailing of the Charlotte. In the sample shown, the body of the top is linen and the contrasting strips are a solid and floral print voile.

FABRIC AND NOTIONS

- 1¾ yards 45" fabric (All sizes); or 1⅓ yards 60" fabric (Sizes S, M), 1⅝ yards 60" fabric (Sizes L, XL, XXL)
- ½ yard any width fabric, for accent strips fabric 1 (one strip 20" × 1¼", one strip 13⅝" × 1⅝", and two strips 10¼" × 1¾")
- ½ yard any width fabric, for accent strips fabric 2 (two strips 11½" × 1", two strips 22" × ¾", two strips 7½" × 1" and two strips 12" × ¾")
- Thread to match fabrics
- Serger thread, if applicable
- 1½ yards of ¼" elastic

TOOLS

- Straight pins
- Scissors
- Tailor's chalk or fabric-marking pencil
- Clear ruler
- Medium safety pin
- Pinking shears

MACHINE(S)

- Standard sewing machine with needle appropriate to fabric choice
- Serger (optional)

APPROXIMATE MEASUREMENTS OF FINISHED GARMENT

	Small	Medium	Large	XL	XXL
Bust measurement	39½"	42"	46"	50"	54"
Hip measurement	45½"	48"	52"	56"	60"

Approximate length of finished garment (Size M) when hemmed, from center back neckline to lower edge: 23" with ¾" hem (Note: The neckline rests several inches below the base of the neck.)

Model height: 5'8"

PATTERN PIECES USED

• C3/C5 Front (traced and cut on the C5 cutting lines)—11

• C3/C5 Back (traced and cut on the C5 cutting lines)—12

• Cap Sleeve—7

CUTTING DIAGRAMS

For 45" fabric, all sizes:

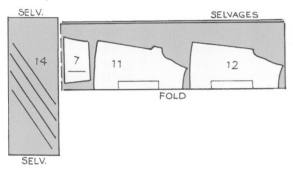

For 60" fabric, sizes L, XL, XXL:

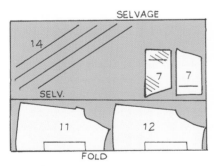

For 60" fabric, sizes S, M:

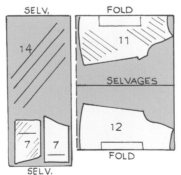

Assembly

1 Pin and cut out the Front, Back, and Cap Sleeve. Mark the darts on the wrong side of the Front.

2 Form the darts by folding the Front with right sides together and aligning the solid lines to the large dot. Pin. Begin at the side edge and stitch to the dot, stitching off the edge of the fold at the dot rather than backstitching.

Cut the thread, leaving a few inches to tie off. Tie and trim the thread. Repeat to form the second dart, then press both darts down.

3 Cut out all accent strips from fabric 1 and fabric 2 on the bias.

4 Take the 13⅝" × 1⅝" strip from fabric 1 and fold it in half lengthwise. On one end, cut diagonally up from the fold to form a point. Open out the strip and pink the long edges

and short diagonal edges if desired. Fold the shirt Front in half lengthwise to find the center and press a light crease. Center this pinked strip on the shirt Front over the crease, aligning the straight short end with the neck edge. Pin and stitch ¼" from both long edges.

5 Take the 20" × 1¼" strip cut from fabric 1 and fold it in half lengthwise. On one end cut diagonally up from the fold to form a point. Open out the strip and machine-baste it down the center of the strip. Pull up the thread to gather slightly. Center this over the pinked strip with the point of the ruffle slightly above the point of the pinked strip. Align the short end with the neck edge. Adjust the gathers to fit. Pin down the center and stitch over the basting stitches. Press the ruffle flat if desired.

6 Measure ⅜" over from the center strip on both sides and place the two strips from fabric 2 that are 11½" × 1". Align one short end with the neck edge and pin down the center. Stitch down the center of both. Take the two strips that are 22" × ¾" and, beginning at the upper edge, measure down 1¼" and mark on the wrong side of the fabric. Continue making marks 1¼" apart. Fold the first mark down to meet the second and press. Fold the third mark down to meet the fourth and press. Continue until no more folds can be made. If desired, vary the depth of the folds for interest. With the folds downward and fabric right side up, align the short end of the strip with the neck edge of the garment, centered over the 11½" flat strips. Pin the folds in place and stitch down the center.

7 Take the two strips from fabric 1 that are 10¼" × 1¾" and pink both long edges. With wrong sides together, fold one side of the strip over ¾" and press a crease. Position these strips ⅜" from the previously stitched strips and pin with the fold on the outside. Use a wide zigzag to stitch vertically through the folded strip.

8 Take the two strips from fabric 2 that are 7½" × 1" and fold them in half lengthwise. On one end, cut diagonally up from the fold to form a point. Position the strips ⅜" beyond the previously stitched strips. Align the flat short end with the neck edge of the garment. Pin down the center and stitch through the center of both strips. Take the remaining two strips from fabric 2 that are 12" × ¾" and fold them in half lengthwise. On one end, cut diagonally up from the fold to form a point. Open out the strip

and machine-baste down the center of the strips. Pull up the thread to gather slightly. Center this over the flat strip with the point slightly above. Align the short flat end with the neck edge. Adjust the gathers to fit. Pin down the center and stitch over the basting stitches. Press the ruffle flat if desired.

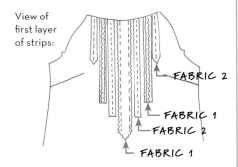

View of first layer of strips:

FABRIC 2
FABRIC 1
FABRIC 2
FABRIC 1

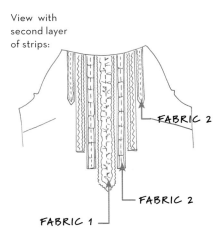

View with second layer of strips:

FABRIC 2
FABRIC 2
FABRIC 1

9 Finish the unnotched long edge of the Cap Sleeve. (The notch indicates the upper edge of the Cap Sleeve.) Press under a ⅝" hem, pin, and machine-stitch to secure it. With right sides together, pin the sleeve to the Front and Back with the single notched edge on the Front and the unnotched edge on the Back. Stitch. Do not trim the seam allowance yet.

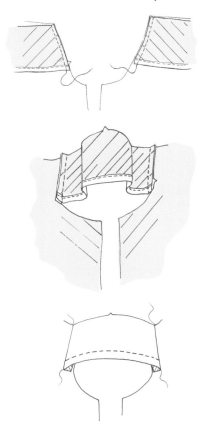

10 To form the bias binding for the lower arm opening, cut two 15" × 2" strips of fabric on the bias from the main shirt fabric. With wrong sides together, fold them in half lengthwise and press a light crease down the center. Fold the long edges in to meet the center crease and press again. Cut the 15" lengths in half to form four 7½" lengths. On one 7½" section, open out one long edge and press under one short edge ½". With right sides together, align the pressed-under short end exactly with the lower edge of the Cap Sleeve and the opened-out raw edge of the bias binding with the raw edge of the arm opening beneath the Sleeve. Pin. Stitch a ⅝" seam, stopping exactly at the lower edge of the Sleeve.

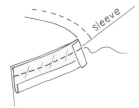

sleeve

Clip the seam allowance to the stitching between the Sleeve and the binding.

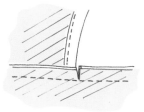

Trim and finish the seam allowance of the Sleeve. Trim slightly the seam allowance of the binding. Press the binding to the wrong side along the stitching and pin. Stitch close to the pressed fold.

Repeat this process on the remaining three arm edges.

MAKE YOUR OWN MAGIC

✂ For a simple top, leave off the embellishments and make Charlotte from fabric yardage, cutting the front piece on the fold of fabric.

✂ If you have a stash of treasured remnants, use them to cut out the bias strips used for the embellishments on the Front, mixing up patterns and textures.

11 With right sides together, pin the Front to the Back along the sides, aligning the notches and the raw edges. Stitch.

Press open seam allowances.

12 Finish the lower edge. Press under a ¾" hem, pin, and machine- or hand-stitch to secure it.

13 For the neck casing, make bias tape from a 2¼" × 50" strip of the main shirt fabric. Piece together if necessary to reach the required length. Fold the strip in half lengthwise with wrong sides together and press lightly. Press the outer edges in to meet the center crease and press again. Fold it in half once again along the center crease and press. Open out one long edge of the bias tape casing and press under one short end ½". Place this pressed-under end at the center back, aligning the raw edge of the bias tape casing with the neck, and pin. When

you reach the beginning, extend beyond 1" and cut. Stitch ½" from the raw edge.

Trim the seam allowance and press it toward the casing. Fold the casing up and over the neckline's raw edge and position the fold just beyond the stitching line. Pin on the right side of the garment, with pins centered under the seam. Stitch in the ditch (page 84, Step 5) to secure it, leaving a small opening to insert the elastic.

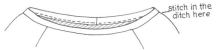

stitch in the ditch here

14 Attach a safety pin to one end of the elastic and pull it through the opening in the neckline casing. Adjust the length of the elastic to attain the desired fit. Overlap the elastic about 1" and cut off any remaining length. Stitch the ends of the elastic securely together. Machine- or hand-stitch the opening in the casing to close.

←A small polka dot adds humor without overwhelming.

Never underestimate the evergreen appeal of a blue and white cotton. →

It's easy to overlook the solid colors at the fabric store, but they often turn into the most-worn garments in a closet! →

6 Suggested Fabrics *for the* Charlotte Shirt

← A chambray shirt goes with everything . . . no, really.

Add highlights to a primarily solid wardrobe by including a small floral print here and there. →

Go darker, and engage a delicate print detail for a more sophisticated look. →

FRESH
AND
FUN!

Model
height:
5'6"

The Chloe

The breezy Chloe halter dress is perfect for those weekends spent out in the garden, but throw on a cardigan and it's also a great piece for the office—it's a chic look, but with plenty of movement and comfort. The A-line dress's halter neck band buttons on the side for ease, and the keyhole neckline in the contrasting front panel allows for just a hint of flirtatiousness!

FABRIC AND NOTIONS

- 1⅛ yards fabric, any width, for contrasting Front Panel, Front Facing, and neck band (All sizes)
- 2⅔ yards 45" fabric for main dress (All sizes); or 1⅔ yards 60" fabric (Sizes S, M), 2¼ yards 60" fabric (Sizes L, XL, XXL)
- ¼ yard interfacing suitable for use with your fabric
- Thread to match dress fabric
- Thread to match front panel (optional for hemming if high-contrast)
- Serger thread, if applicable
- Small ⅝" to ⅞" button
- Package of ¼" bias tape (or ¼" bias tape maker to make bias tape from the dress fabric)

TOOLS

- Straight pins
- Scissors
- Tailor's chalk or fabric-marking pencil
- Clear ruler or seam gauge
- Large safety pin
- Hand-stitching needle
- Loop turner (optional for completing Neck Band)

MACHINE(S)

- Standard sewing machine with a buttonhole foot and needle appropriate to fabric choice
- Serger (optional)

APPROXIMATE MEASUREMENTS OF FINISHED GARMENT

	Small	Medium	Large	XL	XXL
Bust measurement	39½"	42"	46"	50"	54"
Hip measurement	45¼"	48"	52"	56"	60"

Approximate length of finished garment (Size M) from center back neckline to lower edge: 33½" with 2½" hem (Note: The neckline rests several inches below the base of the neck.)

"The becomingness of a frock of this type depends greatly on its individuality, so by making it yourself, you can suit it to your figure."

—The Woman's Institute's *Fashion Service* magazine, 1929

PATTERN PIECES USED

- Front (traced and cut on the C4 cutting lines)—1
- Back (traced and cut on the C4 cutting lines)—2
- C4 Front Panel—10
- Front Facing—8
- Fabric cutting bias strips—14

CUTTING DIAGRAMS

For 45" or 60" fabric, contrasting Front Panel, all sizes:

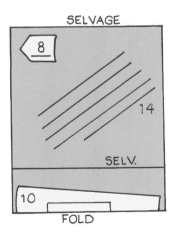

For 45" fabric, main dress, all sizes:

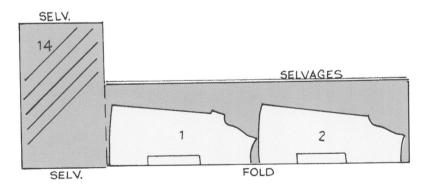

(Continued on next page)

(Continued from previous page)

For 60" fabric, main dress, sizes S, M:

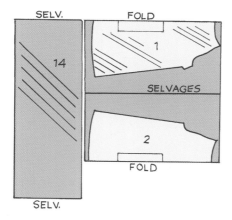

For 60" fabric, main dress, sizes L, XL, XXL:

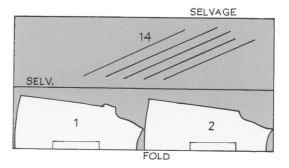

Assembly

NOTES: The dress featured in the photograph was shortened at the lengthen/shorten line by 1¼". If you, too, would like to make a slightly shorter dress, follow the directions provided in Chapter 1, page 30, for shortening garments. (Remember to shorten the Front Panel, too!) If you prefer to construct the dress slightly longer, omit this step and cut out the pattern pieces as they are.

Step 1 instructions are for the C4 individual pattern. If you use Magic Pattern C to make C4, cut away 1" from the upper edge of the Front and the upper edge of the Back.

1 Pin and cut out the Front and Back pattern pieces on the C4 cutting lines. Mark the darts on the wrong side of the Front. Pin and cut the C4 Front Panel and the Front Facing.

2 Form the darts by folding the Front with right sides together, aligning the solid lines to the large dot. Pin. Begin at the side edge and stitch to the dot, stitching off the edge of the fold at the dot rather than backstitching.

Cut the thread, leaving a few inches to tie off. Tie and trim the thread. Repeat to form the second dart, then press both darts down.

3 Fold the Front Panel in half lengthwise and press a light crease down the center. Press under the long sides of the Front Panel ⅜".

4 Fold the dress Front in half lengthwise and press a light crease down the center. Open out the Front and place the Front Panel on top of it, aligning the pressed center creases. (The wrong side of the Front Panel should be on the right side of the Front.) The notched edge of the Front Panel should be aligned with the neck edge of the Front. Pin down the pressed undersides of the panel and stitch close to the long edges.

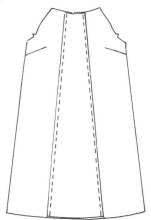

5 Transfer the stitching lines to the wrong side of the Front Facing interfacing piece. Trim away ½" from the neck edge of the interfacing. Carefully cut away the interfacing along the dashed stitching lines as shown.

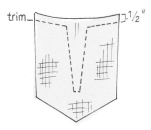

With lower edges aligned, fuse the interfacing to the wrong side of the Front Facing following the manufacturer's directions. Transfer the solid, center line to the wrong side of the Front Facing fabric. Finish the outer edges of the facing, excluding the neck edge.

6 With right sides together, center the Front Facing on the Front, aligning the neck edges and the lower point of the Front Facing to the center crease of the Front Panel. Beginning at the neck edge, pin and stitch along the stitching lines (where you cut away the interfacing). Stitch along the cut edge of the interfacing, pivoting at the bottom of the V. Make 3 or 4 stitches across the lower V, pivot, and stitch up to the neck.

7 After stitching, cut straight down on the solid line stopping just short of the stitching.

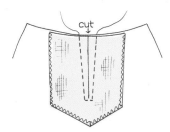

Trim the interior seam allowance to ⅛". Turn the Front Facing to the wrong side of the garment (wrong sides together). Press. Align the upper edges of the Front and the Front Facing, pin, and baste them together.

STYLE SECRET
The straight styling of this dress with slight gathers and a contrasting center panel will create a very slimming silhouette.

8 If you're not using purchased bias tape, cut two 1"-wide strips of dress fabric on the bias approximately 20" long. Form ¼" bias tape with these strips following the manufacturer's instructions if using a bias tape maker. If you do not have a bias tape maker, follow the instructions provided in Chapter 1, page 27, for making double-fold bias tape. Open out one long folded edge of the tape and, with right sides together, align this edge with the armhole edges of the Front and Back. Pin and stitch ¼" from the raw edge.

Trim the seam allowance to ⅛". Press the bias tape to the wrong side and pin it again along the fold. Stitch close to the fold on the wrong side of the garment.

9 With right sides together, pin the Front to the Back along the sides, aligning the notches and the raw edges. Stitch.

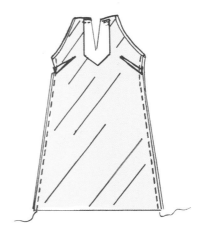

Press open the seam allowances.

10 To make the neck casing for the dress, cut a strip of the dress fabric on the bias that is 3¾" wide and 30" long. Piece together if necessary to attain the needed length. Press under one long edge ¼". Press under one short end ½". With right sides together, place the unpressed long edge of the casing on the raw edge of the neck. The pressed-under short end should be flush with the center front of the dress neck edge. Pin, continuing to pin the casing to the neck

edge. Extend ½" beyond the arm edge of the Front and cut. Press under this cut edge ½" and pin it flush with the edge of the Front. Stitch a ½" seam.

Press the casing and the seam allowance up. Repeat this process on the opposite Front side and across the Back.

11 After pressing the seam allowance and the casing upward, fold the casing to the wrong side of the dress so that the pressed fold is a scant ⅛" below the casing seam. Press the upper fold of the casing. Pin horizontally on the wrong side to keep it in the correct position. Turn the dress right side out and pin the casing to the dress on the right side with the connecting seam centered under the pins. Stitch in the ditch (see page 84, Step 5) to secure it.

stitch in the ditch here

12 To form the neck band, cut a fabric strip on the bias that is 3½" wide and 36" long from the contrasting fabric used for the Front Panel. Piece together if necessary to attain the needed length. With right sides together, fold the strip in half lengthwise, aligning the raw edges. Pin and stitch a ½" seam. Center the seam and press the seam allowance open. Stitch across one short end ¼" from the raw edge. Turn the strip right side out through the open short end, pushing out the corners. Press. Topstitch close to the finished edges. Stitch a buttonhole to fit your button in the finished end, centered 1" from the edge as shown.

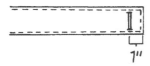

"The straight slim silhouette dominates [for dresses]: 'The straighter the line, the smarter the frock.'"

—Mary Brooks Picken

13 With the dress right side out and the Front facing you, pull the unfinished end of the neck band, seamed side down, through the Left Front Casing as shown. Attach a safety pin if necessary to help guide it through the casing. Continue pulling the neck band through the Right Front Casing and then through the Back Casing. Pull until the finished end of the neck band extends only about 4½" beyond the Left Front Casing.

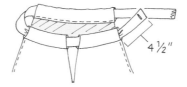

Pin the neck band to the casing at this point to secure it temporarily.

14 Try on the dress and adjust the neck band to fit you. The unfinished end of the neck band should extend 2" under the end with the buttonhole. Cut off the extra length. Finish the cut edge of the neck band. Stitch a button to this end, centered under the buttonhole.

15 Finish the lower edge of the dress. Press under the desired hem and pin. Hand-stitch to secure it, changing the thread color if desired across the contrasting Front Panel.

MAKE YOUR OWN MAGIC

- If you are unable or unwilling to stitch a buttonhole, just add a large snap to the neck band to secure.

- Showcase a special piece of new or vintage fabric as the center Front Panel.

- Use the center Front Panel as a blank canvas to apply hand or machine embroidery.

- Omit Steps 3 and 4 and proceed with the instructions as written for a simplified pattern, without the center panel, in all one fabric.

← To add to the summery effect of the dress, yellow cotton evokes sunshine and warmth.

A large-scale print is just the right proportion on a short dress. →

Bright colors are de rigueur for summer! →

6 Suggested Fabrics
for the
Chloe Dress

← Colored denim helps the transition from winter to spring.

Mix florals with geometric prints for an eclectic element of style. →

Navy and white cotton with a splash of color is classic for casual sportswear. →

The Catherine

The Catherine, a cap-sleeve blouse, can be worn belted or loose, and looks equally smashing worn with skinny jeans and a statement necklace, or tucked into a pencil skirt for a business casual day. Depending on the fabric, it could be the statement piece to complete the outfit or a go-to supporting character that goes with anything.

FABRIC AND NOTIONS

- 1¾ yards 45" fabric (All sizes); or 1⅓ yards 60" fabric (Sizes S, M), 1⅝ yards 60" fabric (Sizes L, XL, XXL)
- Thread to match fabric
- Serger thread, if applicable
- 1½ yards of ¼" elastic

TOOLS

- Straight pins
- Scissors
- Tailor's chalk or fabric-marking pencil
- Clear ruler or seam gauge
- Medium safety pin
- Hand-stitching needle (optional)

MACHINE(S)

- Standard sewing machine with needle appropriate to fabric choice
- Serger (optional)

APPROXIMATE MEASUREMENTS OF FINISHED GARMENT

	Small	Medium	Large	XL	XXL
Bust measurement	39½"	42"	46"	50"	54"
Hip measurement	45¼"	48"	52"	56"	60"

Approximate length of finished garment (Size M) from center back neckline to lower edge: 23" with ¾" hem (Note: The neckline rests several inches below the base of the neck.)

Model height: 5'8"

PATTERN PIECES USED

- C3/C5 Front (traced and cut on the C5 cutting lines)—11
- C3/C5 Back (traced and cut on the C5 cutting lines)—12
- Cap Sleeve—7

CUTTING DIAGRAMS

For 45" fabric, all sizes:

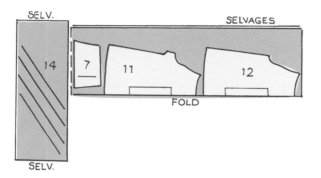

For 60" fabric, sizes S, M:

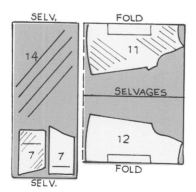

For 60" fabric, sizes L, XL, XXL:

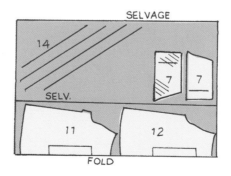

Assembly

1 Pin and cut out the Front, Back, and Cap Sleeve. Mark the darts on the wrong side of the Front.

2 Form the darts by folding the Front with right sides together and aligning the solid lines to the large dot. Pin. Begin at the side edge and stitch to the dot, stitching off the edge of the fold at the dot rather than backstitching.

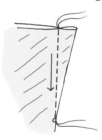

Cut the thread, leaving a few inches to tie off. Tie and trim the thread. Repeat to form the second dart, then press both darts down.

STYLE SECRET

Use fabric remnants to make flowers to accent as a necklace, belt, or pin. Add lace, ribbons, buttons, and tulle to embellish.

3 Finish the unnotched long edge of the Cap Sleeve. (The notch indicates the upper edge of the Cap Sleeve.) Press under a ⅝" hem, pin, and machine-stitch to secure it. With right sides together, pin the sleeve to the Front and Back, with the single notched edge on the Front and the unnotched edge on the Back. Stitch. Do not trim the seam allowance yet.

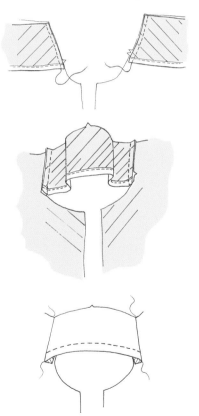

4 To form the bias binding for the lower arm opening, cut two 15" × 2" strips of fabric on the bias. With wrong sides together, fold them in half lengthwise and press a light crease down the center. Fold the long edges in to meet the center crease and press again. Cut the 15" lengths in half to form four 7½" lengths. On one 7½" section, open out one long edge and press under one short edge ½". With right sides together, align the pressed-under short end exactly with the lower edge of the Cap Sleeve and the opened-out raw edge of the bias binding with the raw edge of the arm opening beneath the Sleeve. Pin. Stitch a ⅝" seam, stopping exactly at the lower edge of the Sleeve.

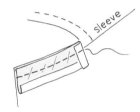

Clip the seam allowance to the stitching between the Sleeve and the binding.

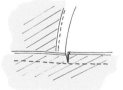

Trim and finish the seam allowance of the Sleeve. Trim slightly the seam allowance of the binding. Press the binding to the wrong side along the stitching and pin. Stitch close to the pressed fold.

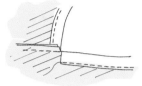

Repeat this process on the remaining three arm edges.

"No longer is it sufficient to be chic in one's clothes. One must be pretty as well. Clothes must be becoming and individual—an easy matter when the list of modes is so voluminous as today."

—Laura McFarlane, the Woman's Institute's *Fashion Service* magazine, 1928

MAKE YOUR OWN MAGIC

✂ Add additional length to front and back to make a darling cap sleeve minidress for summer.

✂ Add one or two of the small pockets from the Blythe skirt (Pattern B1, page 86).

5 With right sides together, pin the Front to the Back along the sides, aligning the notches and the raw edges. Stitch.

Press open seam allowances.

6 Finish the lower edge of the garment. Press under a ¾" hem, pin, and machine- or hand-stitch to secure it.

7 For the neck casing, make bias tape from a 2¼" × 50" strip of fabric. Piece if necessary to reach required length (see page 29). Fold the strip in half lengthwise with wrong sides together and press lightly. Press the outer edges in to meet the center crease and press again. Fold it in half once again along the center crease and press. Open out one long edge of the bias tape casing and press under one short end ½". With right sides together, place this pressed-under end at the center back, aligning the raw edge of the bias tape casing with the neck, and pin. When you reach the beginning, extend beyond 1" and cut. Stitch ½" from the raw edge.

Trim the seam allowance slightly and press toward the casing. Fold the casing up and over the neckline's raw edge and position the fold just beyond the stitching line. Pin on the right side of garment, with pins centered under the seam. Stitch in the ditch (see page 84, Step 5) to secure

it, leaving a small opening to insert the elastic.

stitch in the ditch here

8 Attach a safety pin to one end of the elastic and pull it through the opening in the neckline casing. Adjust the length of the elastic to attain the desired fit. Overlap the elastic approximately 1" and cut off any remaining length. Stitch the ends of the elastic securely together. Machine- or hand-stitch the opening in the casing to close.

"Choose trimmings with a view to smart effect, avoiding those whose quality is so fine that the contrast with the material will emphasize its age."

—Mary Brooks Picken's *Inspiration* newsletter, 1924

←Add sophistication to a pastel gingham by mixing it with a darker color like gray.

Go small scale with a chevron print—you get the style without being overwhelmed by it. →

The simple silhouette makes patterned fabric an easy choice. →

6 Suggested Fabrics *for the* Catherine Blouse

←Heavy cotton adds more structure, while a fun print keeps things light.

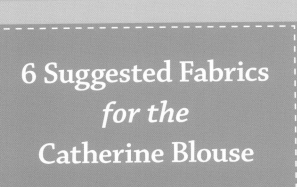

Floral cotton lawn fabric lends easy elegance to this simple top. →

Pastels plus voile make for an ethereal combination (balance it out by pairing your top with basic denim on the bottom). →

MOVE OVER LBD! IT'S A LITTLE GRAY DRESS TO STEAL THE SHOW.

Model height: 5'9"

The Candace

T he crisp silhouette of the Candace dress, with its ruffled flourish at the elbow, is a versatile look that can be dressed up or down. Though it's shown here in a sophisticated wool/silk tweed, this little gray dress could be charming in any hue. Fashion the optional flower pin with tulle and netting accents to add an extra burst of excitement and flare—to really top it off, transform the flower pin into a fascinator using a few hairclips, and you'll have a true statement piece!

FABRIC AND NOTIONS

- 3⅓ yards 45" fabric (Sizes S, M, L), 3½ yards 45" fabric (Sizes XL, XXL); or 2⅓ yards 60" fabric (Sizes S, M), 2⅝ yards 60" fabric (Sizes L, XL, XXL)
- Thread to match fabric
- Serger thread, if applicable
- 1½ yards of ¼" elastic
- 1 to 2 large pin backs (optional)
- 4" circle of felted wool or other sturdy backing (optional)
- ¼ yard of tulle and/or netting in one or more complementary colors (optional)
- Fabric scraps from the dress including selvages (optional)

TOOLS

- Straight pins
- Scissors
- Tailor's chalk or fabric-marking pencil
- Clear ruler or seam gauge
- Medium safety pin
- Hand-stitching needle
- Pinking shears (optional)

MACHINE(S)

- Standard sewing machine with needle appropriate to fabric choice
- Serger (optional)

APPROXIMATE MEASUREMENTS OF FINISHED GARMENT

	Small	Medium	Large	XL	XXL
Bust measurement	39½"	42"	46"	50"	54"
Hip measurement	45¼"	48"	52"	56"	60"

Approximate length of finished garment (Size M) from center back neckline to lower edge: 31⅝" with 4" hem (Note: Neckline rests several inches below the base of the neck.)

PATTERN PIECES USED

• Front (traced and cut on the C6 cutting lines)—1

• Back (traced and cut on the C6 cutting lines)—2

• Sleeve (traced and cut on the C6 cutting lines)—3

• Ruffle—13

CUTTING DIAGRAMS

For 45" fabric, all sizes:

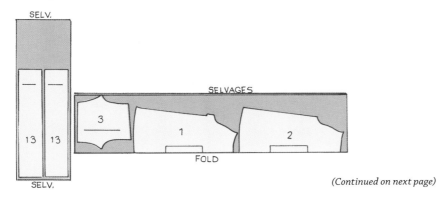

(Continued on next page)

> *"A designer may create a beautiful gown, [but] he needs the collaboration of a charming woman to wear it with distinction before it becomes a perfect work of art."*
>
> —Laura McFarlane, the Woman's Institute's *Fashion Service* magazine, 1930

Assembly

1 Pin and cut out the Front, Back, Sleeve, and Ruffle. Mark the darts on the wrong side of the Front.

2 Form the darts by folding the Front with right sides together, aligning the solid lines to the large dot. Pin. Begin at the side edge and stitch to the dot, stitching off the edge of the fold at the dot rather than backstitching.

(Continued from previous page)

For 60" fabric, sizes S, M:

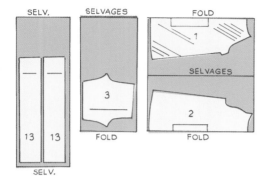

For 60" fabric, sizes L, XL, XXL:

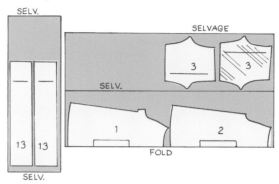

Cut the thread, leaving a few inches to tie off. Tie and trim the thread. Repeat to form the second dart, then press both darts down.

3 With right sides together, pin the Front to the Back along the sides, aligning the notches and the raw edges. Stitch.

Press open the seam allowances.

4 Remove 1" from the lower edge of both Sleeves.

With right sides together, pin and stitch the underarm seam of both Sleeves.

Press the seam allowances open.

5 With right sides together, fold the Ruffle in half, aligning the notched edges, and pin. Stitch.

Trim and press open the seam allowance. Turn it right side out. Fold the Ruffle in half with wrong sides together, aligning the seams and the raw edges.

Pin together. Beginning at the seam, machine-baste the two layers together ⅝" from the raw edges. Baste again ¼" inside the first stitching. Lightly press the fold.

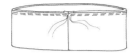

Pull up the basting threads to gather.

6 With the Sleeve right side out, pin the Ruffle to the lower edge with right sides together, aligning the seams and the raw edges. Adjust the gathers to fit. Stitch.

Trim and finish the seam allowance and press upward.

7 With right sides together, matching the Front and Back notches and the underarm and side seams, pin and stitch the Sleeves to the dress. Clip the curves. Press the seam allowance toward the Sleeve.

8 To form the elastic casing around the neck opening, press under ½" twice to the wrong side and pin. Stitch close to the inside folded edge, leaving a small opening at the center back for pulling through the elastic.

9 Attach a safety pin to one end of the elastic and pull it through the neckline casing. Adjust the length of the elastic to attain your desired fit. Overlap the elastic approximately 1" and cut off any remaining length. Stitch the ends of the elastic securely together.

Machine- or hand-stitch the opening in the casing to close.

10 Finish the lower edge of the dress. Press under the desired hem and pin. Hand-stitch to secure it. The dress featured has a 4" hem.

Flower Pin (optional)

1 Gather any fabric that you have left that includes the selvage. If you do not have any selvage fabric left, cut the edges of the fabric strips with pinking shears. If you do not have pinking shears, cut fabric strips on the bias to prevent frayed edges.

2 Cut three strips of fabric—2" × 30", 4" × 30", and 6" × 30", tapering down to a point on one end. If possible, orient the fabric so that one long edge of each strip is along the selvage. Pink the other long edge.

SELVAGE

Cut a strip of tulle (single or double thickness) and place it on the wrong side of each strip.

Fold each strip lengthwise over the tulle, but do not align the long edges. Baste along the fold.

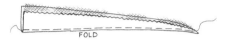

3 Prepare a double-threaded needle and keep it nearby. Beginning with the narrowest strip of fabric, wrap it in a tight coil, twisting the strip two or three times during the course of each coil, and gradually loosening it as you move outward. Hand-stitch the layers together as you twist. Tie off the thread and get a new length of thread as needed. Add the second strip of fabric and coil it around the first, folding over the edges and twisting to make a natural blossom look. Add the third and widest strip last. Leave a point of fabric visible at the end for a leaf effect.

4 Cut a 2" wide strip of tulle the width of your tulle yardage. Form it into loops about 3" to 4" long. Stitch them together with needle and thread at the base. Place them behind the flower on one side and stitch them to the underside.

5 If desired, fold and gather a strip of netting and place it behind the flower on the upper right. Pin and stitch it to the underside of the flower.

6 Cut an approximately 4" circle of felted wool or other sturdy material and pink the edges if desired. Hand-stitch it to the center of the underside of the flower.

7 Hand-stitch a large pin back to the circle base. Stitch a second pin back for extra stability if your pin is heavy.

MAKE YOUR OWN MAGIC

✂ Make the Candace dress out of a fun cotton but fashion the sleeve Ruffle from a contrasting fabric for a colorful punch.

✂ Rather than gathering the fabric of the Ruffle sleeve, follow the directions in Step 5 but form pleats on its upper edge so that it fits the lower sleeve. Stitch a narrow bias band to the lower sleeve before stitching on the pleated embellishment.

✂ Shorten the dress to make a tunic. Depending on your fabric choice, the tunic can be dressed up or down.

"Ease [of] motion, sturdiness of fabric, and a certain gaiety of color are essentials for such frocks, features that take away not a whit from their attractiveness and appeal for a variety of other occasions."

—The Woman's Institute's *Fashion Service* magazine, 1930

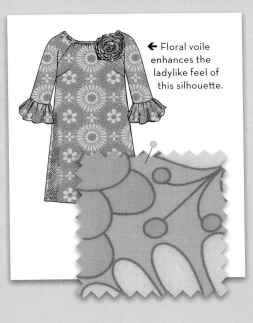
← Floral voile enhances the ladylike feel of this silhouette.

Gingham charms in any garment. →

An Asian-inspired print adds refinement to any garment. →

6 Suggested Fabrics *for the* Candace Dress

← A dark print adds a subtle elegance.

Take a smart turn with cool hues and classic plaid. →

Look polished in green linen—an earth mother style for the 21st century. →

CHAPTER 5
The Cardigan

~~~^^^^^~~~

MAGIC PATTERN D

What do Diana, Delia, Daisy, Davina, Daphne, and Dorothy all have in common? Each girl is all cozily wrapped up in a delightful piece of light outerwear. From a sleek jersey knit sweater to a sturdy corduroy jacket, the cardigan pattern can be redefined in an array of lengths and silhouettes to provide comfort and style.

There's a cropped, waist-length Jackie O style, an embellished, fluttery wrap number, as well as a knee-length sweater knit affair tied loosely in front. All of the looks are unlined, except the nifty classic men's-style vest with mismatched vintage buttons that add a feminine flourish. The cardigan designs offer long, straight sleeves, a long sleeve with turned-back cuff, or a slightly flared bracelet length sleeve, and the range of fabrics will provide unlimited creativity in construction. We've used an Italian wool sweater knit, fine wale corduroy, vintage linens, menswear suiting, a wool/Lycra solid, and a soft-as-a-feather bamboo knit. But whether your goal is warmth, a bit of coverage, or a fashion accent, you're all set to transform this pattern into the right finishing garment.

Meet the Family

PATTERN D1
THE DIANA
Page 174

PATTERN D2
THE DELIA
Page 179

PATTERN D3
THE DAISY
Page 184

PATTERN D4
THE DAVINA
Page 190

PATTERN D5
THE DAPHNE
Page 196

PATTERN D6
THE DOROTHY
Page 202

Magic Pattern D Notes

✂ Please read thoroughly all directions for the pattern before you start cutting or sewing.

✂ All seams in the D patterns are ⅝" unless stated otherwise. There will be variations in seam allowances so please read carefully.

✂ When constructing the Dorothy jacket (Pattern 6, page 202), be certain to measure the Sleeve pattern piece against your own arm length. It must be altered at the lengthen/shorten line in order for the Cuff and Sleeve Facing pieces to fit the lower edge of the Sleeve properly.

"Wherever she is or whatever her activities, good taste dictates an appropriate type of costume with fitting accessories for every hour of the day."

—The Woman's Institute's *Fashion Service* magazine, 1926

MAGIC PATTERN PIECES D

In the cutting diagrams, each pattern piece is labeled with a number, and the key, with the corresponding number, is listed below. Be sure to refer to this list when laying out the pattern pieces on your fabric.

1. D1/D4 Front
2. D1/D4 Back
3. Sleeve
4. D2/D4 Front Facing
5. D2/D4 Back Facing
6. D4 Tie
7. Back Yoke
8. Lower Back

9. Collar
10. Pocket
11. Cuff
12. Sleeve Facing
13. D3/D6 Front Facing
14. D3/D6 Back Facing
15. D2/D3/D6 Front
16. D2/D3 Back

17. D3 Sleeve
18. D3 Tie
19. D5 Front
20. Center Back
21. Side Back
22. Belt
23. Pocket Flap

Indicates wrong side of fabric

THE COMFORT CARDI

Model height: 5'8"

The Diana

Compassion is key to Diana's personality—she's a fiercely loyal gal who cares about people, working as a human rights lawyer by day, and rolling up her sleeves to man the soup kitchen every month. This slouchy cardigan is perfect for those holiday weekends spent in the company of other do-gooder pals. Gently rounded in front, it tapers to below the hip in the back with a flattering curve. The fabric you see here, a fine bamboo jersey knit, showcases another of Diana's passions—her care for the environment. It's a wardrobe staple that you'll want to wear everywhere.

FABRIC AND NOTIONS

- 2⅔ yards of 45" fabric (Sizes S, M, L), 2¾ yards of 45" fabric (Sizes XL, XXL); or 2⅓ yards of 60" fabric (Sizes S, M, L), 2½ yards of 60" fabric (Sizes XL, XXL)
- 2 spools identical thread to match fabric (use polyester if using knit fabrics)
- One box of ½" Steam-A-Seam Lite or other light, adhesive fusible web
- Serger thread, if applicable

TOOLS

- Straight pins
- Scissors
- Tailor's chalk or fabric-marking pencil
- Clear ruler or seam gauge

MACHINE(S)

- Standard sewing machine with a twin needle suitable for fabric used
- Serger (optional, if using wovens)

NOTE: If your machine will not hold two spools of thread simultaneously, then complete Steps 6 and 11 using a single needle. Apply two separate lines of stitching (space the rows approximately ¼" apart) to achieve the same look as seen in the illustrations.

APPROXIMATE MEASUREMENT OF FINISHED GARMENT

	Small	Medium	Large	XL	XXL
Bust measurement	42"	43½"	45½"	47½"	49½"

Approximate length of finished garment (Size M) from center back neck to lower edge: 33¾" with 1" hem

PATTERN PIECES USED

• D1/D4 Front (traced and cut on the D1 cutting lines)—1

• D1/D4 Back (traced and cut on the D1 cutting lines)—2

• Sleeve—3

CUTTING DIAGRAMS

For 45" fabric, all sizes:

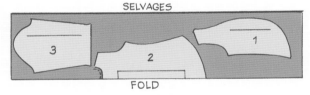

For 60" fabric, all sizes:

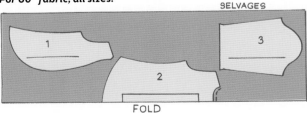

Assembly

NOTE: The cardigan shown has been created with the sleeve narrowed. If necessary, adjust the length of the sleeve on the pattern piece before cutting. The pattern piece has a dashed line indicating the cutting line for the size small D1 sleeve. For subsequent sizes, you will need to draw your own cutting line. If you desire a wider sleeve, then just use the pattern piece as is. Cut out the Sleeve using the original pattern piece. Place the Sleeve on your work surface with the fabric wrong side up. You will notice that the sides flare out slightly near the bottom. At the point where it begins to flare, measure in 1" and make a mark with chalk. Then make a mark 1" in from both lower points. Use a ruler to draw a line connecting these two marks. Now draw a line from the top of this line to the upper point of the side edge. See the illustration.

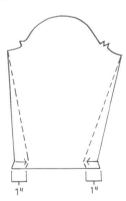

This is your new cutting line. Trim the sleeves along these lines. Follow the assembly instructions as written.

1 Pin and cut the Front pattern piece for your size. Pin the Back pattern piece; measure ⅜" beyond the neck edge only and cut, following the D1 cutting lines for the rest of the Back.

Pin and cut out the Sleeves, following the instructions on page 175.

2 With right sides together, pin the Front pieces to the Back on the shoulder edges. Stitch. Press the seam allowances open.

3 With right sides together, pin the sides of the Fronts and the Back, aligning the raw edges. Stitch.

Press open the seam allowances.

4 Press all the outer edges under 1" to form a crease.

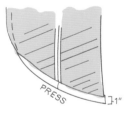

If desired, on the wrong side of the fabric, first measure in 2" from the raw edges and lightly mark it with the chalk, then fold the raw edges in to meet this line. If sewing with cotton or other woven fabric, it may be helpful to use a long machine-stitch around the garment, 1" from the edge, and press under on the stitching. Remove the stitching when complete.

5 Open out the pressed-under edges and, following the manufacturer's directions, apply the ½" Steam-A-Seam Lite to the edge of the garment on the wrong side.

Turn under along the pressed crease again and press until the hem is fused.

6 Insert the twin needle in your machine and thread with two spools of thread. Begin at one shoulder seam and stitch around the front, the lower edge and neck of the garment ⅝" from the edge.

7 With a single needle, baste ⅝" beneath the upper edge of the Sleeve between the notches. Baste again ¼" inside the first stitching.

8 With right sides together, pin and stitch the underarm edge of the Sleeves. Press open the seam allowances.

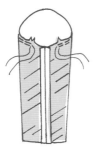

9 Press the hem edge under 1" to form a crease. If desired, on the wrong side of the fabric, first measure in 2" from the raw edges and lightly mark it with chalk. Fold the raw edges in to meet this line.

10 Open out the hem and, following the manufacturer's directions, apply the ½" Steam-A-Seam Lite to the edge of the Sleeve on the wrong side. Turn under along the pressed crease again and press until the hem is fused. Repeat with the other Sleeve.

"A little jacket, magic in its making, has been designed to wear."

—The Woman's Institute's *Fashion Service* magazine, 1930

11 Insert the twin needle in your machine and thread with two spools of thread. Begin at the seam and stitch around the Sleeve ⅝" from the lower edge.

Repeat with the other Sleeve.

12 With the Sleeve right side out and the armhole facing you, pin the sleeve to the garment with right sides together, aligning the side seam of the garment with the underarm seam of the Sleeve. Align the notches and the raw edges and align the large dot of the Sleeve to the shoulder seam of the garment. Pull up the basting threads slightly to ease the fit. Stitch.

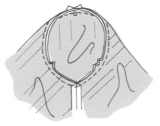

Trim the seam allowance and press toward the Sleeve.

MAKE YOUR OWN MAGIC

- ✂ Use a cotton knit print for a fun look with jeans.

- ✂ Make the cardigan out of black wool knit for the perfect fall topper.

- ✂ Add small ties at the front for a simple closure. (See the Davina, Pattern D4, page 190, for Tie pattern piece and instructions.)

← A cardigan is the perfect canvas for a large-scale barkcloth print.

Velour offers the softness of velvet with a little extra swing. →

A cozy flannel cardi will see you through the chilliest months. →

6 Suggested Fabrics *for the* Diana Cardigan

Find a classic wool plaid for a dose of all-natural warmth. →

A soft denim cardigan recalls the classic jean jacket with the movement of a chambray. →

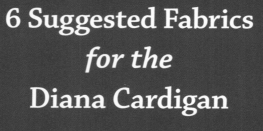

← A diaphanous gauze fabric converts the cardigan layer to decorative accessory.

The Delia

LOOKING SHARP!

The Delia is as buttoned-up as they come—without actually employing any buttons! This unlined, Jackie O–style cropped jacket features gentle curving seams in front for a delicate twist on a classic shape, and narrow sleeves that can be rolled or worn long. Featured in a wool/Lycra blend (but easily worked in any other structured material, too), the tailored Delia jacket exudes polish and purpose. Accessorize with a vintage pin to add a little flair!

FABRIC AND NOTIONS

- 2⅛ yards 45" fabric (Sizes S, M, L), 2⅓ yards 45" fabric (Sizes XL, XXL); or 1⅞ yards 60" fabric (Sizes S, M, L), 2 yards 60" fabric (Sizes XL, XXL)
- ¾ yards interfacing suitable for fabric used
- Thread to match fabric
- Serger thread, if applicable

TOOLS

- Straight pins
- Scissors
- Tailor's chalk or fabric-marking pencil
- Clear ruler or yardstick
- Hand-stitching needle

MACHINE(S)

- Standard sewing machine with needle appropriate to fabric choice
- Serger (optional)

APPROXIMATE MEASUREMENT OF FINISHED GARMENT

	Small	Medium	Large	XL	XXL
Bust measurement	42"	43½"	45½"	47½"	49½"

Approximate length of finished garment (Size M) from center back neck to lower edge: 19¼" with 2¼" hem

Model height: 5'9"

PATTERN PIECES USED

- D2/D3/D6 Front (traced and cut on the D2 cutting lines)—15
- D2/D3 Back (traced and cut on the D2 cutting lines)—16
- Sleeve—3
- D2/D4 Front Facing—4
- D2/D4 Back Facing—5

CUTTING DIAGRAMS

For 45" fabric, all sizes:

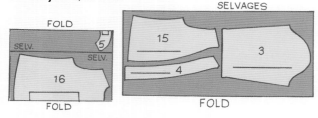

For 60" fabric, all sizes:

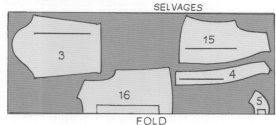

"Although the new ensembles are tailored in effect, they have taken on much of the softened silhouette that characterizes all the new fashions."

—Mary Mahon, the Woman's Institute's *Fashion Service* magazine, 1930

Assembly

NOTE: The cardigan shown has been created with the sleeve narrowed. The pattern piece has a dashed line indicating the cutting line for the size small D2 Sleeve. For subsequent sizes, you will need to draw your own cutting line. If you desire a wider sleeve, then just use the pattern piece as is. Pin and cut out the Sleeve using the original pattern piece. Place the Sleeve on your work suface with the fabric wrong side up. You will notice that the sides flare out slightly near the bottom. At the point where it begins to flare, measure in ¾" and make a mark with chalk. Use chalk to make a mark ¾" in from both lower points. Use a ruler to draw a line connecting these two marks. Now draw a line from the top of this line to the upper point of the side edge. See the illustration.

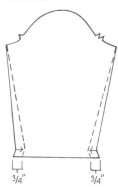

This is your new cutting line. Trim the Sleeves along these drawn lines. Follow the assembly instructions as written.

1 Pin and cut out the Front, Back, Sleeve, Front Facing and Back Facing pattern pieces using the D2 cutting lines. If necessary, adjust the length of the Sleeve on the lengthen/shorten line before cutting them out.

2 With right sides together, pin the Front pieces to the Back on the shoulder edges. Stitch. Press the seam allowances open.

3 With right sides together, pin the sides of the Fronts and the Back, aligning the raw edges. Stitch.

Press open the seam allowances.

4 Apply the interfacing to the wrong side of the Front Facing and the Back Facing. With right sides together, pin the Front Facing pieces to the Back Facing on the shoulder edges. Stitch. Press open the seam allowances. Finish the outer edge of the completed facing.

5 With right sides together, pin the facing to the garment, aligning the raw edges and the shoulder seams. Stitch.

Trim the seam allowance and clip the curves as necessary. Turn the facing to the wrong side and press.

6 With right sides together, turn the lower edge of the Front Facing to the outside and pin. Stitch straight across the facing 2¼" above the lower edge. Then trim beneath the stitching. Finish the lower edge of the garment.

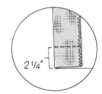
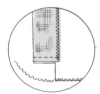

Turn the facing to the wrong side and press.

7 With the garment wrong side out, press under and pin a 2¼" hem even with the lower edge of the facing. Pin the facing to the garment around the finished outer edge of the facing, aligning the shoulder seams. Beginning at the center back, stitch the facing to the garment through the finished edge. Pivot at the upper edge of the hem and stitch through the finished edge of the hem. Pivot at the opposite side when you reach the Front Facing and stitch through the outer edge of the Front Facing until you reach the center back again.

8 Baste ⅝" beneath the upper edge of the Sleeve between the notches. Baste again ¼" inside the first stitching.

9 With right sides together, pin the underarm edge of the Sleeve. Stitch. Press open the seam allowance.

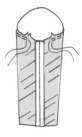

Finish the lower edge of the Sleeve. Repeat with the other Sleeve.

10 Press under a 1" hem and pin. Hand-stitch to secure it.

Repeat with the other Sleeve.

11 With a Sleeve right side out and the armhole facing you, pin the Sleeve to the armhole with right sides together, aligning the side seam of the garment with the underarm seam of the Sleeve. Align the notches and the raw edges and align the large dot of the Sleeve to the shoulder seam of the garment. Pull up the basting thread slightly to ease the fit. Stitch.

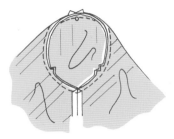

Trim the seam allowance and press toward the Sleeve. Repeat with the other Sleeve.

MAKE YOUR OWN MAGIC

✂ Make it out of beautiful tweed and add a braid down the front of the jacket and around the sleeves for a Chanel-like touch.

✂ Make it out of a rich raw silk.

✂ Make it out of new or recycled denim to layer over a longer T-shirt or blouse.

← Made from raw silk, this jacket goes from day into eveningwear.

A busy print fabric can be the statement piece in an otherwise quiet outfit. →

For a tailored, polished look, try men's suiting fabric. →

6 Suggested Fabrics *for the* Delia Jacket

← Cotton isn't always airy and delicate—heavyweight cotton is perfect for lightweight jackets.

A light wool jacket can be worn inside as an accessory or layered as outerwear. →

Woven fabrics come in many weights and textures—find one that's different from anything else in your wardrobe. →

REPURPOSED MAGIC: FROM TABLE TO WARDROBE

The Daisy

REPURPOSED LOOK

L ike its namesake flower, the Daisy top is like a cheerful best friend— up for a bright summer day bicycle adventure or a quiet evening on the porch with a pint of ice cream. The tie-front shacket (shirt-plus-jacket hybrid), shown here constructed from a vintage tablecloth with an embellished border, falls midhip and is the perfect complement to a fitted mini or a skinny tuxedo pant. The bracelet-length sleeves, with a slight flare, beg to be accessorized.

FABRIC AND NOTIONS

To construct from repurposed fabric as shown:

- Medium-to-large decorative-edge tablecloth or other linens

To construct from fabric yardage:

- 2¼ yards 45" fabric; or 2 yards 60" fabric (All sizes)
- 1 yard interfacing suitable for the fabric used
- Thread to match fabric
- Serger thread, if applicable

TOOLS

- Straight pins
- Scissors
- Tailor's chalk or fabric-marking pencil
- Clear ruler or seam gauge

MACHINE(S)

- Standard sewing machine with needle appropriate to fabric choice
- Serger (optional)

APPROXIMATE MEASUREMENT OF FINISHED GARMENT

	Small	Medium	Large	XL	XXL
Bust measurement	42"	43½"	45½"	47½"	49½"

Approximate length of finished garment (Size M) from center back neck to lower edge: 25⅝" unhemmed, as shown, or 24⅝" hemmed

PATTERN PIECES USED

- D2/D3/D6 Front (traced and cut on the D3 cutting lines)—15

- D2/D3 Back (traced and cut on the D3 cutting lines)—16

- D3 Sleeve—17
- D3 Tie—18
- D3/D6 Front Facing—13
- D3/D6 Back Facing—14

CUTTING DIAGRAMS

For 45" fabric, all sizes:

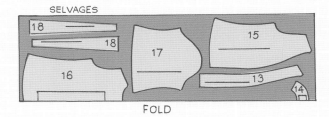

For 60" fabric, all sizes:

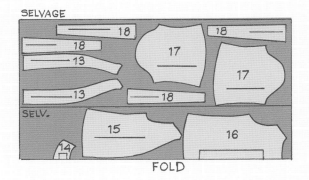

"In planning decoration, one should keep definitely in mind that decoration should be for beauty, for balance, for subduing or for brightening a fabric."

—Mary Brooks Picken's *Inspiration* newsletter, 1923

Assembly

NOTE: Instructions following are for constructing the cardigan with vintage linens as shown. At the end of these instructions, additional information will be provided for constructing from fabric yardage.

1 Place the D2/D3/D6 Front, D2/D3 Back, and D3 Sleeve pattern pieces on the fabric, but straighten the lower edge, removing the curve of the lower Front, lower Back and Sleeve hem by folding the pattern pieces straight across from point to point, or by cutting straight across if desired. Place the lower edge of the Sleeve and the lower edge of the Front and Back pattern pieces even with the outer, decorative edge of the tablecloth. Pin and cut out the pieces. Pin and cut out the D3 Tie and the D3/D6 Front and Back Facings. Using chalk and a clear ruler, mark the darts and Tie placement on the wrong side of the Front pieces. Mark the darts on the wrong side of the Back. Mark the large dot on the wrong side of the Sleeve.

2 With right sides together, fold the Back along the solid dart line. Stitch along the dashed stitching line. Do not backstitch at the beginning and end. Leave a 3" or 4" tail of thread to tie off. Tie and trim the threads. Repeat for the second Back dart. Press the darts toward the center.

3 With right sides together, pin two of the Tie pieces together on the unnotched edges. Stitch a ⅜" seam, pivoting at the corners and leaving the notched edge open.

Clip the corners. Turn the Tie right side out, gently pushing out the corners. Press. Repeat to create the second Tie. Set aside.

4 With right sides together, fold the Front pieces along the solid dart line and press. With the Tie and Front piece right side up, slide the notched end of the Tie into the fold between the Tie placement markings.

The notched edge should be against the fold. Pin. Stitch along the dashed stitching line.

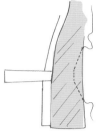

Do not backstitch at the beginning and end. Leave a 3" or 4" tail of thread to tie off. Tie and trim the threads. Repeat for the second Tie. Press the darts toward the center.

5 With right sides together, pin the Fronts to the Back on the shoulder edges. Stitch. Press the seam allowances open.

6 With right sides together, pin the sides of the Fronts and the Back, aligning the raw edges. Stitch.

Press open the seam allowances.

7 Apply the interfacing to the wrong side of the Front Facing and Back Facing. With right sides together, pin the Front Facing pieces to the Back Facing on the shoulder edges. Stitch. Press open the seam allowances. Finish the outer edge of the completed facing.

8 With right sides together, pin the facing to the garment, aligning the raw edges and shoulder seams. Stitch.

Trim the seam allowance and clip the curves as necessary. Turn the facing to the wrong side and press.

9 With the garment wrong side out, pin the facing to the garment around the finished outer edge of the facing, aligning the shoulder seams. Trim the lower front edge of the facing to match the hem of the garment if necessary. Beginning at

one Front hem, stitch the facing to the garment through the finished edge. Continue around facing to the opposite Front hem.

10 Baste ⅝" beneath the upper edge of the Sleeve between the notches. Baste again ¼" inside the first stitching.

Repeat with the other Sleeve.

11 With right sides together, pin the underarm edge of the Sleeve. Stitch. Press open the seam allowance.

Repeat with the other Sleeve.

12 With the Sleeve right side out and the garment armhole facing you, pin the Sleeve to the armhole with right sides together, aligning the side seam of the garment with the underarm seam of the Sleeve. Align the notches and the raw edges and align the large dot of the Sleeve to the shoulder seam of the garment. Pull up the basting thread slightly to ease the fit. Stitch.

Trim the seam allowance and press toward the Sleeve.

"'Maximum of wear' does not mean the continued use of a garment that has lost its style value, but rather an intelligent adjustment of a partly worn dress or suit so that both its beauty and usefulness are increased and it may become a worthwhile addition to even an already well-supplied wardrobe."

—Mary Brooks Picken's *Inspiration* newsletter, 1925

Assembly with Woven Fabrics (Optional)

1 Pin and cut out the pattern pieces from the fabric yardage. Mark the darts and Tie placement on the wrong side of the Front pieces. Mark the darts on the wrong side of the Back. Mark the large dot on the wrong side of the Sleeve. **NOTE:** you may wish to add 1" to Sleeve length at the lengthen/shorten line to provide a hem allowance.

2 Follow Steps 2 through 8 from the previous instructions.

3 With right sides together, turn the lower edge of the Front Facing to the outside and pin. Stitch straight across the facing 1" above the lower edge as shown.

Trim beneath the stitching as shown.

Finish the lower edge of the garment.

4 Turn the facing to the inside and press up a 1" hem, even with the lower edge of the facing.

5 With the garment wrong side out, pin up the hem and pin the facing to the garment around the finished outer edge of the facing, aligning the shoulder seams. Beginning at the center back, stitch the facing to the garment through

the finished edge. Pivot at the upper edge of the hem and stitch through the finished edge of the hem. Pivot at the opposite side when you reach the Front Facing and stitch through the outer edge of the facing until you reach the center back again.

6 Follow Steps 10 and 11 from the previous instructions.

7 Press under a 1" hem on the Sleeve. Pin. Hand- or machine-stitch to secure it.

8 With the Sleeve right side out and the garment armhole facing you, pin the Sleeve to the armhole with right sides together, aligning the side seam of the garment with the underarm seam of the Sleeve. Align the notches and the raw edges and align the large dot of the Sleeve to the shoulder seam of the garment. Pull up the basting thread slightly to ease the fit. Stitch.

Trim the seam allowance and press toward the Sleeve.

MAKE YOUR OWN MAGIC

- ✂ Using a border-print fabric, cut out so that the border is on the lower edge of the sleeves and the bottom of the jacket.

- ✂ Make this silhouette out of a midweight linen for a more casual look.

- ✂ Extend the length to just above the knee to create a singular spring coat.

← A delicate cotton print celebrates the feminine silhouette of this cardigan.

Add more substance to the cardigan with a homespun woven fabric. →

Batik fabrics are playful and fun— and can make an eclectic statement garment. →

6 Suggested Fabrics *for the* Daisy Cardigan

← A preppy chambray is BFFs with this structured jacket.

A lightweight floral cotton cardi is carefree and relaxed. →

Darker, geometric prints are chic and stately. →

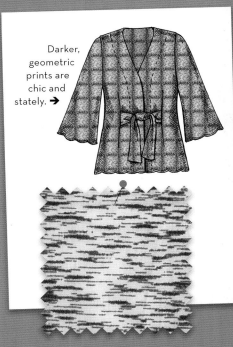

COZY AND CHIC

Model height: 5'10"

The Davina

Approachable and charismatic, Davina is a self-diagnosed computer nerd. She codes by day and, having studied piano since she was seven, plays in her community symphony by night. This knee-length sweater can be swept behind her on the piano bench, and the front fabric ties will keep it in place, just below the bust. Shown here in embellished Italian wool knit, this unlined cardi, with its long straight sleeves, would be just as perfect in a breezy cotton knit for a summer cover-up.

FABRIC AND NOTIONS

NOTE: If using a woven (rather than a knit) fabric, add ¼ yard fabric for 60" fabrics, and ⅓ yard for 45" fabrics, to allow for enough yardage to cut out the Ties on the bias.

- 3 yards 45" fabric (Sizes S, M, L), 3¼ yards 45" fabric (Sizes XL, XXL); or 2⅔ yards 60" fabric (All sizes)
- 1½ yards Pellon Easy-Knit interfacing or similar product or an interfacing suitable for the fabric used
- Thread to match fabric
- Serger thread, if applicable

TOOLS

- Straight pins
- Scissors
- Tailor's chalk or fabric-marking pencil
- Clear ruler or seam gauge
- Hand-stitching needle
- Loop turner for front ties (optional)

MACHINE(S)

- Standard sewing machine with needle appropriate to fabric choice
- Serger (optional)

APPROXIMATE MEASUREMENT OF FINISHED GARMENT

	Small	Medium	Large	XL	XXL
Bust measurement	42"	43½"	45½"	47½"	49½"

Approximate length of finished garment (Size M) from center back neck to lower edge: 36⅝" with 1" hem

PATTERN PIECES USED

- D1/D4 Front (traced and cut on the D4 cutting lines)—1
- D1/D4 Back (traced and cut on the D4 cutting lines)—2

- Sleeve—3
- D2/D4 Front Facing—4
- D2/D4 Back Facing—5
- D4 Tie—6

CUTTING DIAGRAMS

For 45" fabric, all sizes:

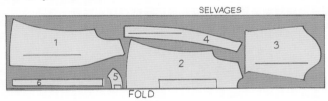

For 60" fabric, all sizes:

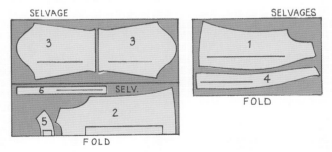

"The ever-increasing popularity of the ensemble is mounting to a high peak this season, for practically every costume, to be fashionable, adds a coat of some sort."

—Mary Mahon,
the Woman's Institute's
Fashion Service magazine, 1929

Assembly

NOTES: 1" was added to the length of the sample shown at the lengthen/shorten line. If you would like to add extra length to your cardigan, see Chapter 1, page 29, for detailed instructions on lengthening garments. Be certain to add the additional length to the Front, Back, and Front Facing.

The D1/D4 Back pattern piece has an optional dart. This is not necessary for knits, but it is recommended that you add these back darts if you are using a woven fabric.

1 Pin and cut out the D1/D4 Back and D1/D4 Front. Using chalk and a clear ruler, mark the placement of the Ties on the Front. Mark the placement of the darts on the Back (if using a woven fabric). If necessary, adjust the length of the Sleeves on the lengthen/shorten lines before pinning and cutting them out. Mark the large dot of the Sleeve on the wrong side of the fabric. For knits, cut the D4 Ties lengthwise on the fabric. For wovens, cut the Ties on the bias.

2 To form the darts on the Back, fold the Back, with right sides together, along the solid center line of the dart. Pin. Stitch along the diagonal lines.

Do not backstitch at the beginning and end of the dart but rather leave a few inches of thread to tie off. Tie and trim the threads. Repeat to form the second dart. Press darts toward the center.

3 With right sides together, pin the shoulder of the Front pieces to the Back. Stitch. Press open the seam allowances.

4 With right sides together, pin the sides of the Front pieces and the Back, aligning the raw edges. Stitch.

For knits, trim and serge the seam allowances together and press them to the back. For wovens, press the seam allowances open.

5 With right sides together, fold the Tie in half lengthwise and align the long edges. Pin. Stitch a ½" seam. Trim the seam allowance to ⅛". For knits, use a loop turner and pull the Tie right side out. For wovens, center the seam and stitch across one short end a scant ¼" from the raw edge. Turn the Tie right side out. Repeat to form the second Tie.

6 With right sides together and seam side up, pin one end of a Tie to the Front at the marking (for wovens, the unfinished end of the Tie). Baste. With the seam side up, pin the second Tie to the opposite Front at the marking. Baste.

7 Following the manufacturer's directions, apply the interfacing to the wrong side of the Front Facing and Back Facing. With right sides together, pin the shoulder edges of the Front Facing to the Back Facing, aligning the notches. Stitch. Press the seam allowances open. Finish the outer unnotched edge of the completed facing.

8 With right sides together, pin the facing to the garment over the Ties, aligning the shoulder seams and raw edges. Stitch.

Trim the seam allowance and press the facing to the wrong side.

9 With right sides together, fold the Front Facing to the outside along the lower edge. Pin and stitch straight across the facing 1" above the lower edge of the garment.

Trim the facing as shown.

Turn the facing to the inside, gently pushing out the lower corners. Finish the lower edge of the garment. Press up a 1" hem even with the lower edge of the facing. Pin. Hem by hand, easing in the fullness.

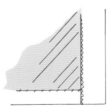

10 With the garment wrong side out, pin the facing to the garment around the finished outer edge, aligning the shoulder seams. Beginning at the hem on one side, stitch the facing to the garment beneath through the finished edge, continuing until you reach the hem on the opposite Front.

11 Baste ⅝" beneath the upper edge of one Sleeve between the notches. Baste again ¼" inside the first stitching.

Repeat with the other Sleeve.

12 With right sides together, pin the underarm seam of one Sleeve. Stitch. For knits, trim and serge the seam allowances together and press to the back. For wovens, press the seam allowance open.

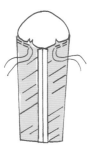

Finish the lower edge of the Sleeve. Press under a 1" hem and pin. Hand-stitch to secure it.

Repeat with the other Sleeve.

13 With the Sleeve right side out and the garment armhole facing you, pin the Sleeve to the armhole with right sides together, aligning the side seam of the garment with the underarm seam of the Sleeve. Align the notches and the raw edges and the large dot of the Sleeve to the shoulder seam of the garment. Pull up the basting thread slightly to ease the fit. Stitch. Trim the seam allowance and press toward the Sleeve. Repeat with the other Sleeve.

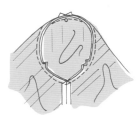

MAKE YOUR OWN MAGIC

✂ Add a row of lace around the bottom of the sleeves and hem.

✂ Make the Davina out of silk dupioni and wear with leggings or cigarette pants.

✂ Use a large-scale print for a dramatic, showstopping look.

"Vibrant colors, often in vivid contrast, rough, open textures, smart little jackets, tiny sleeves, plaits, buttons, and stitchings work together effectively to produce sports costumes capable of both dressing and creating a merry mood."

—The Woman's Institute's *Fashion Service* magazine, 1931

← Silk makes a sumptuous evening wear cardigan.

Classic menswear patterns like houndstooth work well in this somewhat structured jacket style. →

Polyester has a great drape (in any color) for this style cardi. →

6 Suggested Fabrics *for the* Davina Cardigan

← Go with a bright linen for a smart, classic statement.

Wool felt is not only warm but easy to work with. →

Channel the 1950s with a retro-style fabric. →

DARLING
AND
DAPPER

The Daphne

The Daphne vest is a menswear-inspired yet strikingly female silhouette—a midhip number that tapers to a point on the lower fronts, this twist on men's style also has two belts that tie in the back for a flattering cinch. The lady who wears it is quirky and engaging, and it echoes in her style choices, like the five mismatched vintage buttons stitched down the front of the vest! You might wear it to a coffee shop for a day of creative writing, but you could wear it anywhere—it suits the office just as well as the farmers' market.

FABRIC AND NOTIONS

- 1¾ yards 45" fabric (All sizes); or 1⅝ yards 60" fabric (All sizes)
- 1½ yards lining fabric, any width (All sizes)
- ⅝ yard fusible interfacing
- 4 snaps (30mm)
- 5 mismatched 1¼" to 1⅝" vintage or new buttons for front
- Thread(s) to match outer vest and lining
- Serger thread, if applicable

TOOLS

- Straight pins
- Scissors
- Tailor's chalk or fabric-marking pencil
- Clear ruler or seam gauge
- Hand-stitching needle

MACHINE(S)

- Standard sewing machine with needle appropriate to fabric choice
- Serger (optional)

APPROXIMATE MEASUREMENT OF FINISHED GARMENT

	Small	Medium	Large	XL	XXL
Bust measurement	42"	43½"	45½"	47½"	49½"

Approximate length of finished garment (Size M) from center back neck to lower edge: 23⅝"

PATTERN PIECES USED

• D5 Front—19

• Center Back—20

• Side Back—21

• Belt—22

• Pocket Flap—23

• D5 Interfacing Guide

CUTTING DIAGRAMS

For 45" or 60" fabric, all sizes:

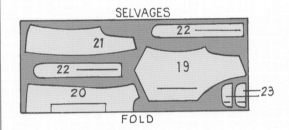

For 45" or 60" lining fabric, all sizes:

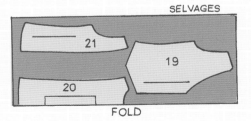

Assembly

1 Pin and cut out the D5 Front, Center Back, Side Back, Belt, Pocket Flap, and D5 Interfacing Guide. Using chalk and a clear ruler, mark the placement of the belts on the Center Back. Mark the Pocket Flap placement on the Fronts.

2 Using the D5 Interfacing Guide to cut the interfacing, trim away the ⅝" seam allowance from the neck, Front, and lower edges. Following the manufacturer's directions, apply the fusible interfacing to the wrong side of the Fronts, positioning the outer edge of the interfacing along the seam line.

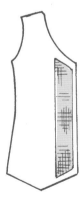

3 With right sides together, pin two Pocket Flaps together on the unnotched edges. Stitch a ¼" seam.

Clip the curves. Turn the flap right side out. Press. Repeat with the remaining two Pocket Flaps.

4 Baste the notched edges together and finish the raw edge.

Fold under the finished, notched edge on the fold line and press, forming a crease.

With right sides together, pin the Pocket Flap to the vest Front, aligning the pressed fold line crease of the flap with the placement line as shown.

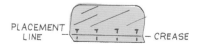

(The placement line is for size small. Move the flap slightly toward the side edge for larger sizes if desired.) Stitch through the crease on the fold line, backstitching at the beginning and end to secure it.

Cut diagonally on the corners as shown.

Fold the Pocket Flap over and pin just below the fold. Topstitch ¼" from the fold across the flap.

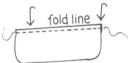

Repeat with the other Pocket Flap.

5 With right sides together, pin two Belt pieces together aligning the raw edges. Stitch a ¼" seam, leaving the notched end open.

Clip the curves. Turn the Belt right side out. Press. Topstitch ¼" from the finished edges. Repeat with the remaining two Belt pieces.

6 With right sides together, pin the notched end of one Belt to the side edge of the Center Back at the marking. Repeat with the other Belt on the opposite side. Baste through the Belt ½" from the side edge of the Center Back.

7 With right sides together, pin the Center Back to the Side Backs, aligning the raw edges and the notches. Stitch. Press open the seam allowances. Clip the curves as necessary.

8 With right sides together, pin the Fronts to the completed Back at the shoulders. Stitch. Press open the seam allowances. Note: Do not stitch the side seams.

9 Repeat Steps 7 and 8 for the lining.

10 With right sides together, pin the lining to the vest, aligning the seams and the raw edges. Stitch the lining to the vest around the neck, down the Fronts, across the lower edge and around the armholes as shown, leaving the sides open for turning the vest right side out. Trim the seam allowances and clip the curves as necessary. Press open as many seam allowances as possible that you can reach with your iron.

11 Turn the vest right side out as follows: Hold the vest with the Back facing you. Reach into one of the side openings and pull the corresponding Front section through the shoulder and out the side opening.

Repeat on the opposite side. After the vest is turned right side out, complete pressing where needed, gently pushing out the corners and lower points.

"The most perfect outing clothes are made of cotton because you feel so free in them and they require so little in the way of care."

—The Woman's Institute's
Fashion Service magazine, 1931

12 With right sides together, pin the vest to the lining on the sides, aligning the raw edges, the lower seams, and the armhole seams. Begin stitching on the lining approximately 1½" above the armhole seam as shown and continue stitching to approximately 1½" below the lower edge seam onto the lining. Backstitch at the beginning and end of the stitching to secure it.

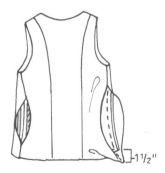

Repeat on the opposite side.

13 Press open the side seam allowances of the vest. Press under the ⅝" seam allowances of the lining between the stitching and slipstitch together securely with invisible stitch. Press.

14 Pull the snaps apart. Stitch one half to the left vest Front using the Snap Placement Guide if desired. On the vest side of the Right Front, stitch the five mismatched buttons where desired. On the lining of the Right Front, stitch the remaining half of the snaps, being careful not to catch in the outer fabric.

15 Tie the Belts at the Center Back, adjusting the fit as desired.

MAKE YOUR OWN MAGIC

✂ For a more fitted look (and before adding the Pocket Flaps), add vertical darts to the fronts, centered over the waist. Be sure to add identical darts to the lining Fronts, too!

✂ Make the vest using a bold fabric design for a dramatic statement piece.

✂ Use tapestry or decorator fabric for a more structured piece.

✂ Instead of tying in the back, shorten the length of the Belts and add a new or vintage belt buckle to cinch the vest in the back.

"Looking as cool as the proverbial cucumber is merely a matter of selecting the right outfit to wear."

—The Woman's Institute's *Fashion Service* magazine, 1932

← Large prints make a loud addition to an ensemble!

Gray denim works well with any wardrobe piece. →

Layer a large floral print vest over small geometric prints to punctuate an eclectic look. →

6 Suggested Fabrics *for the* Daphne Vest

← A small, dark print adds a touch of whimsy without going overboard.

Blue is a nearly universally flattering color—find the right shade and mix liberally in your wardrobe. →

Brown velvet is a stately, stylish choice.→

CREATE A WARDROBE STAPLE

Model height: 5'9"

The Dorothy

Made here in light brown fine wale corduroy, with inseam pockets and a long straight sleeve, the Dorothy jacket is a softer (and machine-washable!) stand-in for a leather or suede jacket. An oversized collar and turned-back, vented cuffs provide structure—and are perfect details when paired with a flirty, feminine fabric like a silk dress or breezy cotton tunic. Made in a classic shade, the Dorothy can easily transition from a day at the office to a casual night at the movies with a pair of skinny jeans.

FABRIC AND NOTIONS

- 3⅛ yards 45" fabric (Sizes S, M), 3¼ yards 45" fabric (Sizes L, XL, XXL); or 2⅓ yards 60" fabric (All sizes)
- ¾ yard interfacing suitable for fabric used
- Thread to match fabric
- Serger thread, if applicable

TOOLS

- Straight pins
- Scissors
- Tailor's chalk or fabric-marking pencil
- Clear ruler or seam gauge
- Point turner (optional)

MACHINE(S)

- Standard sewing machine with needle appropriate to fabric choice
- Serger (optional)

APPROXIMATE MEASUREMENT OF FINISHED GARMENT

	Small	Medium	Large	XL	XXL
Bust measurement	42"	43½"	45½"	47½"	49½"

Approximate length of finished garment (Size M) from center back neck to lower edge: 23⅝" with 1½" hem

"Every frock must have its coat, whether it's the little piqué or gingham for morning shopping, the afternoon silks for church and social affairs, or the printed chiffon for evening functions."

—The Woman's Institute's *Fashion Service* magazine, 1929

PATTERN PIECES USED

- D2/D3/D6 Front (traced and cut on the D6 cutting lines)—15
- Back Yoke—7
- Lower Back—8
- Sleeve—3
- Sleeve Facing—12
- Cuff—11
- Collar—9
- Pocket—10
- D3/D6 Front Facing—13
- D3/D6 Back Facing—14

CUTTING DIAGRAMS

For 45" fabric, all sizes:

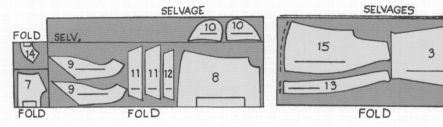

For 60" fabric, all sizes:

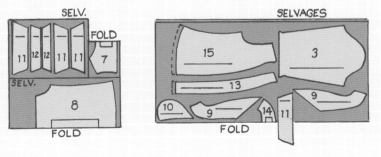

Assembly

1 Pin and cut out the D2/D3/D6 Front pattern piece ½" below the lower edge of the pattern as shown. Pin and cut out the D3/D6 Front Facing ½" below the lower edge of the pattern piece as shown.

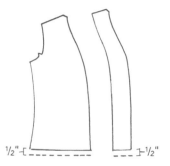

Using chalk, transfer the large dots for the Pocket placement on the Front pattern piece onto the wrong side of the Fronts. If necessary, adjust the length of the Sleeves on the lengthen/shorten lines before placing the pattern piece on the fabric. Pin and cut out the Back Yoke, Lower Back, Sleeve, Sleeve Facing, Cuff, Collar, Pocket, and D3/D6 Back Facing. Using chalk, transfer the large dots from the Pocket pattern piece onto the wrong side of the Pocket fabric. Mark the pleat lines on the wrong side of the Lower Back.

2 With right sides together, fold the Lower Back in the direction of the arrows, aligning the solid lines to form pleats.

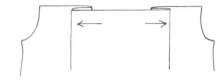

Press and pin. Baste across the pleats on the upper notched edge of the Lower Back.

3 With right sides together, pin the Back Yoke to the Lower Back on the notched edges. Stitch.

Trim the seam allowance and press toward the Yoke.

4 Finish the outer, curved edges of the two Pocket pieces. Stitch ⅝" from the side edge of the Fronts through the large dots, extending about 1" above and below each dot.

Carefully clip to the stitching at the large dots.

Press the side edges of the Front to the wrong side along the stitching between the clips.

STYLE SECRET

This pattern is a great look when worn over T-shirts, blouses, or tank tops. The pattern length can be changed to best flatter your body type.

Press ¼" to the wrong side along the raw edge of the pressed-under sections and pin.

On the right side, topstitch ¼" from the finished edge as shown.

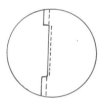

Pin the right side of the Pockets to the wrong side of the Fronts, aligning the large dots and the raw edges.

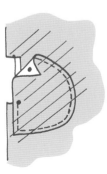

Beginning and ending at the large dots, baste the Pocket in place as shown.

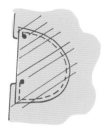

On the right side of the Fronts, topstitch along the basting.

Remove the basting threads. (Note: Pockets not shown in subsequent construction illustrations.)

5 With right sides together, pin the shoulder of the Fronts to the Back. Stitch. Press open the seam allowances.

6 With right sides together, pin the sides of the Fronts and the Back,

aligning the raw edges. Stitch, being careful not to catch in the stitched-under Pocket section.

Press the seam allowances open.

7 With right sides together, pin the double-notched edge of two Collar pieces together. Stitch.

Press open the seam allowance. This will be your collar lining. Apply the interfacing to the wrong side of the two remaining Collar pieces. With right sides together, pin the double-notched edges together and stitch. Press open the seam allowance.

This will be your outer Collar. With right sides together, pin the Collar to the Collar lining along the unnotched edges, aligning the raw edges and seams. Stitch around the edge, from one lower point along the outer edge and down to the point on the other side, pivoting at the corners, and leaving the inside edge of the Collar open.

Trim the seam allowance and clip the corners. Turn it right side out and gently push out the corners. Press. Topstitch ¼" from the finished edges. Baste the open, single-notched edges together. (The single-notched edge denotes the inner edge of the Collar and does not align to a notch on the garment.)

8 With the lining side against the garment, pin the Collar to the neck edge, aligning the seam with the center back. The small dots are at the shoulder seam. Baste the Collar to the neck edge, keeping the raw edges even.

9 Apply the interfacing to the wrong side of the Front Facing and Back Facing. With right sides together, pin the Front Facing pieces to the Back Facing on the shoulder edges. Stitch. Press open the seam allowances. Finish the outer edge of the completed facing.

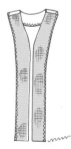

10 With right sides together, pin the facing to the garment over the Collar, aligning the raw edges and the shoulder seams. Stitch.

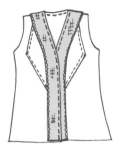

Trim the seam allowance and clip the curves as necessary. Turn the facing to the wrong side and press.

11 With right sides together, turn the lower edge of the Front Facing to the outside and pin. Stitch straight across the facing 1½" above the lower edge as shown.

Trim beneath the stitching as shown. Finish the lower edge of the garment.

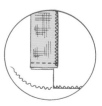

12 Turn the facing to the inside and press up a 1½" hem, even with the lower edge of the facing. Pin.

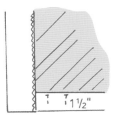

1½"

13 With the garment wrong side out, pin the facing to the garment around the finished outer edge of the facing, aligning the shoulder seams. Beginning at the center back, stitch the facing to the garment beneath through the finished edge. Pivot at the upper edge of the hem and stitch through the finished edge of the hem. Pivot at the opposite side when you reach the Front Facing and stitch through the outer edge of the facing until you reach the center back again. Be careful not to catch in the Collar.

collar

14 Baste ⅝" beneath the upper edge of the Sleeve between the notches. Baste again ¼" inside the first stitching.

15 With right sides together, pin the underarm edge of the Sleeve. Stitch. Press open the seam allowance.

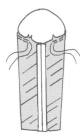

Repeat with the other Sleeve.

16 Apply the interfacing to the wrong side of two Cuff pieces. These will be your Cuffs. The remaining two will be the Cuff lining. With right sides together, pin one Cuff to one Cuff lining on the unnotched edges, aligning the raw edges.

Stitch, pivoting at the corners, leaving the notched edge open.

Trim the seam allowance and clip the corners. Turn the Cuff right side out, gently pushing out the corners. Topstitch ¼" from the finished edges, leaving the notched edge open.

Repeat with the other Cuff.

17 Lay the Sleeve flat on the ironing board with the underarm seam straightened along the lower edge. Press a crease along the Sleeve on the shoulder edge all the way down to the hem.

crease

underarm seam

STYLE SECRET
The simple silhouette is sophisticated when paired with a great scarf or jewelry.

With the lining side down and the raw edges even, place one end of the Cuff at the crease and pin around the Sleeve edge until the Cuff ends meet at the crease. Baste the Cuff to the Sleeve ¼" from the edge.

Repeat with the other Sleeve and Cuff.

18 With right sides together, pin the short ends of the Sleeve Facing together. Stitch. Press open the seam allowance. Finish the long unnotched outer edge.

With right sides together, pin the notched edge of the Sleeve Facing to the Sleeve over the Cuff, aligning the seams. Stitch a ¼" seam.

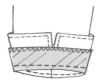

Press the facing to the wrong side. With the Sleeve wrong side out, slipstitch the finished edge of the Sleeve Facing to the Sleeve. Turn the Sleeve right side out and fold up the Cuff. Repeat with the other Sleeve.

19 With the Sleeve right side out and the garment armhole facing you, pin the Sleeve to the armhole with right sides together, aligning the side seam of the garment with the underarm seam of the Sleeve. Align the notches and the raw edges and the large dot of the Sleeve to the shoulder seam of the garment. Pull up the basting thread slightly to ease the fit. Stitch.

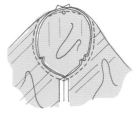

Trim the seam allowance and press toward the Sleeve. Repeat with the other Sleeve.

MAKE YOUR OWN MAGIC

- Add embroidery to the large collar corners or back yoke.

- Add a large fabric flower made out of corduroy scraps. See Candace, (Pattern C6, page 164) for ideas.

- Pair a loop closure with a large button for function and interest.

- Add a row of small decorative buttons on each side of the front opening.

- Construct Dorothy from a Pendleton wool plaid for a '40s/'50s retro look.

- Render Dorothy in a graphic print and cut the yoke and cuffs cross grain to reverse the print for visual flair.

← Add sparkle to the silhouette with sumptuous metallic leather.

Velvet is a rich fabric that dresses up this classic coat.→

↑ You will *always* reach in your closet for a classic denim jacket.

6 Suggested Fabrics
for the
Dorothy Jacket

←The touch of a loose weave adds a bohemian look to this structured jacket.

Fine linen is always fashionable in the summer months.→

↑ Use raw silk for a stunning evening jacket.

CHAPTER 6

The Coat

A h, those brisk fall days! They're the perfect weather after the dog days of sweltering summer, and they have been known to inspire a wardrobe crisis. But fear not! With this Magic Pattern, you'll be prepared to weather the change of the seasons in any outfit—from a midhip jacket (there are two) to a longer coat that lands just above the knee. And here's the thing about a coat—it's a big canvas for a rich fabric, and you can add myriad details to the finished look for an extra dose of character.

The pattern begins as an Asian-inspired swing silhouette and is reinvented into six distinctive styles—four of which embrace the Mandarin collar. One jacket has a turn-back oversized lapel. A slightly flared long sleeve can be shortened easily to a bracelet or three-quarter length. All but an asymmetrically tied jacket are secured with hidden extra-large snaps. Join Estelle, Emma, Eloise, Edith, Evelyn, and Evangeline and wrap yourself in style with these six pattern variations.

Meet the Family

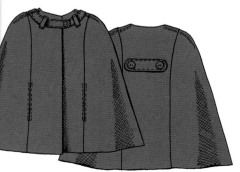

Magic Pattern E Notes

✂ Please read thoroughly all directions before you start cutting or sewing.

✂ All seams in the E pattern are ⅝" unless stated otherwise. There will be variations in seam allowances so please read carefully.

✂ Lengthen or shorten any of the six styles for a wide range of looks. All the sleeves, too, can be easily shortened to a bracelet or three-quarter length by altering the pattern on the lengthen/shorten line following the directions in Chapter 1 (page 29).

✂ All the coats, with the exception of Eloise (Pattern E3), are fastened with large hidden snaps. If you prefer, apply traditional buttonholes to the right front of any of the styles and stitch buttons to the left front in the corresponding location.

✂ Any of the coats can be made without the collar for a clean, rounded neckline.

"Have you ever made a coat? If so, you've enjoyed the satisfaction of a real accomplishment. If not, you've missed one of the most interesting kinds of sewing."

—The Woman's Institute's *Fashion Sewing* magazine, 1929

MAGIC PATTERN PIECES E

In the cutting diagrams, each pattern piece is labeled with a number, and the key, with the corresponding number, is listed below. Be sure to refer to this list when laying out the pattern pieces on your fabric.

1. Front
2. Back
3. Sleeve
4. Front Facing
5. Back Facing
6. Collar
7. E1 Belt
8. E1 Back Carrier
9. E1 Front Carrier
10. E1 Pocket
11. E4 Belt
12. E4 Pocket
13. E3 Front Extension
14. E3 Tie
15. Back Yoke
16. Cuff
17. Loop
18. E5 Front
19. Side Front
20. Side Back
21. Center Back
22. E5 Belt
23. Right Neckline Belt
24. Left Neckline Belt
25. E5 Neckline Belt Carrier

Indicates wrong side of fabric

SNAP IT, BELT IT, AND GO!

The Estelle

The oversize pockets on this coat (they fit an iPad!) are perfect for a dedicated journo, student, or busy mom who needs her notebook—electronic or otherwise—with her at all times. This classic trench also boasts a fabric tie belt, center back pleat, wide mandarin collar, flared sleeves, and three accent buttons. Channel your inner Harriet the Spy with a dark, solid-color fabric or go with a lighter khaki blend for a Lois Lane–inspired spring trench.

FABRIC AND NOTIONS
- 4⅝ yards 45" fabric (Sizes S, M), 4⅔ yards 45" fabric (Sizes L, XL, XXL); or 3⅜ yards 60" fabric (All sizes)
- 1 yard interfacing suitable for fabric
- 3 snaps (30 mm)
- 3 buttons 1¼" to 1⅝" for Front
- Thread to match fabric
- Serger thread, if applicable

TOOLS
- Straight pins
- Scissors
- Tailor's chalk or fabric-marking pencil
- Ruler or seam gauge
- Hand-stitching needle
- Point turner (optional)

MACHINE(S)
- Standard sewing machine with needle appropriate to fabric choice
- Serger (optional)

Model Height: 5'9"

APPROXIMATE MEASUREMENT OF FINISHED GARMENT

	Small	Medium	Large	XL	XXL
Bust measurement	42"	43½"	45½"	47½"	49½"

Approximate length of finished garment (Size M) from center back neckline to lower edge: 32⅝" with 2" hem

PATTERN PIECES USED

- Front (traced and cut on the E1 cutting lines)—1
- Back (traced and cut on the E1 cutting lines)—2
- Sleeve—3
- Front Facing (traced and cut on the E1 cutting lines)—4
- Back Facing—5
- Collar—6
- E1 Belt—7
- E1 Back Carrier—8
- E1 Front Carrier—9
- E1 Pocket—10

> *"To produce a coat you'll be proud of, you'll have to stitch accurately, press thoroughly, and finish every part neatly."*
>
> —The Woman's Institute's *Fashion Service* magazine, 1929

CUTTING DIAGRAMS

For 45" fabric, all sizes:

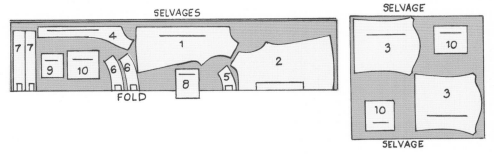

For 60" fabric, all sizes:

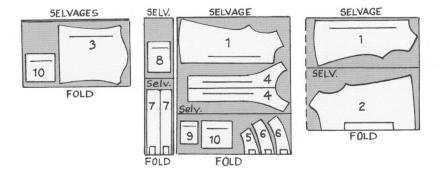

Assembly

1 Pin and cut out the Front, Back, and Front Facing following the E1 cutting lines. Pin and cut out the Sleeve, Back Facing, Collar, E1 Belt, E1 Back Carrier, E1 Front Carrier, and the E1 Pocket. Mark the placement of the snaps on the Fronts and the large E1 dot on the Back. Mark the Pocket placement guidelines on the Fronts. Mark the guidelines for the Front Carriers on the Fronts. Mark the large dot on the wrong side of the Sleeve.

2 With the Back right sides together, fold the fabric in half along the center back and align all the edges. Pin and stitch along the solid line from the neck to the large dot. Backstitch at the large dot to secure.

3 Press the Back piece flat, and center the stitching.

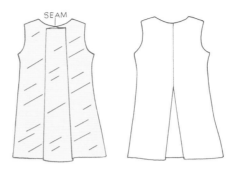

Beneath the stitching, fold the fabric on the solid line to the center to form a pleat. Press. Baste ½" from the neck edge over the folds, as shown.

Beginning at the neck edge, topstitch 1½" to the right of the center seam to the large dot. Beginning at the neck edge, topstitch 1½" to the left of the center seam to the large dot.

4 With right sides together, fold the belt Back Carrier in half, aligning the notches. Pin along the notched edge and stitch a ⅜" seam, but leave a small opening in the center to turn.

 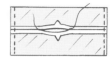

With the Back Carrier still wrong side out, center and press open the seam allowance. Stitch the short ends in a ⅜" seam allowance. Turn the Back Carrier right side out through the opening in the center seam. Press. Slipstitch the opening to close it. Repeat this process for the two belt Front Carriers.

5 With the seam horizontal and against the coat, center the Back Carrier on the Back over the large dot. Pin the upper and lower edges. Stitch close to the upper and lower edges.

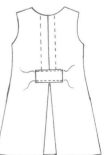

6 With the seam horizontal and against the coat, place the Front Carriers on the Fronts with the lower edge on the markings. The marking is for size small—move the carrier toward the side edge to adjust the placement for each larger size. Pin and stitch close to the upper and lower edges.

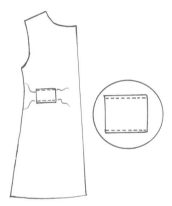

7 With right sides together, pin two Pocket pieces together on the outer edges. Stitch, pivoting at the corners, leaving an opening on the lower edge to turn.

Clip the corners and trim the seam allowance. Turn the fabric right side out

through the opening in the lower edge, gently pushing out the corners. Press. Slipstitch the opening to close it. Position the pocket using the guidelines on the Fronts. The guideline is for size small. Move the pocket toward the side edge for larger sizes. Pin. Stitch close to the outer edge, backstitching at the upper corners to secure it.

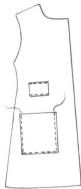

Repeat to make and place the second Pocket.

8 With right sides together, pin the Fronts to the Back on the shoulder edges. Stitch.

Press open the seam allowances.

9 With right sides together, pin a Sleeve to the armhole edge, aligning the notches and placing the large dot at the shoulder seam. Stitch.

Finish and trim the seam allowance. Press the seam allowance toward the Sleeve. Repeat with the remaining Sleeve.

10 With right sides together, pin the Fronts to the Back along the sides, aligning the Sleeve edges and the seams. Beginning at the Sleeve, stitch one continuous seam to the lower edge.

Trim the seam allowance on the curve of the underarm and clip the curves. Press the seam allowance open.

11 Finish the lower edge of the Sleeves. Press under the hem of the Sleeves and pin. Hand- or machine-stitch to secure it.

12 Apply the interfacing to the wrong side of one Collar section.

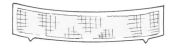

(This will be referred to now as the Collar and the remaining Collar piece as the lining.) If you are using cotton or other lightweight fabric and you would like the Collar to stand up straighter, apply the interfacing to the lining as well.

13 With right sides together, pin the Collar and Collar lining together, leaving the lower notched edge open. Stitch, pivoting at the corners.

Trim the seam allowance and clip the corners. Turn the Collar right side out, gently pushing out the corners. Press. Baste the lower notched edges together.

14 Stay stitch the neck edge of the garment ½" from the edge.

"In planning clothes for yourself, first read all the authentic fashion news available and observe style drawings, shop windows, and well-dressed women."

—Mary Brooks Picken, 1923

15 With right sides together, pin the notched edge of the Collar to the neck, aligning the center of the Collar with the center back. Baste the Collar to the neck, clipping the fabric along the curve to fit as necessary. There should be ⅝" of neck edge remaining beyond the front Collar edge as shown.

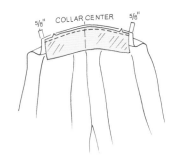

16 Apply the interfacing to the wrong side of the Front Facing and the Back Facing. With right sides together, pin the Front Facings to the Back Facing at the shoulders. Stitch.

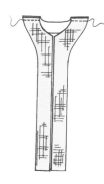

Press open the seam allowances. Finish the outer edge of the completed facing.

17 With right sides together, pin the facing to the garment over the Collar, aligning the shoulder seams and the raw edges. Stitch, pivoting at the upper corner and being careful not to catch in the front edge of the Collar beneath.

Clip the corners and trim the seam allowance. Turn the facing right side out, gently pushing out the upper corners. Press.

18 Align the shoulder edges of the garment and the facing and pin. Hand-tack the facing to the shoulder seam allowance of the garment. If desired, with the garment wrong side out, hand-tack the back facing to both back folds as shown.

19 With right sides together, fold the Front Facing to the outside along the lower edge. Pin and stitch straight across the facing 2" above the lower edge of the garment. Trim the facing as shown.

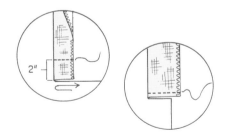

Turn the facing to the inside, gently pushing out the lower corners. Finish the lower edge of the garment. Press up a 2" hem even with the lower edge of the

facing. Pin. Hem by hand, easing in the fullness.

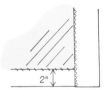

20 Separate the three snaps and stitch one half of each to the Left Front at the markings, stitching through the facing beneath. Stitch the remaining halves to the Right Front Facing at the corresponding marks, being careful to not stitch through the outer fabric.

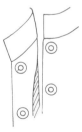

21 On the outside of the Right Front, stitch the three buttons where desired.

22 With right sides together, pin and stitch the short notched ends of the Belt pieces together in a ⅜" seam. Press open the seam allowance.

With right sides together, fold the Belt in half lengthwise, aligning the raw edges. Pin along the long edge. Stitch a ⅜" seam, leaving a small opening near the center to turn.

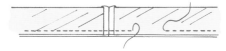

With the Belt still wrong side out, center the seam and press the seam allowance open.

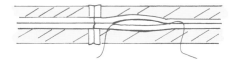

Stitch the short ends together in a ¼" seam. Turn the Belt right side out through the small opening. Push out the corners. Slipstitch the opening to close it. Slide the Belt, seamed side down, through the carriers of the coat.

MAKE YOUR OWN MAGIC

✂ Another option for this retro coat is to create it using wide wale corduroy in a rich color.

✂ A contemporary fabric such as an animal print or other graphic pattern would make a fun statement piece as well.

✂ Stitch five vertical buttonholes down the Right Front and add buttons to the Left Front for a traditional closure.

✂ Add 4" or 5" in length for a knee-skimming coat.

← Velvet easily takes sportswear into evening wear.

This pattern makes an easy transition into solid wool—a must-have for the cooler seasons. →

← A classic men's suit fabric like herringbone adds serious style.

6 Suggested Fabrics *for the* Estelle Coat

← Large print fabric in a coat is an easy way to add some fun to an outfit without having to commit to a print all day.

Create a coat out of laminate for a touch of fun and practicality—it's waterproof! →

Thin wale corduroy is perfect for layering over heavier sweaters. →

LIGHT AND
LIVELY

Model
height:
5'8"

The Emma

The name Emma means "whole" or "universal," and this silhouette follows suit, with universal appeal. It's easy to wear, generous and forgiving, and incredibly versatile. Over a long maxiskirt, skinny pencil pants, or to complement a fitted mini, this coat is so young and fresh that you might be inspired to go jump in some puddles! Here you see it fashioned in a modern decorator-weight fabric, with three loop-and-toggle closures, narrow mandarin collar, and narrow, gathered cuff at the wrist.

FABRIC AND NOTIONS

- 3½ yards 45" fabric (Sizes S, M), 4½ yards 45" fabric (Sizes L, XL, XXL); or 3 yards 60" fabric (All sizes)
- 1 yard interfacing suitable for fabric
- 3 large toggle buttons
- 2 snaps (30 mm), optional
- Thread to match fabric
- Serger thread, if applicable

TOOLS

- Straight pins
- Scissors
- Tailor's chalk or fabric-marking pencil
- Clear ruler or seam gauge
- Hand-stitching needle
- Point turner (optional)

MACHINE(S)

- Standard sewing machine with needle appropriate to fabric choice
- Serger (optional)

APPROXIMATE MEASUREMENT OF FINISHED GARMENT

	Small	Medium	Large	XL	XXL
Bust measurement	42"	43½"	45½"	47½"	49½"

Approximate length of finished garment (Size M) from center back neckline to lower edge: 32⅜" with 2¼" hem

PATTERN PIECES USED

- Front (traced and cut on the E2 cutting lines)—1
- Back Yoke—15
- Back (traced and cut on the E2 cutting lines)—2
- Sleeve—3
- Front Facing (traced and cut on the E2 cutting lines)—4
- Back Facing—5
- Collar—6
- Cuff—16
- Loop—17

"Ensemble coats vary in length from the short box coat to full-length, including the fingertip, the three-quarters, and the seven-eighths lengths. In general one may say that the formality of the costume increases with the length of the coat."

—The Woman's Institute's *Fashion Service* magazine, 1929

CUTTING DIAGRAMS

For 45" fabric, sizes S, M:

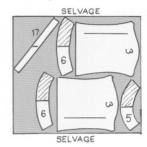
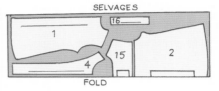

For 45" fabric, sizes L, XL, XXL:

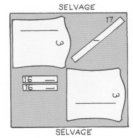
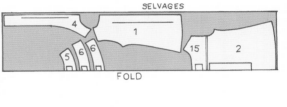

For 60" fabric, all sizes:

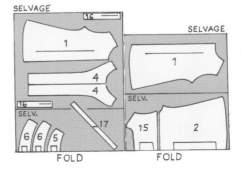

Assembly

1 Pin and cut out the Front, Back, Sleeve, Front Facing, Back Facing, Collar, Cuff, Loop, and Back Yoke. If desired, cut out the Back Yoke across the grain so that the direction of the pattern is reversed and contrasts with the lower back. Mark the position of the loops on the Front. Mark the large dot on the Sleeve. Cut away 1⅝" from the upper, unnotched edge of the Collar pieces (not the short ends).

2 Measure in 7" from both sides of the Back and mark on the wrong side of the fabric. Baste between these marks ⅝" from the upper edge of the Back. Baste again ¼" inside the first stitching between the marks.

Pull up the basting threads to gather them. With right sides together, pin the lower notched edge of the Back Yoke to the upper edge of the Back, aligning the raw edges and pulling up the gathers of the Back to fit the width of the Back Yoke. Stitch.

Press the seam allowance upward toward the Back Yoke. Topstitch ¼" from the connecting seam across the Back Yoke.

3 With right sides together, pin the Fronts to the Back on the shoulder edges.

Stitch. Press open the seam allowances.

4 With right sides together, pin a Sleeve to the armhole edge, aligning the notches and placing the large dot at the shoulder seam. Stitch.

Finish and trim the seam allowance. Press the seam allowance toward the Sleeve. Repeat for the remaining Sleeve.

5 With right sides together, pin the Fronts to the Back along the sides, aligning the seams and the raw edges of the Sleeves and the sides. Beginning at the Sleeve, stitch one continuous seam.

Trim the seam allowance on the underarm curve. Clip the curves as necessary. Press seam allowances open.

6 Apply the interfacing to the wrong side of one Collar piece. (This will be referred to now as the Collar and the remaining Collar piece as the lining.) If you are using cotton or other lightweight fabric and you would like the Collar to stand up straighter, apply the interfacing to the lining as well.

7 With right sides together, pin the Collar and Collar lining together, leaving the lower notched edge open. Stitch, pivoting at the corners.

Trim the seam allowance and clip the corners. Turn the Collar right side out, gently pushing out the corners. Press. Baste the lower notched edges together.

8 Stay stitch the neck edge of the garment ½" from the edge.

9 With right sides together, pin the notched edge of the Collar to the neck edge, aligning the center of the Collar with the center back. Baste the Collar to the neck edge, clipping the fabric along the curve to fit as necessary. There should be ⅝" of neck edge remaining beyond the front Collar edge.

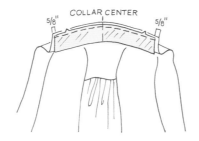

10 Apply the interfacing to the wrong side of the Front Facing and the Back Facing. With right sides together, pin the Front Facings to the Back Facing at the shoulders. Stitch.

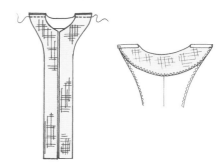

Press seam allowances open. Finish the outer edge of the completed facing. Set aside.

11 With wrong sides together, fold the Loop in half lengthwise, aligning the raw edges, and press a light crease down the center. Fold the outer raw edges in to meet the center crease. Press again. Fold the Loop in half lengthwise, aligning the folds, press, and pin. Stitch close to the outer folded edges. Cut the Loop into three equal sections.

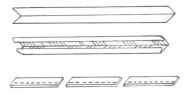

12 Fold each Loop in half and overlap the short ends, aligning the raw edges. Baste the short ends together.

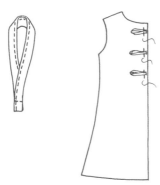

At the markings on the Right Front, align the short ends of the three Loops with the raw edge of the Front. Pin and baste ½" from the edge. Adjust the length of the Loops if necessary to fit your toggles.

13 With right sides together, pin the facing to the garment over the Collar and Loops, aligning the shoulder seams and the raw edges. Stitch, pivoting at the upper corner and being careful not to catch in the front edge of the Collar beneath.

Clip the corners and trim the seam allowance. Turn the facing right side out, gently pushing out the upper corners. Press.

14 With right sides together, fold the Front Facing to the outside along the lower edge. Pin and stitch straight across the facing 2¼" above the lower edge of the garment.

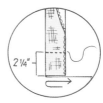

Trim the facing as shown.

Turn the facing to the inside, gently pushing out the lower corners. Finish the lower edge of the garment. Press, pressing under a 2¼" hem even with the lower edge of the facing. Pin. Hem by hand, easing in the fullness.

"Work for harmony in color and for becomingness in line, and be ever alert for distinctiveness. There are enough subdued colors, enough soft materials, enough of every kind so that every woman may have something right in every way."

—Mary Brooks Picken, 1923

15 Align the shoulder seams of the facing and the garment. Pin and hand-tack the facing to the shoulder seam allowance of the garment.

16 Beginning and ending at the underarm seam, baste around the lower edge of the Sleeve ½" from the raw edge. Baste again ¼" inside the first stitching.

Pull up the basting threads to gather.

17 With right sides together, pin and stitch the short ends of the Cuff together.

Trim the seam allowance and press it open. Press under the unnotched edge ½". With right sides together, pin the notched edge of the Cuff to the gathered edge of the Sleeve, aligning the seams and pulling up the gathering stitches of the Sleeve to fit. Stitch.

Press the seam allowance toward the Cuff. Fold the Cuff to the wrong side so that the pressed fold of the Cuff is just even with the seam. Hand-stitch the Cuff to the seam allowance. Press.

18 If desired, topstitch ¼" from the front edges of the coat.

19 Wrap the Right Front over the Left and mark the placement of the toggles beneath the ends of the Loops. Stitch the toggles to the Left Front. If desired, you can stitch two or three snaps to the garment according to the pattern markings. Follow the instructions from E1, Step 20.

MAKE YOUR OWN MAGIC

- ✂ Instead of gathering the center back, make pleats.
- ✂ Velvet fabric in black or a sumptuous color would make this coat even more elegant for evening.
- ✂ Antique contrasting buttons would be all you need to make this a showstopper.

← Create this coat in wool to achieve both structure and warmth.

A cotton jacket in a classic pattern can be worn as an indoor top in winter. →

← Laminate adds shine and practicality to any garment.

6 Suggested Fabrics *for the* Emma Coat

← Pretty pink floral cotton offers up a 1960s vibe.

A busy print and many colors give you endless options for coordinating. →

← Classic blue ikat coordinates well with all the denim in your closet.

The Eloise REPURPOSED LOOK

A true dreamer at heart, reliable Eloise will go to bat for any cause she believes in. This cozy midhip-length jacket—shown here from a repurposed woolen army blanket—is a dead giveaway of the sweet laid-back side that fuels her convictions. It's constructed of a single two-sided piece of fabric and complete with delightful details like an asymmetrical side cinch, bright contrasting thread detail, and large, turned-back collar. When she's not heading up a volunteer group, Eloise loves hosting potluck dinners and nights in with the girls.

ALL WRAPPED UP

Model height: 5'8"

FABRIC AND NOTIONS

To construct from repurposed fabric as shown:
- 62" × 80" vintage wool army blanket

To construct from standard two-sided fabric yardage:
- 3 yards 45" fabric (All sizes); or 2⅓ yards 60" fabric (All sizes)
- Thread to match fabric
- Serger thread to match or contrast with fabric

TOOLS
- Straight pins
- Scissors
- Tailor's chalk or fabric-marking pencil
- Clear ruler
- Yardstick or tape measure
- Tape
- Drafting tape (optional)

MACHINE(S)
- Standard sewing machine with needle appropriate to fabric choice
- Serger

APPROXIMATE MEASUREMENT OF FINISHED GARMENT

	Small	Medium	Large	XL	XXL
Bust measurement	42"	43½"	45½"	47½"	49½"

Approximate length of finished garment (Size M) from center back neckline to lower edge: 26⅛" unhemmed

PATTERN PIECES USED

- Front (traced and cut on the E3 cutting lines)—1
- Back (traced and cut on the E3 cutting lines)—2
- E3 Front Extension—13
- Sleeve—3
- E3 Tie—14

CUTTING DIAGRAMS

For 45" fabric, all sizes:

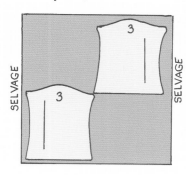
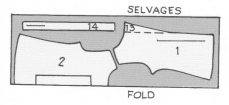

For 60" fabric, all sizes:

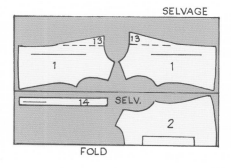

Assembly

NOTE: Step 1 instructions are for the E3 individual pattern. If you use Magic Pattern E to make E3, cut or fold the Back pattern piece on the E3 fold line and pin and cut out the Back.

1 Align the notch on the front edge of the Front pattern piece with the notch of the E3 Front Extension pattern piece and tape.

Pin and cut out two Fronts using this new piece. Cut out the Back pattern piece on the fold. If you prefer a bracelet length Sleeve, fold the pattern piece at the lengthen/shorten line before pinning and cutting. Pin and cut the E3 Tie pieces.

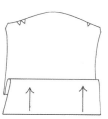

2 Finish all of the unnotched edges of the Ties with serging. Set aside.

3 With right sides together, pin the Fronts to the Back at the shoulders. Stitch.

Press open the seam allowances.

4 With right sides together, pin a Sleeve to the armhole edge, aligning the notches and placing the large dot at the shoulder seam. Stitch.

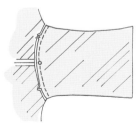

Finish and trim the seam allowance. Press the seam allowance toward the Sleeve. Repeat with the remaining Sleeve.

5 With right sides together, pin the Right Front to the Back at the side, aligning the seams and the raw edges of the Sleeve and sides. Beginning at the bottom of the Sleeve, stitch one continuous seam. Trim the seam allowance on the underarm curve. Clip the curve as necessary.

Press open the seam allowance.

6 With right sides together, pin the Left Front to the Back along the side, aligning the seams and the raw edges of the Sleeve and side. Beginning at the hem of the Sleeve, stitch one continuous seam, but once you have gone approximately 2" beyond the underarm seam, change to a machine-basting stitch until you reach the lower edge of the garment.

— BASTE

Trim the seam allowance on the underarm curve. Clip the curve as necessary. Lightly press open the seam allowance. Turn the coat right side out.

7 Try on the coat and wrap the Right Front over the Left. You will need to mark on the left side seam where you would like the Tie to emerge. Determine this by aligning the lower edge of the Fronts and moving directly across from the point where the E3 Front Extension folds back on the Right Front. Remove the basting stitch at this point. Slide the notched short end of one Tie into the opening until the notched edge is even with the side edge.

Repin the opening and stitch the side seam over the basting.

8 Carefully finish all the edges of the coat with serging, including the lower edge of the Sleeves.

9 Slide the notched end of the remaining Tie under the Right Front where the Front Extension folds back about ¾" and pin it on the right side.

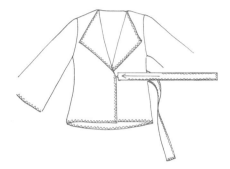

From the right side, stitch a narrow rectangle through the Front and tie beneath to secure it.

"Whatever we select, it should be just right for ourselves, harmonious with the rest of our wardrobes, and correct for when we shall wear it."

—Laura McFarlane, the Woman's Institute's *Fashion Service* magazine, 1930

MAKE YOUR OWN MAGIC

✄ If you do not have a serger or if you would simply like an alternative method of finishing the edges, apply bias tape to the cut edges of this coat constructed of any two-sided fabric. It will look good on both sides of the garment. You can purchase bias tape, but by making your own, following the directions in Chapter 1, page 27, you can add a brilliant visual detail. Make it to match or to highly contrast with your fabric. Don't shy away from prints or textures, and consider different widths, from a petite ¼" to a much wider statement-making bias tape.

✄ Because this particular coat takes advantage of the two-sided fabric and the serged edges with contrasting thread, look for two-sided decorator-designed fabrics that could be easily swapped in.

← A twill is for the in-between: heavier than cotton, but lighter than denim.

↗ An unusual print makes for a fantastic one-of-a-kind coat.

Brighten up the winter fashion landscape with pink wool! ↑

6 Suggested Fabrics *for the* Eloise Coat

← Plush velvet makes for a posh coat.

Create this coat in black stripe flannel for a cozy and office-appropriate look. →

Colored denim comes in all colors and adds a flattering structure to a layering top. →

SIMPLE
AND
ELEGANT

The Edith

The Edith, a midthigh-length coat with long, flared sleeves and inseam pockets embodies the wearer's rich lust for life and optimistic sensibility. Shown here in a decorator fabric with matching covered buttons, the fabric options are infinite (see the variation in Make Your Own Magic on page 240 for a practical take on this stunner).

FABRIC AND NOTIONS
- 3½ yards 45" fabric (Sizes S, M),
  4½ yards 45" fabric (Sizes L, XL, XXL);
  or 2½ yards 60" fabric (All sizes)
- 1 yard interfacing suitable for fabric
- 2 or 3 snaps (30 mm)
- 2 covered buttons, 1⅞", and 3 covered
  buttons, 1½" (or 5 matching buttons,
  1½" to 1⅝")
- Thread to match fabric
- Serger thread, if applicable

TOOLS
- Straight pins
- Scissors
- Tailor's chalk or fabric-marking pencil
- Clear ruler or seam gauge
- Hand-stitching needle

MACHINE(S)
- Standard sewing machine with needle
  appropriate to fabric
- Serger (optional)

APPROXIMATE MEASUREMENT OF FINISHED GARMENT

	Small	Medium	Large	XL	XXL
Bust measurement	42"	43½"	45½"	47½"	49½"

Approximate length of finished garment (Size M) from center back neckline to lower edge: 30⅝" with 4" hem

Model
height:
5' 9"

PATTERN PIECES USED

- Front (traced and cut on the E4 cutting lines)—1
- Back (traced and cut on the E4 cutting lines)—2
- Sleeve—3
- Front Facing (traced and cut on the E4 cutting lines)—4
- Back Facing—5
- Collar—6
- E4 Pocket—12
- E4 Belt—11

CUTTING DIAGRAMS

For 45" fabric, sizes S, M:

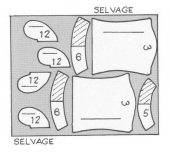
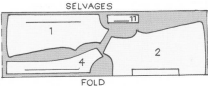

For 45" fabric, sizes L, XL, XXL:

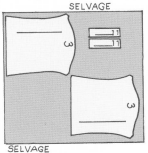
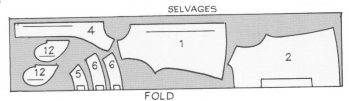

For 60" fabric, all sizes:

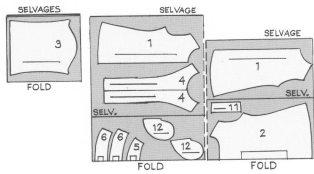

Assembly

1 Pin and cut out the Front, Back, Sleeve, Front Facing, Back Facing, Collar, Cuff, Pocket, and Belt. Use chalk and a clear ruler to mark the snap placement on the Fronts, the stitching line and E4 large dot on the Back, the small dots on the sides of the Fronts and Back for Pocket placement, the small dots on the wrong sides of the Pockets, the large dot on the Sleeve, and the button marks on the Belt.

2 With right sides together, fold Back in half along the center and align all the edges. Backstitching at the beginning and end, stitch along the solid line from the neck to the E4 large dot.

3 Press the Back piece flat, and center the stitching.

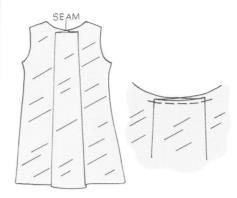

Beneath the stitching, fold the fabric on the solid line to the center to form a pleat. Press. Baste ½" from the neck edge over the folds as shown.

4 Finish the outer, curved edges of all four Pocket pieces. Aligning the dots, and with right sides together, pin the straight edge of one Pocket to each side of the Front and Back. Stitch the Pockets to the sides along the straight edge in a ⅜" seam.

Press the Pockets outward.

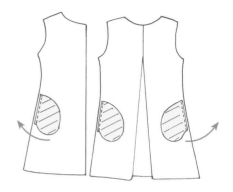

5 With right sides together, pin the Fronts to the Back at the shoulders. Stitch.

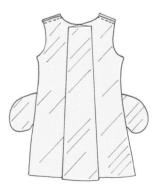

Press open the seam allowances.

6 With right sides together, pin a Sleeve to the armhole edge, aligning the notches and placing the large dot at the shoulder seam. Stitch.

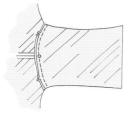

Finish and trim the seam allowance. Press the seam allowance toward the Sleeve. Repeat with the remaining Sleeve.

7 With right sides together, pin the Fronts to the Back at the sides, aligning the Sleeve edges, Pockets, and seams. Beginning at the bottom of the Sleeve, stitch one continuous seam, pivoting at the dot and continuing around the outer edge of the Pocket. When you come to the lower dot of the Pocket, pivot again and continue down the side of the garment. Repeat on the opposite side.

8 Clip the Back seam allowance to the stitching above and below the Pockets.

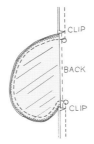

Trim the seam allowance on the underarm curve. Clip the curves as necessary. Press the seam allowances open.

9 Finish the lower edges of the Sleeves. Press under the hem of the Sleeve and pin it. Machine-stitch close to the finished edge. Topstitch again ¼" beneath the first stitching. Repeat on the other Sleeve.

10 Apply the interfacing to the wrong side of one Collar piece.

(This will be referred to now as the Collar and the remaining Collar section as the lining.) If you are using cotton or other lightweight fabric and you would like the Collar to stand up straighter, apply the interfacing to the lining as well.

11 With right sides together, pin the Collar pieces together, leaving the lower notched edge open. Stitch, pivoting at the corners.

Trim the seam allowance and clip the corners. Turn the Collar right side out, gently pushing out the corners. Press. Baste the lower notched edges together.

12 Stay stitch the neck edge of the garment ½" from the edge.

"[Make use of] trimmings in harmonizing, rather than contrasting, colors so that they will not stand out boldly from the garment."

—Mary Brooks Picken, c. 1920s

13 With right sides together, pin the notched edge of the Collar to the neck edge, aligning the center of the Collar with the center Back. Baste the Collar to the neck edge, clipping the fabric along the curve to fit as necessary. There should be ⅝" of neck edge remaining beyond the front Collar edge as shown.

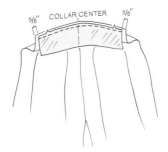

14 Apply the interfacing to the wrong side of the Front Facing and the Back Facing. With right sides together, pin the Front Facings to the Back Facing at the shoulders. Stitch.

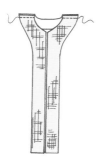

Press the seam allowances open. Finish the outer edge of the completed facing.

15 With right sides together, pin the facing to the garment over the Collar, aligning the shoulder seams and the raw edges. Stitch, pivoting at the upper corner and being careful not to catch in the front edge of the Collar beneath.

Clip the corners and trim the seam allowance. Turn the facing right side out, gently pushing out the upper corners. Press.

16 Align the shoulder seams of the facing and the garment. Pin and hand-tack the facing to the shoulder seam allowance of the garment. If desired, with the garment wrong side out, hand-tack the Back Facing to both back folds as shown.

17 With right sides together, fold the Front Facing to the outside along the lower edge. Pin and stitch straight across the facing 4" above the lower edge of the garment. Trim the facing as shown.

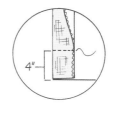
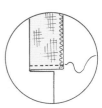

Turn the facing to the inside, gently pushing out the lower corners. Finish the lower edge of the garment. Press under a 4" hem even with the lower edge of the facing. Pin. Hem by hand, easing in the fullness.

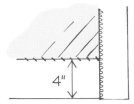

18 Separate the two or three snaps and stitch one half of each to the Left Front at the markings, stitching through the facing beneath. Stitch the remaining halves to the Right Front Facing at corresponding marks, being careful to not stitch through the outer fabric.

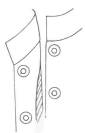

19 Cover three 1½" buttons with the coat fabric following the manufacturer's instructions and stitch them to the Right Front where desired.

20 Apply the interfacing to the wrong side of one Belt piece. With right sides together, pin the Belt pieces together. Stitch a ⅜" seam, pivoting at the corners, leaving a small opening to turn it right side out.

Clip the corners and turn the Belt right side out. Press. Slipstitch the opening to close it. Topstitch ¼" from all edges, pivoting at the corners. Center the completed Belt over the top point of the Back pleat. Pin it in place. Cover two 1⅞" buttons with the coat fabric following manufacturer's instructions and stitch them centered over each end of the Belt at the marking to secure the Belt to the back of the coat.

MAKE YOUR OWN MAGIC

✂ Make your coat out of a water-resistant fabric for a light raincoat (shown here with two buttons rather than three).

✂ Extend the Asian inspiration to the closures, and craft button loops (see the Emma, Pattern E2, page 222) or frogs instead of using snaps.

✂ Add a little pop of color with a contrasting color thread: Begin at one lower front corner of the coat and topstitch ¼" from the edge along the front, continuing up the front of the collar. Pivot at the corner of the collar, continue around the collar, pivot and stitch down the front of the collar on the opposite side and down the opposite front of the coat.

✂ Dress up this coat as well as the next (see the Evelyn, Pattern E5, page 242) with embroidery on the back belt. If using a solid fabric, try adding embroidery or decorative machine stitches to the fabric used to cover the buttons and/or the collar.

✂ Leave off the collar, omitting Steps 10, 11, and 13, and construct the coat with a clean, rounded neckline.

← You can cultivate a whole fall wardrobe around a brown corduroy coat.

Try an all-over print for a true statement piece. →

Mustard is an incredibly versatile color, and a must-have in any closet. →

6 Suggested Fabrics
for the
Edith Coat

← A quirky print in a jacket is easy to wear because you can balance it out with solids.

Go for grunge-chic with blue check flannel. →

Brighten up those rainy days with large-scale floral laminate. →

CAPES AREN'T JUST FOR SUPERHEROES.

Model height: 5'10"

The Evelyn

Polished . . . yet free-spirited and quirky. Buttoned-up, but go-with-the-flow. Chic, but down-to-earth, Evelyn's the best of both worlds. This magnificent, lined cape boasts details like a hidden snap closure, asymmetric closure belt, upper back accent belt with button details, and, of course, openings in the front for your arms. Prepare for your own boost to superhero status!

FABRIC AND NOTIONS

- 3⅔ yards 45" fabric (All sizes); or 2¾ yards 60" fabric (All sizes)
- 2⅔ yards 45" lining fabric (Sizes S, M, L), 2¾ yards 45" lining fabric (Sizes XL, XXL); or 2¼ yards 60" lining fabric (All sizes)
- 1 yard interfacing suitable for fabric
- 1 button for Neckline Belt, ⅞" to 1"
- 2 buttons for Back Belt, 1½" to 1⅞"
- 2 snaps (30 mm) for hidden front closure
- Thread(s) to match outer fabric and lining
- Serger thread, if applicable

TOOLS

- Straight pins
- Scissors
- Tailor's chalk or fabric-marking pencil
- Clear ruler or seam gauge
- Hand-stitching needle
- Point turner (optional)

MACHINE(S)

- Standard sewing machine with a buttonhole foot and needle appropriate to fabric choices
- Serger (optional)

APPROXIMATE MEASUREMENT OF FINISHED GARMENT

	Small	Medium	Large	XL	XXL
Bust measurement	42"	43½"	45½"	47½"	49½"

Approximate length of finished garment (Size M) from center back neckline to lower edge: 29⅝" with 1¾" hem

PATTERN PIECES USED

- E5 Front—18
- Side Front—19
- Center Back—21
- Side Back—20
- Front Facing—4
- Back Facing—5
- E5 Belt—22
- Right Neckline Belt—23
- Left Neckline Belt—24
- E5 Neckline Belt Carrier—25

CUTTING DIAGRAMS

For 45" fabric, all sizes:

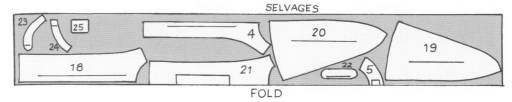

For 60" fabric, all sizes:

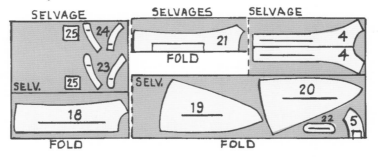

For 45" lining fabric, all sizes:

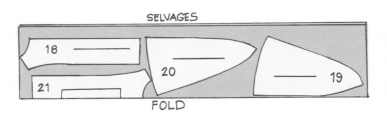

For 60" lining fabric, all sizes:

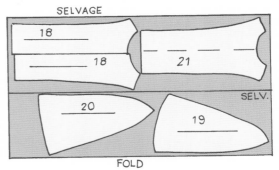

Assembly

1 Pin and cut the Front Facing and the Back Facing out ½" from the outer curved edges as shown.

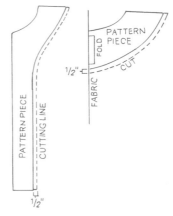

Pin and cut the E5 Front, Side Front, Center Back, Side Back, E5 Belt, Right Neckline Belt, Left Neckline Belt, and E5 Neckline Belt Carrier. Pin and cut out the E5 Front, Side Front, Center Back, and Side Back from the lining fabric also. Using chalk and a clear ruler, mark the button placement on the E5 Belt fabric. Mark the large dots on the E5 Front. Mark the buttonhole placement on the Right Neckline Belt pieces. Finish the cut edges of the fabric and lining Fronts, Side Fronts, Center Back and Side Backs, excluding the neck edges and lower edges.

2 With right sides together, pin the Side Back pieces to the Center Back, aligning the notches and the raw edges. Stitch from the top down on both sides. Press open the seam allowances, clipping the curves as necessary.

3 With right sides together, pin the Side Front pieces to the Fronts aligning the notches and the raw edges. Stitch, leaving the space between the large dots open. Backstitch at the large dots to reinforce.

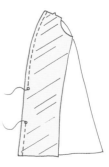

Press open seam allowances, clipping the curves as necessary.

4 With right sides together, pin and stitch the two Right Neckline Belts together along the unnotched edges in a ⅜" seam.

Trim the seam allowance slightly. Turn the Right Neckline Belt right side out and press. Topstitch ¼" from the finished edges. Stitch a 1" buttonhole centered on the Belt at the marking. Place the notched end of the Right Neckline Belt on the Right Front shoulder edge, aligning the notches. Pin and baste the notched end to the shoulder edge. With right sides together, pin and stitch the two Left Neckline Belts together along the unnotched edges in a ⅜" seam, pivoting at the corners.

Trim the seam allowance slightly and clip the corners. Turn the Left Neckline Belt right side out, gently pushing out the corners. Press. Topstitch ¼" from the finished edges, pivoting at the corners. Place the notched end of the Left Neckline Belt on the Left Front shoulder edge, aligning the notches. Pin and baste the notched end to the shoulder edge.

5 With right sides together, align the long, notched edges of a Neckline Belt Carrier, pin, and stitch a ⅜" seam. Center the seam and press the seam allowance open. Turn the Neckline Belt Carrier right side out through one of the open short ends and press flat. Topstitch ⅛" from both long edges. Finish the short ends. Press under the short ends ½" to the seamed side. Repeat for the second Neckline Belt Carrier.

6 Lay the Fronts, right side up, on a table making sure the Neckline Belts are flat against the garment. Center the Neckline Belt Carriers over the Neckline Belts on the curve of the Belt. Pin the upper and lower edges of the carriers.

Remove the Neckline Belt and hand-baste the ends of the Neckline Belt Carriers to the garment Front.

7 Stitch across the pressed-under ends to secure them. Remove basting. Pull the Neckline Belts through the Neckline Belt Carriers.

8 With right sides together, pin the two E5 Belt pieces together, aligning the raw edges. Stitch a ⅜" seam, leaving a small opening along one long edge to turn it right side out.

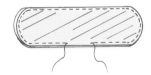

STYLE SECRET
Construct any of these coats (including the cape!) from a laminate to create a unique rain-repellant outer garment.

Trim the seam allowance and turn the Belt right side out through the opening. Press. Slipstitch the opening to close it. Topstitch ¼" from the finished edges. Center the Belt on the Back where desired and secure it to the Back with two buttons at the markings.

NOTE: You can wait until the end to do this step, but you will have to reach up under the lining to stitch on the buttons.

9 With right sides together, pin the completed Front to the completed Back of the cape on the shoulder/side edges. Stitch.

Press open the seam allowances, clipping the curves as necessary. Finish the lower edge of the cape.

10 Apply the interfacing to the wrong side of the Front Facing and the Back Facing. With right sides together, pin the Front Facing to the Back Facing on the shoulder edges. Stitch.

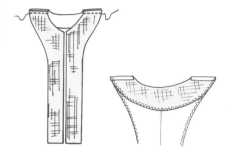

Press open the seam allowances. Finish the outer edge of the completed facing.

11 If you have not done so already, finish the cut edges of the lining except the neck edges and the hems. Follow Steps 2, 3, and 9 for the lining pieces, but remove 1" from the hem of the cape before finishing the lower edge.

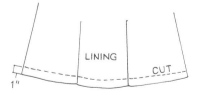

Press under a 1½" hem on the lining and pin. Hand-stitch to secure it.

12 With the wrong side of the completed facing on the right side of the cape lining, align all the seams and raw edges of the neck and Front. The facing will extend beyond the lower edge of the hemmed lining. Pin around the neck and the front edges. Baste together along the front and the neck edges.

Pin the outer edges of the facing to the lining. Stitch through the finished edge of the facing.

Remove the basting stitches around the neck and front edge. Turn the cape facing/lining wrong side out and trim away the lining that is under the facing close to the stitching.

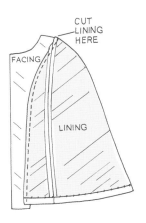

13 With right sides together, pin the lining with the attached facing to the cape around the neck and the front edges, aligning the seams and the edges. Keep the Neckline Belt out of the way. Stitch, pivoting at the upper corner. Trim the seam allowance and clip the upper corner. Turn the facing right side out, gently pushing out the upper corners. Press.

14 With right sides together, fold the Front Facing to the outside along the lower edge. Pin and stitch straight across the facing 1¾" above the lower edge of the garment.

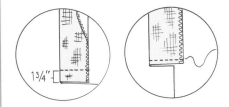

Trim the facing as shown. Turn the facing to the inside, gently pushing out the lower corners. Press under a 1¾" hem even with the lower edge of the facing. Pin. Hand-stitch to secure it.

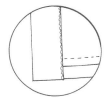

15 Separate the two snaps and stitch one half of each to the Left Front, stitching through the facing beneath. The first should be centered on the Left Neckline Belt on the front edge of the garment.

The second snap half should be stitched at the marking on Left Front. Stitch the remaining halves to the Right Front Facing at the corresponding mark, being careful to not stitch through the outer fabric.

16 Stitch a button to the Left Neckline Belt beneath the buttonhole on the end of the Right Neckline Belt.

17 Secure the snaps and the button and place the cape on a hanger with the shoulders straightened. Align the openings for the arms in the front seam of the cape and the lining beneath. Pin them together at the upper and lower point of the opening. Turn the cape wrong side out and press the lining seam allowance around the arm opening so that it is approximately ¾" instead of ⅝". With an invisible hand-stitch, stitch the lining to the cape on the long sides of the opening, leaving ⅛" of cape fabric visible. You do not need to stitch all the way around the opening.

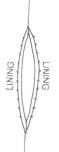

MAKE YOUR OWN MAGIC

✂ If your fabric choice is suitable, construct the cape without the lining for a lightweight outer garment. Press under the seam allowances around the front arm openings and from the wrong side, apply an invisible stitch to secure them to the cape or topstitch around the arm openings from the right side.

✂ If you are unable or unwilling to make a buttonhole on the Right Neckline Belt, simply stitch a snap beneath it to secure and stitch a decorative button on top if desired.

✂ This cape would look stunning made from recycled men's suit coats. Look for patterns and textures that go well together, such as herringbone and soft plaids, and don't forget to make use of the pocket flap on the front panel!

✂ Use a simple solid fabric such as pinwale corduroy for the cape with a vivid color lining on the inside for a fun surprise.

"Capes lend a softening influence and are at work for afternoon, sports, and evening."

—The Woman's Institute's
Fashion Service magazine, 1928

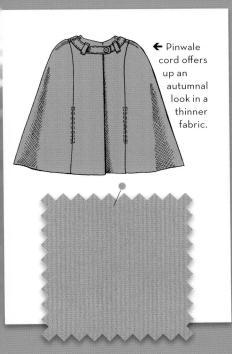

← Pinwale cord offers up an autumnal look in a thinner fabric.

Ditch the traditional raingear for a snazzy laminate cape. →

Channel your inner Janis Joplin with tie-dyed velvet. →

6 Suggested Fabrics *for the* Evelyn Cape

← Black and white woven wool makes for an evening-ready cape.

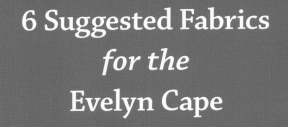

Use plaid flannel for a cozy and classic cape. →

Make a timeless statement with a black-and-white print. →

HOW TO BE
CASUALLY
SENSATIONAL

Model
height:
5'6"

PATTERN E6

The Evangeline

Evangeline means "good news" and good news it is: Perfect for a spring layer, or for wearing indoors as a creative alternative to a blazer, this midhip jacket rises to any occasion. But it reaches fashion nirvana with its contrasting Left Front (featured in vintage bark cloth) and symmetrical back pleating.

FABRIC AND NOTIONS

To construct as shown:
- For all but Left Front: 3⅓ yards 45" fabric (All sizes); or 2⅓ yards 60" fabric (All sizes)
- For contrasting Left Front: ⅞ yard 45" fabric (All sizes); or ⅞ yard 60" fabric (All sizes)

To construct from one fabric:
- 4⅝ yards 45" fabric (All sizes); or 2⅓ yards 60" fabric (Sizes S, M, L), 2⅔ yards 60" fabric (Sizes XL, XXL)
- 1 yard interfacing suitable for fabric
- 2 covered or regular buttons, 1½"

- 3 snaps, 30 mm
- Thread to match fabric
- Serger thread, if applicable

TOOLS
- Straight pins
- Scissors
- Tailor's chalk or fabric-marking pencil
- Clear ruler or seam gauge
- Hand-stitching needle
- Point turner (optional)

MACHINE(S)
- Standard sewing machine with needle appropriate to fabric choice
- Serger (optional)

APPROXIMATE MEASUREMENT OF FINISHED GARMENT

	Small	Medium	Large	XL	XXL
Bust measurement	42"	43½"	45½"	47½"	49½"

Approximate length of finished garment (Size M) from center back neckline to lower edge: 23⅞" with 2¼" hem

PATTERN PIECES USED

- Front (traced and cut on E6 cutting lines)—1
- Back (traced and cut on E6 cutting lines)—2
- Sleeve—3
- Front Facing—4
- Back Facing—5
- Collar—6

CUTTING DIAGRAMS

For 45" fabric (all but Left Front), all sizes:

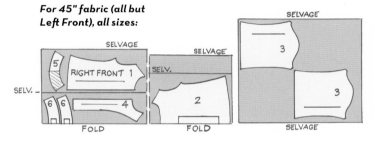

For 60" fabric (all but Left Front), all sizes:

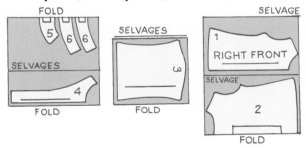

For 45" or 60" fabric (contrasting Left Front), all sizes:

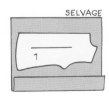

For 45" fabric (all one fabric), all sizes:

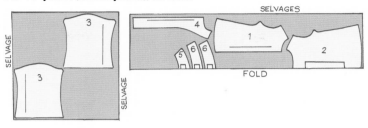

For 60" fabric (all one fabric), sizes S, M, L:

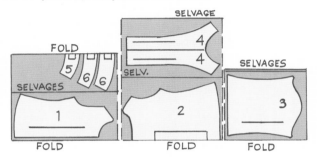

For 60" fabric (all one fabric), sizes XL, XXL:

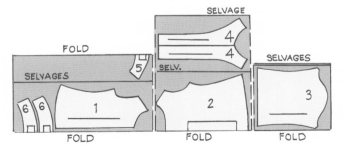

Assembly

1 Pin and cut out the Front and Back, cutting the Left Front from a contrasting fabric as shown if desired. Pin and cut out the two Collar pieces from the fabric, cutting away 1" from the upper unnotched edge (not the short edges).

For three-quarter-length sleeves, remove the desired length from the Sleeve by folding the pattern piece on the lengthen/shorten line. (See Chapter 1, page 30, for detailed instructions on shortening.)

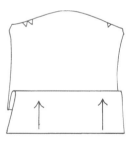

Using chalk and a clear ruler, mark the large dot and stitching line on the right side of the Back, the snap placement on the Fronts, and the large dot on the wrong side of the Sleeves.

2 With the wrong sides together, fold the Back fabric in half along the center back and align all the edges. Backstitching at the beginning and end, stitch along the solid line from the neck to the large dot.

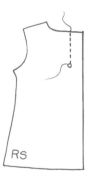

3 Press the Back piece flat, and center the stitching.

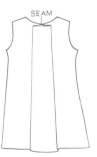

Beneath the stitching, fold the fabric on the solid line to the center to form a pleat. Press. Baste ½" from the neck edge over the folds, as shown.

4 With the Back right side out, pin along both folds from the neck to the large dot. Topstitch ¼" from the fold on both sides as shown.

5 With right sides together, pin the Front to the Back at the shoulders. Stitch. Press open the seam allowances.

6 With right sides together, pin a Sleeve to the armhole edge, aligning the notches and placing the large dot at the shoulder seam. Stitch.

Finish and trim the seam allowance. Press the seam allowance toward the Sleeve. Repeat with the other Sleeve.

7 With right sides together, pin the Front to the Back along the sides, aligning the Sleeve edges and the seams. Beginning at the bottom of the Sleeve, stitch one continuous seam.

Trim the seam allowance on the underarm curve. Press open the seam allowance. Repeat on the opposite side.

8 Finish the lower edge of the Sleeves. Press under the hem of the Sleeves and pin. Machine-stitch close to the finished edge.

9 Apply the interfacing to the wrong side of one Collar piece. (This will now be referred to as the Collar and the remaining Collar section as the lining.)

If you are using cotton or other lightweight fabric and would like the Collar to stand up straighter, apply the interfacing to the lining as well.

10 With right sides together, pin the Collar and Collar lining pieces together, leaving the lower notched edge open. Stitch, pivoting at the corners.

Trim the seam allowance and clip the corners. Turn the Collar right side out, gently pushing out the corners. Press. Baste the lower notched edges together.

11 Stay stitch the neck edge of the garment ½" from the edge.

"Every costume, whether for sports, travel, afternoon or evening, has a coat and quite unmistakably its own coat."

—The Woman's Institute's *Fashion Service* magazine, 1929

12 With right sides together, pin the notched edge of the Collar to the neck edge, aligning the center of the Collar with the center back. Baste the Collar to the neck edge, clipping the fabric along the curve to fit as necessary. There should be ⅝" of neck edge remaining beyond the front Collar edge.

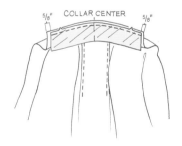

13 Apply the interfacing to the wrong side of the Front Facing and the Back Facing. With right sides together, pin the Front Facings to the Back Facing at the shoulders. Stitch.

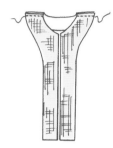

Press the seam allowances open. Finish the outer edge of the completed facing.

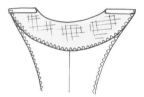

14 With right sides together, pin the facing to the garment over the Collar, aligning the shoulder seams and the raw edges. Stitch, pivoting at the upper corner and being careful not to catch in the front edge of the Collar beneath.

Clip the corners and trim the seam allowance. Turn the facing right side out, gently pushing out the upper corners. Press.

15 Align the shoulder seams of the facing and the garment. Pin and hand-tack the facing to the shoulder seam allowance of the garment. If desired, hand-tack the Back Facing to the center back, being careful not to stitch through all layers.

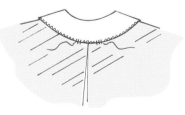

Another option is to apply a small piece of fusible web to the wrong side of the Back Facing so that it adheres to the wrong side of the center back.

16 With right sides together, fold the Front Facing to the outside along the lower edge. Pin and stitch straight across the facing 2¼" above the lower edge of the garment.

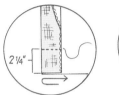

Trim the facing as shown. Turn the facing to the inside, gently pushing out the lower corners. Finish the lower edge of the garment. Press under a 2¼" hem even with the lower edge of the facing. Pin.

STYLE SECRET
All of these jackets can be made longer or shorter, so you can decide how long you want them to be based on what flatters your body type.

17 Beginning ¼" from the Front edge, stitch 2" from the lower edge around the lower edge of the garment. When you reach the opposite side, pivot and stitch up the Front ¼" from the edge, continuing around the collar, pivoting at the corners. Stitch down the opposite Front until you meet the starting point of the stitching.

18 Separate the three snaps and stitch one half of each to the Left Front at the mark, stitching through the facing beneath. Stitch the remaining halves to the Right Front facing at the

corresponding mark, being careful to not stitch through the outer fabric.

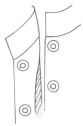

19 Following the manufacturer's directions, use scraps of fabric from the contrasting Left Front to cover the two buttons. Stitch the buttons to the Right Front where desired.

"Work at being truly lovely. Find as much pleasure as you can and as much interest. You are required and privileged to express as much beauty as you can manifest, so be up and about it and enhance your assets by the real joy you get out of it."

—Mary Brooks Picken, 1924

MAKE YOUR
OWN MAGIC

✂ Construct the Evangeline jacket in a single color in wool, linen, or corduroy. Accent it with 5 to 6 matched or mismatched (but all the same shape, size, or color so they coordinate) buttons.

✂ Try the Evangeline in cotton and add buttonholes to the right front for closure, and you have an all-day shirt alternative.

✂ After cutting out the Collar and the Collar lining, place them on top of each other with right sides together. Carefully cut a curve beneath the top points. Proceed with directions given but stitch ⅝" from this curve around collar. This will give you a second Asian-inspired design detail with a rounded collar.

A standard cotton print brings your winter outerwear into daywear. ➜

↗ Create a light cotton jacket in a subtle print for breezy evenings.

A solid wool jacket is the perfect canvas for fun buttons! ➜

6 Suggested Fabrics *for the* Evangeline Jacket

← Orange is a happy and versatile hue that works in fall *and* spring.

Small prints can appear neutral when used on large-scale garments. ➜

Pink floral says feminine and fun. ➜

CHAPTER 7
The Accessory

MAGIC PATTERN F

I f you've flipped through this chapter to see what accessories are in store, you may be wondering: How can a single pattern be made into a hat and a tote bag . . . *and* a scarf? The answer? Well, that's simple. It's magic!

This pattern includes three hat styles—a wide-brimmed sunhat, a newsboy cap, and a classic beret. But wait . . . What if you're not a self-diagnosed hat person? The good news is that the accessory pattern is, perhaps, the most magical pattern of all. The silhouette changes so dramatically between the looks, that you can create something for everyone: Beyond the hats, there's an artisanal scarf, an elegant pouch purse, and a roomy tote bag with plenty of pockets for organizing your haul. As you make your way through this pattern, you may find that a well-executed accessory is one of the most transformative wardrobe staples of all.

Meet the Family

PATTERN F1
THE FREDDIE
Page 262

PATTERN F2
THE FIONA
Page 267

PATTERN F3
THE FAITH
Page 272

PATTERN F4
THE FRIDA
Page 276

PATTERN F5
THE FARRAH
Page 281

PATTERN F6
THE FRANCESCA
Page 290

Magic Pattern F Notes

✂ Please read thoroughly all directions before you start cutting or sewing.

✂ All seams in the F pattern are ½" unless stated otherwise. There will be variations, so please read carefully.

✂ All the projects in the Accessory chapter emanate from two original pattern pieces, the F1/F4 Crown and the F3/F5 Top. A touch of creative magic transfigures these two simple shapes into three hats, two handbags, and a scarf. If your accessory is frugal at its inception, using recycled materials, or lavish, with high-end designer fabric, the distinctive basic style of each pattern will transcend your handiwork. Each of the six patterns has fabric suggestions and variations.

✂ Though the Faith beret-style hat (Pattern F3) is the repurposed look in this pattern family, each of these looks lends itself well to selections from your fabric scrap stash. The Frida hat (Pattern F4) can be pieced together from old denim, the Fiona scarf (Pattern F2) can be constructed from two or more old T-shirts, and the Freddie cap (Pattern F1) can be created from any number of wool suiting or cotton quilting combinations. Because the core pattern pieces are so small, they could each be sourced from a different piece of fabric.

> *"Though small things in themselves, the accessories spell the difference between a costume and mere clothes."*
>
> —Mary Mahon,
> the Woman's Institute's
> *Fashion Service* magazine, 1929

MAGIC PATTERN PIECES F

In the cutting diagrams, each pattern piece is labeled with a number, and the key, with the corresponding number, is listed below. Be sure to refer to this list when laying out the pattern pieces on your fabric.

1. F1/F4/F6 Crown/Base
2. F4 Brim
3. F1 Band
4. F1 Visor
5. F3/F5 Top
6. F3 Crown

7. F3/F5 Band
8. F2 Extension
9. F6 Body
10. F5 Outer Pocket
11. Pocket Accent
12. F5 Front and Back

13. F5 Casing
14. Drawstring Accent
15. F5 Interior Pocket 1
16. F5 Interior Pocket 2
17. F5 Base
18. F5 Outer Pocket Band

Indicates wrong side of fabric

A SMART-
LOOKING
CROWN

The Freddie

As its androgynous name suggests, the Freddie cap mixes tomboyish spunk with classic feminine charm—and the resourceful gal who wears it appreciates the way the newsboy style keeps her looking smart in any outfit. Made of woolen menswear suiting, as shown here, the lined, pieced crown holds a trim and tailored appeal, while the jaunty front brim and asymmetrically placed covered button add a wink of fun. Though it's quite a classic in tweed, try it in black canvas for a more punk, utilitarian vibe, or a pinstripe for another professional look.

FABRIC AND NOTIONS

- ¼ yard each of two complementary fabrics, any width
- ⅜ yard fabric, any width, for the lining
- 1 sheet of Craf-Tex Plus (15" × 18") or similar product to add heavyweight stability to the Visor
- 1 covered or regular button, 1⅛"
- ½ yard interfacing suitable for fabric
- Thread to match fabric

TOOLS

- Straight pins
- Scissors
- Tailor's chalk or fabric-marking pencil
- Hand-stitching needle

MACHINE(S)

- Standard sewing machine with needle appropriate to fabric choice

APPROXIMATE MEASUREMENT OF FINISHED GARMENT

One size fits most

PATTERN PIECES USED

- F1/F4/F6 Crown/Base
  (traced and cut on the F1 cutting lines)—1
- F1 Band—3
- F1 Visor—4

CUTTING DIAGRAMS

For Fabric 1, any width fabric:

For Fabric 2, any width fabric:

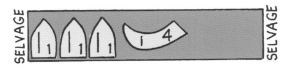

For lining, any width fabric:

"In designing a successful hat, the principle requirements are that it shall be comfortable, easy to wear, well balanced from every angle, appropriate for the occasion, and suited to the figure of the wearer."

—Mary Mahon, the Woman's Institute's *Inspiration* newsletter, 1928

Assembly

1 Cut out the pattern pieces on F1 cutting lines. From fabric 1, cut three crown pieces, one visor, and one band. From fabric 2, cut three crown pieces and one visor. From fabric 3 (the lining), cut six crown pieces and one band. Be sure to cut opposites of the Visor, piece 4. With fabric 1 right side up, cut a Visor with the pattern piece right side up. With fabric 2 right side up, cut a Visor with the pattern piece face down.

2 Apply the fusible interfacing to the wrong side of all six fabric Crown pattern pieces. Use chalk to transfer the large dot from the pattern piece to the interfacing.

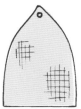

3 With right sides together, pin and stitch three Crown pieces (from alternating fabrics) together beginning at the outer edge and ending at the large dot.

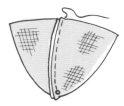

(When stitched together, no two Crowns of the same fabric will be next to each other.) Press open the seam allowances. Repeat for the remaining three crown pieces.

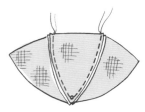

With right sides together, pin the two stitched sections together and stitch a ½" seam. Press open the seam allowance. Turn the Crown right side out.

4 With right sides together, pin the Visor (fabric 1) to the Visor lining (fabric 2). Stitch, leaving the inner curved edge open.

Trim the seam allowance. Turn the Visor right side out. Press. Find the center of the visor on the inner curved edge and make a small notch to mark.

5 Cut one visor from the Craf-Tex Plus. Cut away the ½" seam allowance on all edges. Slide it into the completed fabric Visor. If necessary, trim the outer edge of the Craf-Tex a little more for a good fit.

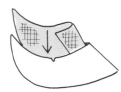

Baste the raw edges of the Visor together.

6 Apply the interfacing to the wrong side of the Band. With right sides together, pin the short ends of the band. Stitch to form the center back seam. Press open the seam allowance. Repeat for the Band lining. Find the center front of the Band by folding it in half and marking the point opposite the center back seam.

MARK CENTER

7 With right sides together, pin the visor to the Band, matching the center front of the Band to the center of the visor. Baste.

8 With right sides together, pin the Band lining to the Band (over the Visor), aligning the centers and the seams. Stitch around the lower edge. Trim the seam allowance to ⅜", press, and understitch the lining.

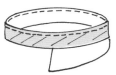

9 Turn the lining to the inside and press. Pin and baste the raw edges together.

10 Find the center of one Crown piece and mark. This will be the center front.

The center of the opposite Crown piece will be the center back. Mark this also. Across the lower edge of the center back section, baste ½" from the edge. Baste again ¼" inside the first stitching.

11 With right sides together, pin the Band to the lower edge of the Crown, matching the center fronts and the seams. If necessary, pull up the basting threads on the center back to ease the fit.

Stitch. Trim the seam allowance and press toward the Crown.

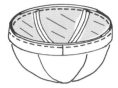

12 Transfer the large dot from the pattern piece to the wrong side of the Crown lining pieces. Repeat Step 3 for the Crown lining pieces.

13 Press under the lower edge of the completed Crown lining ½". Aligning the seams, place the lining in the crown of the hat with wrong sides together. The pressed-under edge of the lining should just cover the seam. Hand-stitch the Crown lining to the Band lining with an invisible stitch.

14 Turn up the point of the Visor using the photos as a guide. Hand-stitch to the cap through all the layers. Center the covered button beneath the point of the Visor and stitch to the hat through all the layers to secure it. Hand-stitch the underside of the Visor to the Band as needed.

"Consider what is becoming to you as an individual. If you are not sure, study and experiment until you find out what you can and cannot wear."

—Mary Brooks Picken, 1924

MAKE YOUR OWN MAGIC

✂ Can't get to a fabric store? No problem. You can get a similar look using repurposed wool from two menswear garments—one pair of trousers and one sport coat! The lining can be made from an old soft cotton shirt.

← A small-print fabric complements a small accessory.

A multistripe twill adds a splash of color to a classic accessory. ↓

A gray plaid wool cap is perfect for the cool winter months. ↓

6 Suggested Fabrics *for the* Freddie Cap

A dark denim hat is perfect for every day, every season. ↙

A thin corduroy plus a fun print equals an irreverent, memorable accessory. →

↑ Cotton has enough structure for a hat, but is light enough to wear all year.

A WARM- OR COOL-WEATHER SOLUTION

PATTERN F2

The Fiona

The Fiona scarf, a lovely layering piece to keep out the air-conditioned chill in summer or the cool breezes in autumn, drapes easily without being too bulky or hot. It's shown here made from two cotton knits, but it would also work well constructed from repurposed T-shirts—perfect for those oversize tees that you might have stashed at the back of a drawer. Make it for yourself or give it as a gift—the subtle detailing (each shape is stitched together, end to end) and embellishments (beading and reverse appliqué) are endearing touches that will warm the heart.

FABRIC AND NOTIONS

- ⅝ yard each of two complementary or contrasting 100 percent cotton knits (or other nonraveling fabric) in any width
- Regular machine thread to match fabric
- Contrasting thread for decorative stitching (Sample shown uses a heavy variegated quilting thread. Button thread will also work.)
- 55 beads (optional)

TOOLS

- Straight pins
- Regular fabric scissors

- Appliqué scissors or similar small sharp scissors for cutting out stencil shapes
- Fabric paint pen, Sharpie marker, or similar item for tracing the stencil onto fabric (Sample shown uses a bronze metallic Sharpie.)
- Sturdy material to use as stencil such as poster board or a manila folder
- Craft knife and cutting mat for cutting stencil
- Hand-stitching needle for use with heavy thread

MACHINE(S)

- Standard sewing machine

APPROXIMATE MEASUREMENT OF FINISHED GARMENT

About 73¼" long; one size fits all

PATTERN PIECES USED

- F1/F4/F6 Crown/Base—1
- F2 Extension—8
- Stencil (printed as pattern piece), to be transferred to suitable sturdy material for tracing

CUTTING DIAGRAM

For Fabric 1 and Fabric 2; any width fabric:

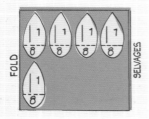

"Of course, you will wear scarfs [sic] with everything, especially coats, suits, and sports dresses."

—The Woman's Institute's *Fashion Service* magazine, 1932

Assembly

1 Trace the F1/F4/F6 Crown/Base pattern piece onto paper along the F1 cutting line and cut it out. Be sure to trace the grainline and the notch as well. Cut out the F2 Extension pattern piece and tape it to the straight edge of the crown piece, aligning the notches.

This will provide your leaf shape. Cut out 10 leaves from fabric 1. Cut out ten leaves from fabric 2. Keep the grainline of the pattern piece straight as you pin to the fabric.

2 Make the stencil in the following manner: Trace over all the lines of the stencil pattern heavily with chalk or a soft lead pencil. Place the traced side of the stencil pattern facedown on the material to be used for the stencil. Firmly rub the back of the stencil pattern with a ruler or another hard, flat edge so that the chalk or pencil mark transfers to the surface. Carefully cut out the stencil along the transferred lines.

3 For instructional purposes, the lower fabric will be referred to as fabric 1. The upper fabric will be referred to as fabric 2. Place the stencil on a leaf of fabric 2, aligning the raw edges. Use the marker or paint pen to trace around the inside edges of all the stencil shapes onto the fabric. It is okay if the lines vary slightly in thickness. Repeat this process on four more fabric 2 leaves (five total). Do not cut out the shapes.

4 Place an unmarked fabric 2 leaf on top of a fabric 1 leaf, aligning the edges. The fabric 1 leaves should be right side up. The fabric 2 leaves should be right side down. Draw a line with chalk down the center of the top leaf from the upper point to the lower edge. Pin the leaves together along this line. Machine-stitch down this center line connecting the two leaves. Repeat this for four more sets of unmarked fabric 2 and fabric 1 leaves (five sets total).

5 On three stitched leaf sets, press the left side of the top leaf to the right along the stitching.

On the remaining two completed sets, press the right side of the top leaf to the left along the stitching.

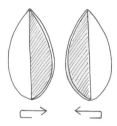

You now have five remaining fabric 1 leaves and five fabric 2 leaves with stencil markings.

6 Place a fabric 2 leaf on a fabric 1 leaf, aligning the edges. Both should be right side up. Secure them with a couple of pins. Double a length of heavy hand-stitching thread and tie off with a double knot, leaving an approximately ½" tail. All knots should be on top of the scarf for the running stitch. Use the stitching guide as a reference. Be careful that the stitches on the underside are satisfactory as well,

because the wrong side of the leaves will be visible when the scarf is worn. With the knot on top, begin a running stitch through both thicknesses around the long center shape. Stitching should be a scant ¼" from the inside of the drawn line. When you return to the beginning, make a double knot in the thread on top of the fabric to tie off. Push the knot down with your fingers to make it flush with the fabric. Try to keep your stitches approximately ⅛" to ¼" in length.

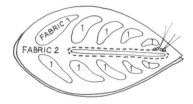

7 Tie a double knot in the thread and with the knot on top, begin on the outer edge of the remaining shapes and stitch a scant ¼" from the inside of the drawn line around the entire shape. When you near the beginning of the stitching, pull the thread through a single bead, make one more stitch and tie off the thread with a double knot on top of the fabric. Beads will be on the outer edge of all the shapes. See the stitching guide. Beads are optional.

8 After all the stitching is completed, carefully pinch up fabric 1 from

fabric 2 in the center of each shape and cut a slit in the upper fabric 2 only. Insert small scissors into the slit and carefully cut around the drawn line, exposing fabric 1 beneath. If desired, leave a small amount of fabric paint showing.

9 On a flat surface, arrange the ten leaves as shown. Measure in 3½" from the end of each leaf and mark with a pin. Overlap the leaves up to this marking. Pin together. Using your hand-stitching thread, stitch the leaves together as shown. If desired, stitch a bead to the point of the appliquéd leaves.

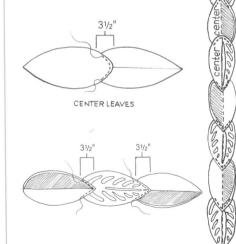

MAKE YOUR OWN MAGIC

✂ Dig into the closet and use two men's 100 percent cotton heavyweight T-shirts in place of traditional yardage! Deconstruct the T-shirt as follows: Remove the neck band by cutting close to the stitching. Cut across the shoulder seam to the sleeve and cut around the entire sleeve seam, removing the sleeves. Cut straight up from the lower edge to the lower center of one arm opening. Open out the T-shirt and press flat. Repeat for the second shirt. This will provide fabric 1 and fabric 2.

✂ Use pinking shears to cut out some of the leaves around the outer edges.

✂ Use pinking shears, cut fabric on the bias, or serge the edges when you make the scarf from woven fabrics like those shown on the opposite page.

"Accessories increase the smartness of new ensembles of cotton or linen."

—The Woman's Institute's *Fashion Service* magazine, 1929

← Linen creates graceful and flowing lines.

Green felt makes for a warm, structured, and textured scarf. →

← Take a page from a classic menswear lookbook and use wool suiting.

6 Suggested Fabrics *for the* Fiona Scarf

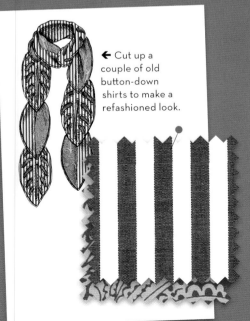

← Cut up a couple of old button-down shirts to make a refashioned look.

For a breezy effect, use light and airy voile. →

Pink is, famously, the navy blue of India—use it in silk to add a punch of elegant color. →

FOUND: THE PERFECT SLOUCH!

The Faith

REPURPOSED LOOK

Y ou gotta have Faith! This classic beret, shown here in a sweet repurposed cashmere cardigan (the perfect project for when a single moth hole makes a sweater unwearable!), is constructed to embrace the ultimate slouch: A pieced top is joined to the lower band by a circular crown. The cashmere is delightful, but you can fashion the beret from any soft, unstructured fabric (a jersey knit goes more casual, a lined velvet more upscale). Whether you're channeling a French oil painter or simply wanting a little touch of boho chic, a little Faith is all you'll need to keep your head warm in the most stylish way.

FABRIC AND NOTIONS

To construct from repurposed fabric as shown:

- ½ yard deconstructed cashmere fabric, any width
- ½ yard fabric, any width (or deconstructed lightweight linen or cotton blouse, featherweight T-shirt, old coat lining, or slip or camisole) for lining (optional)

To construct from fabric yardage:

- ½ yard 45" fabric, or ⅜ yard 60" fabric

- ½ yard 45" fabric, or ⅜ yard 60" fabric for lining (optional)
- Thread to match fabric

TOOLS

- Straight pins
- Scissors
- Tailor's chalk or fabric-marking pencil
- Hand-stitching needle

MACHINE(S)

- Standard sewing machine with needle appropriate to fabric choice

APPROXIMATE MEASUREMENT OF FINISHED GARMENT

One size fits most

PATTERN PIECES USED

- F3/F5 Top (traced and cut on the F3 cutting lines)—5
- F3 Crown—6
- F3/F5 Band—7

CUTTING DIAGRAMS

For 45" fabric, Main Hat:

For 45" fabric, Lining:

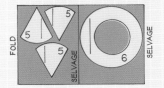

For 60" fabric, Main Hat:

For 60" fabric, Lining:

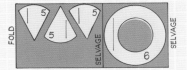

Deconstruct Sweater

1 Cut off the neck band and the ribbed lower band, if applicable.

2 Cut across the shoulder seam to the sleeve. Cut around each sleeve just inside the seam.

3 Cut along the side seams to the arm openings to create two panels of sweater fabric.

4 Cut along the underarm seam of each sleeve, or, if there is not an underarm seam, cut straight from the lower edge to the underarm curve. Cut off any ribbed wristbands.

5 Carefully press all the sweater sections flat.

"A right hat, a right dress, correctly worn, can really do wonders as a tonic. Try it. It truly is a good prescription."

—Mary Brooks Picken, c. 1920s

Assembly

NOTE: For an unlined beret, omit Steps 5 and 6.

1 Pin and cut out six F3/F5 Top pieces. Pin and cut out the F3 Crown and F3/F5 Band pieces. Using chalk, mark the large dot on the pattern piece on the wrong side of the beret Top pieces.

(If lining the beret, transfer the large dot to the wrong side of the Top lining pieces.)

2 Stay stitch the inner edge of the beret Crown ⅜" from the edge.

3 With right sides together, pin three Top pieces together. Beginning at the outer edge, stitch a ½" seam to the large dot.

Press open the seam allowances. Pin and stitch the remaining three Top pieces together in the same manner. With right sides together, pin the two sections together and stitch a ½" seam. Press open the seam allowance.

4 With right sides together, pin the outer edge of the crown to the beret top, aligning the raw edges. If necessary, trim the outer edge of the Top to be flush with the Crown. Stitch.

Trim the seam allowance. Turn the beret right side out. Press.

5 Repeat Steps 3 and 4 for the lining pieces if applicable.

6 If applicable, with wrong sides together, place the lining in the beret, aligning the seams and the raw edges. Pin and baste them together close to the lower edge.

7 With right sides together, pin the short ends of the beret band together. Stitch a ½" seam. Press open the seam allowance.

8 Find the center of one of the six Top pieces on the curved outer edge and mark. This will be the center back.

With right sides together, pin one long edge of the Band to the Crown with the seam aligned with this center back mark. Pin around the entire Crown. Stitch. Trim the seam allowance and press toward the Band.

9 Press ¼" of the long edge of the Band to the wrong side.

Fold the Band toward the wrong side so that the pressed fold just covers the connecting seam of the Band and the Crown. Hand-stitch the Band to the lining in an invisible stitch. If you're not using the lining, use an invisible stitch to connect the Band to the seam allowance.

MAKE YOUR OWN MAGIC

✂ Since the Faith hat takes so little yardage to complete, why not splurge on a high-end fabric for dramatic results?

A slouchy beret becomes a statement piece when it's made in a fun print! ↓

Tan and white ticking stripes add a touch of interest while still maintaining a neutral wardrobe position. ↓

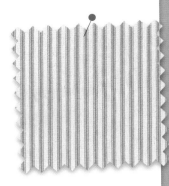

Soft velvet is elegant and snug for winter. ↓

6 Suggested Fabrics *for the* Faith Beret

Plaid is a classic for fall. ↓

A hot pink wool hat is a welcome pop of color in a sea of dark winter outerwear—and cozy, too! ↘

A hat gets a less-slouch, more-structure makeover when made in corduroy fabric. ↓

KEEP THE SUN OFF!

The Frida

A touch of Mediterranean flair, or a weekend in the park . . . pristine white sand beaches, or a soft blanket parked in the shade. Wherever you are, whatever the summer activity, a girl needs something to keep the sun off her face! Meet the Frida sunhat—a graceful solution for keeping out the rays on the most sun-soaked days. The two versions shown here (one in a subdued ticking stripe, page 279, the other in a lush floral print) showcase this pattern's versatility—choose a subtle fabric that will go with any outfit, or opt for something bold that will *make* the outfit—but whatever pattern (or solid color) you use, this summery piece will keep you extra cool with both function and style.

FABRIC AND NOTIONS

- 1⅛ yards 45" fabric; or ⅔ yard 60" fabric
- ¼ yard lining fabric, any width
- 1½ yards fusible interfacing
- Thread to match fabric, thread to match lining

TOOLS

- Straight pins
- Scissors
- Tailor's chalk or fabric-marking pencil
- Clear ruler or seam gauge
- Hand-stitching needle

MACHINE(S)

- Standard sewing machine with needle appropriate to fabric choice

APPROXIMATE MEASUREMENT OF FINISHED GARMENT

Diameter of brim is about 17"; one size fits most

PATTERN PIECES USED

- F1/F4/F6 Crown/Base (traced and cut on the F4 cutting lines)—1
- F4 Brim—2

CUTTING DIAGRAMS

For 45" fabric:

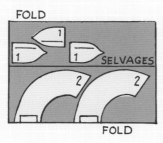

For 60" fabric:

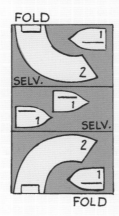

For the lining; any width fabric:

Assembly

1 Pin and cut out the F1/F4/F6 Crown/Base and F4 Brim pieces. Cut out the F1/F4 Crown pieces from the lining fabric.

2 Apply the fusible interfacing to the wrong side of all six Crown pieces. Using chalk, transfer the large dot from the pattern piece to the interfacing.

3 With right sides together, pin and stitch three Crown pieces together beginning at the outer edge and ending at the large dot.

Press open the seam allowances. Repeat for the remaining three Crown pieces.

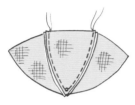

With right sides together, pin the two stitched sections together and stitch a ½" seam. Press open the seam allowance.

4 Apply the interfacing to the wrong side of the outer Brim only if you would like a softer look. Apply the interfacing to the wrong side of the Brim and Brim lining if you would like a more substantial Brim. With right sides together, pin the ends of the Brim together, aligning the raw edges and the notches. Stitch.

Press open the seam allowance. Repeat for the Brim lining.

5 With right sides together, pin the brim to the brim lining on the outer edge, aligning the seams. Stitch a ¼" seam.

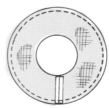

Turn the Brim right side out. Press. Pin the inner edges together, aligning the seams, and baste. If desired, topstitch ¼" from the outer curved edge.

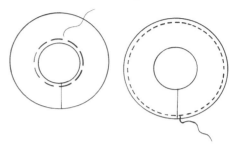

6 Find the center of one Crown piece on the lower edge and mark. This will be the center back.

With right sides together, pin the Brim to the Crown with the seam at the center back mark. Clip the Brim if necessary. Stitch a ½" seam.

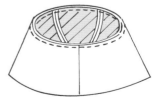

Trim the seam allowance and press toward the Crown.

7 Transfer the large dot from the pattern piece to the wrong side of the six crown lining pieces. Follow Step 3's instructions for the lining.

8 Press under the lower edge of the completed Crown lining ½".

Aligning the seams, place the lining in the Crown of the hat with wrong sides together. The pressed-under edge of the lining should just cover the seam. Hand-stitch the lining to the hat with an invisible stitch.

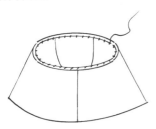

"For surety, make a definite rule to assemble your attire and decide on every detail before you start to dress."

—Mary Brooks Picken, 1924

MAKE YOUR OWN MAGIC

✂ Trace the Brim pattern piece onto another piece of paper. Extend the outer edge an inch or two to make a dramatically draping hat or draw in a bit for a smaller brimmed hat. Cut out your new pattern and proceed with the directions as written.

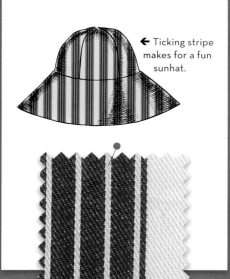

← Ticking stripe makes for a fun sunhat.

The weight of home decor fabric works well for hats with structure. ➔

Linen classes up any look—even an accessory. ⬇

6 Suggested Fabrics *for the* Frida Hat

⬆ A pink print cotton is light and stylish for summer.

Bright colors and energetic prints make a lively summer hat. ➔

⬆ Use a dark fabric for maximum sun protection.

The Farrah

The Farrah tote was designed for the practical planner—the girl who likes to be ready for anything wherever she goes—a book in case she gets a spare moment to read, a water bottle to stay hydrated. . . . You name it, she's got it tucked away somewhere. The Farrah tote features over-the-shoulder straps and a drawstring to keep everything contained. There are four outside pockets and two interior pockets to keep everything sorted and accessible (because no one wants to be that girl rooting around in her bag for keys or a loudly ringing phone—not that you'd ever forget to put it on "vibrate"). Because of all these qualities, the Farrah is easily cast as a book bag, a grocery tote, or an everyday carryall. Choose a cotton quilting fabric for something lightweight and colorful or a sturdy canvas if you're expecting a heavy haul.

FABRIC AND NOTIONS

- Fabric 1: 1¾ yards 45" fabric; or 1⅝ yards 60" fabric
- Fabric 2: 1¼ yards any width fabric
- 1½ yards interfacing suitable to fabric
- Thread to match fabrics

TOOLS

- Straight pins
- Scissors

- Tailor's chalk or fabric-marking pencil
- Clear ruler
- Hand-stitching needle
- Large safety pin
- Pencil
- 1 sheet tracing paper

MACHINE(S)

- Standard sewing machine with needle appropriate to fabric choice

APPROXIMATE DIMENSIONS OF FINISHED BAG

16½" wide x 15¼" high x 6" deep

PATTERN PIECES USED

NOTE: Cut 8 pieces of fabric for the straps (piece F3/F5 Band). Do not cut on the fold. For instructional purposes, designate 4 of the pieces as the outer strap and 4 as the strap lining. Cut 2 on the fold for the main drawstrings. See instructions in Step 23 before cutting!

- F3/F5 Top (traced and cut on the F5 cutting line)—5
- F5 Front and Back—12
- F5 Outer Pocket—10
- F5 Outer Pocket Band—18
- Pocket Accent—11
- F5 Base—17
- F5 Casing—13
- F5 Interior Pocket 1—15
- F5 Interior Pocket 2—16
- Drawstring Accent—14
- F3/F5 Band—7

CUTTING DIAGRAMS

For Fabric 1, 45" fabric:

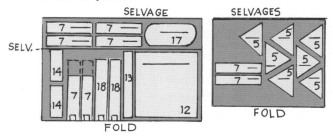

For Fabric 1, 60" fabric:

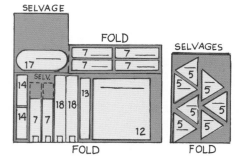

For Fabric 2, 45" or 60" fabric:

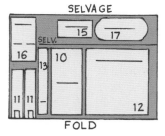

"Carry your purse as though it contains something of value, you are proud of it, and it has a decorative as well as a utilitarian function."

—Mary Brooks Picken, c. 1920s

Assembly

1 Pin and cut the F3/F5 Top pieces, F5 Front and Back, F5 Base, F5 Casing, F3/F5 Band pieces, Drawstring Accent, and F5 Outer Pocket Band from fabric 1. Pin and cut F5 Front and Back, F5 Base, F5 Casing, F5 Interior Pocket 1, F5 Interior Pocket 2, F5 Outer Pocket, and Pocket Accent from fabric 2. Using chalk, transfer alignment markings such as the large dots on the F5 Base and the F3 Top pieces to the wrong side of the cut fabric.

2 Line up seven F3/F5 Top pieces with the middle triangle point up. With right sides together, begin at one end and pin and stitch the triangles together in ¼" seams to form the front outer pocket. Press open the seam allowances as you

go. Set aside. Repeat for the remaining 7 Top pieces to form the Back Outer Pocket.

3 With wrong sides together, fold the Pocket Accent in half lengthwise, aligning the long edges. Press.

Center and place the raw edges of the folded Pocket Accent strip on the long upper edge of the Front Outer Pocket. Pin. Baste ¼" from the edge.

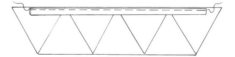

Repeat on the Back Outer Pocket.

4 With right sides together, center the Outer Pocket Band on the Front Outer Pocket and pin the long edges together over the Pocket Accent strip. Stitch a ½" seam.

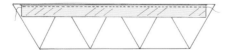

Press the seam allowance upward toward the Band. Repeat on the Back Outer Pocket.

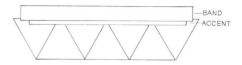

5 Center the F5 Outer Pocket pattern piece over the stitched fabrics, aligning the long edges. Pin the sides and trim off the ends of the fabric flush with the pattern piece. Repeat for the remaining pocket.

6 Apply the interfacing to the wrong side of the Front and Back Outer Pockets. With right sides together, pin the Front Outer Pocket to the Back Outer Pocket on the notched side edges. Stitch a ½" seam down both notched sides. Press open the seam allowances.

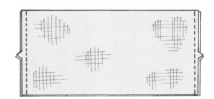

7 With right sides together, pin the Outer Pocket lining pieces together on the notched side edges. Stitch a ½" seam down both notched sides.

Press open the seam allowances.

8 With right sides together, pin the upper edge of the Outer Pocket to the upper edge of the Outer Pocket lining, aligning the side seams. Stitch a ½" seam.

Trim the seam allowance. Turn the lining to the inside. Press. Pin and baste the lower raw edges of the pocket and the lining together. Set aside.

"Choose accessories discriminately and wear or carry them smartly."

—Mary Brooks Picken, c. 1920s

9 Apply the interfacing to the wrong side of the four outer strap (F3/F5 Band) pieces. With right sides together, pin two outer strap pieces together on the short end. Stitch a ¼" seam.

Press open the seam allowance. With right sides together, pin the short ends of two strap lining pieces together and stitch a ¼" seam. Press open the seam allowance. With right sides together, pin the strap to the lining, aligning the seams and the raw edges. Stitch a ½" seam, pivoting at the corners and leaving an opening on one long edge to turn.

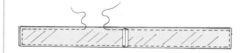

Trim the seam allowance and clip the corners. Turn the strap right side out. Press. Slipstitch the opening to close it, then topstitch ¼" from the finished edges, pivoting at the corners.

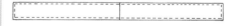

Repeat with the remaining straps and lining. Set aside.

10 Apply the interfacing to the wrong side of the bag front and bag back (the F5 Front and Back pieces). With right sides together, pin the F5 Front to the F5 Back on the notched side edges. Stitch, leaving the space between the dots open. Press open the seam allowances. Mark the center of the lower edge of the Front and Back. Turn right side out.

MARK CENTER

11 Slide the Outer Pocket over the lower bag with the lining side of the pocket on the right side of the bag. Align the side seams and the lower, raw edges. Pin them together on the lower edge and baste.

12 Stitch the pocket to the bag, starting at the lower edge, through the center of four triangles (two on the front, two on the back) to the top of the pocket as shown in the illustration. Backstitch at the upper edge to secure it. This forms four smaller pockets on the bag.

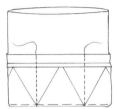

13 With right sides together, pin the notched ends of the F5 Casing together. Stitch a ½" seam down the notched sides.

Press open the seam allowances. With right sides together, and aligning the side seams, pin the Casing to the top of the bag and stitch a ¼" seam.

Press the seam allowance toward the Casing.

14 Apply the interfacing to the wrong side of the bag base (F5 Base). With right sides together, pin the Base to the bag, aligning the side seams of the bag with the large dots on the Base and the center of the Front and the Back with the lines on the Base. Stitch a ½" seam.

Press but do not trim the seam allowance. Make a few clips in the seam allowance on the curves if necessary.

15 To make Interior Pocket 1, fold the upper edge to the right side along the fold line to form the facing. Pin the sides of the facing. Stitch ½" from the sides and lower edge, pivoting at the corners.

Turn the facing to the inside, gently pushing out the corners. Press the pocket under along the stitching below the

facing. Topstitch across the pocket 1¾" below the upper edge.

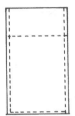

Pin the pocket to the right side of the front lining piece 4" below the upper edge. Stitch close to the outer edge, pivoting at the corners and backstitching at the upper edges to secure it.

16 To make Interior Pocket 2, fold the upper edge to the right side along the fold line to form the facing. Pin the sides of the facing. Stitch ½" from the sides and lower edge, pivoting at the corners.

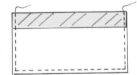

Turn the facing to the inside, gently pushing out the corners. Press the pocket under along the stitching below the facing. Topstitch across the pocket 1¼" below the upper edge. Center and pin the pocket to the right side of the back lining piece 4" below the upper edge.

Stitch close to the outer edge, pivoting at the corners and backstitching at the upper edges to secure it. Stitch from the top to the bottom through the vertical stitching guide indicated on the pattern piece to divide the pocket if desired.

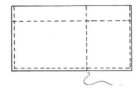

17 Mark the center lower edge of the Front and Back lining. With right sides together, pin the notched side edges of the lining Front and Back. Stitch.

Press open the seam allowances.

18 With right sides together, pin the notched ends of the Casing lining together. Stitch a ½" seam. Press open the seam allowances. With right sides together, and aligning the side seams, pin the Casing lining to the top of the bag lining and stitch a ¼" seam. Press the seam allowance toward the casing.

19 Apply the interfacing to the wrong side of the bag lining base. With right sides together, pin the Base lining to the Front and Back bag lining, aligning the side seams of the bag with the large dots on the Base and the center of the Front and the Back with the small dots on the base. Stitch a ½" seam. Press but do not trim the seam allowance.

Make a few clips in the seam allowance on the curves if necessary.

20 With right sides together, pin the bag to the bag lining along the upper edge of the Casing, aligning the side seams. Stitch a ½" seam, leaving an approximately 8" opening to turn on one side. Trim the seam allowance. Turn the bag right side out through the opening. Slipstitch the opening to close it. Push the lining firmly inside the bag and press.

21 Fold the top of the bag to the inside along the casing seam line. Pin. Stitch close to the edge.

22 To apply the straps, with the bag right side out, measure in 3" from the side seams on the front and back and mark with a pin along the casing stitching. With a strap right side out, place one short end ¾" beneath the casing stitching and the outer edge, even with the mark as shown. Pin and stitch a rectangle in the end of the strap beneath the casing stitching. Repeat on the opposite side and on the other side of the bag.

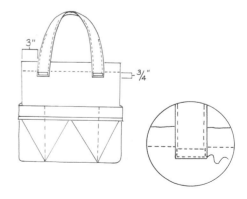

23 To make the drawstrings, use the F3/F5 Band pattern piece. With fabric 1 folded right sides together, place the F3 Band pattern pieces on the fold and pin. Use a ruler to draw out an additional 3" on the opposite end with chalk or a light pencil. Cut two main drawstrings in this manner using the drawn line as shown.

24 With right sides together, pin a Drawstring Accent piece to both ends of the main drawstrings, aligning the short edges. Stitch a ¼" seam.

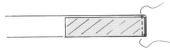

Press open the seam allowances. With right sides together, fold the stitched length of the drawstring in half aligning the long edges. Pin. Stitch a ¼" seam on the long edge, leaving an opening to turn near the center.

With the drawstring still wrong side out, turn so that the seam runs down the center. Press open the seam allowance. Stitch a ¼" seam across the short ends. Turn the drawstring right side out. Press. Slipstitch the opening to close. Topstitch ⅛" from the finished edges.

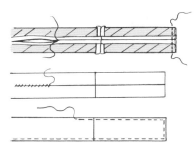

Repeat to create the second drawstring.

25 Attach a safety pin to one end of a drawstring and, with the seamed side against the bag, insert it into one side seam opening of the casing. Pull it through until you reach the original opening again. Pull out the drawstring until the short ends are aligned and the bag is not cinched. On the opposite side of the casing, insert the second drawstring with a safety pin attached and the seamed side against bag. Pull it through until you reach the entry point again. Pull it out until the short ends are aligned and the bag is not cinched.

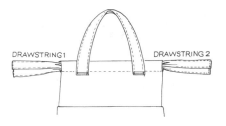

DRAWSTRING 1   DRAWSTRING 2

Tie a knot to connect the drawstring ends, leaving an approximately 1" to 1½" tail.

Pull the knots straight out from bag simultaneously to cinch the bag closed. Place your hands in the upper bag and push outward to open.

MAKE YOUR OWN MAGIC

✂ Alternate fabrics on the triangles comprising the large outer pocket to accentuate the pieced construction detail.

✂ Construct Farrah from a solid fabric and use a high-contrast thread to topstitch along the triangular pieces comprising the outer pockets.

✂ Use the Farrah as a soft portable sewing bag. Place scissors (point down, of course!) into the outer pockets along with rulers, seam gauges, etc. Use the inner pockets for needles, thread, buttons or any other small notion. There's plenty of room for small project essentials in the roomy interior of the bag!

← Black and white stripes are a classic, versatile pattern.

Velvet prints can be hard to find, but are worth it for their rich color. →

Cotton is easy to work with and is a good first fabric to try with a challenging pattern. →

6 Suggested Fabrics *for the* Farrah Totebag

← A border print adds more detail to the bag.

A laminate bag has the added benefit of being easy to clean. →

Thick fabric like corduroy makes for a sturdy bag. →

DON'T LEAVE HOME WITHOUT IT!

The Francesca

The F family of patterns transitions (ahem) *seam*lessly from hat to handbag. The bag is created with four fabrics (here, in velvet and three shades of silk dupioni), all accented with a contrasting binding. For an unencumbered night out, this bag is the ideal accessory: The extra-long, narrow strap allows for hands-free, cross-body wearing.

FABRIC AND NOTIONS

- Fabric 1: ¼ yard fabric, any width, for bottom of outer bag
- Fabric 2: ½ yard lining fabric, any width
- Fabric 3: ⅓ yard fabric, any width, for body of outer bag
- Fabric 4: ⅔ yard fabric, any width, for binding around upper edge of bag, drawstrings, and strap
- 1 yard interfacing suitable to fabric (**NOTE:** For sample shown, sew-in interfacing was used for velvet on the lower bag and fusible interfacing was used on the silk dupioni of the upper bag.)
- ¼ yard sew-in interfacing for straps (**NOTE:** If using sew-in interfacing for the bag, you will probably have enough left over for this application.)
- Thread to match fabrics

TOOLS

- Straight pins
- Scissors
- Tailor's chalk or disappearing fabric-marking pen or pencil
- Clear ruler
- Hand-stitching needle
- Medium safety pin

MACHINE(S)

- Standard sewing machine with needle appropriate to fabric choice

APPROXIMATE DIMENSIONS OF FINISHED BAG

22½" circumference at widest point; 14½" tall from bottom point of bag to upper edge when straightened

PATTERN PIECES USED

- F1/F4/F6 Crown/Base (traced and cut on the F1 cutting line)—1
- F6 Body—9

CUTTING DIAGRAMS

For Fabric 1; any width fabric:

For Fabric 2; any width fabric:

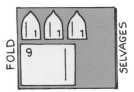

For Fabric 3; any width fabric:

For Fabric 4; any width fabric:

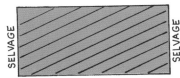

"Bags are of every shape, size, and color, of metal, beads, silk, lace, cloth, and leather. But do not depend entirely on an elaborate bag. Have at least two others for service."

—Mary Brooks Picken, c. 1920s

Assembly

1 From fabric 1, pin and cut six F1/F4/F6 Crown/Base pieces on the F1 cutting line. From fabric 2, pin and cut six F1/F4 Crown pieces, also on the F1 cutting line, and two F6 Body pieces. From fabric 3, pin and cut two F6 Body pieces. From fabric 4, cut a 24" × 1½" strip on the bias for the binding. Cut a 48" × 2" strip on the bias for the strap (this may be pieced together to form this length; see Chapter 1, page 27, for instructions). Cut two 26" × 1½" strips on the bias for the drawstrings (these may be pieced if necessary to form this length).

2 To make the bottom of the bag, apply the interfacing to the wrong side of all six Crown pieces cut from fabric 1. Using chalk, transfer the large dot from the pattern piece to the interfacing on each piece.

With right sides together, pin three Crown pieces together, aligning the raw edges. Beginning at the outer edge and ending at the large dot, stitch a ½" seam.

Press open seam allowances. Stitch the remaining three Crown pieces cut from fabric 1 together in the same manner.

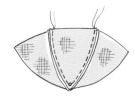

With right sides together, stitch the two completed sections together in a ½" seam. Press open the seam allowances.

3 Find the center of the lower edge of the Body pieces (both outer and lining) and mark with a single notch. See illustration below. Apply the interfacing to the wrong side of the two Body pieces cut from fabric 3. Using chalk, transfer the dots from the pattern to the wrong side of the fabric pieces. With right sides together, pin and stitch the double-notched edges of these two Body pieces in a ½" seam, leaving the space between the dots open. Press open the seam allowances.

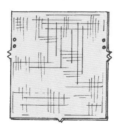

4 Find the center of one of the six bottom pieces on the upper edge and mark. Mark the center of the piece that is opposite also. With right sides together, align these marks with the single notches

on the Body and pin them together around the perimeter of the bag.

Stitch a ½" seam.

Press the seam allowance upward toward the Body.

5 Repeat Step 2 for the six Crown pieces cut from fabric 2, which will form the lining of the bag bottom.

6 Using chalk or a disappearing fabric ink pen, transfer the casing stitching lines to the right side of the two Body pieces cut from fabric 2.

With right sides together, pin and stitch the double-notched edges of the Body pieces cut from fabric 2 in a ½" seam, leaving open the space between the casing lines. Press open the seam allowances.

7 Repeat Step 4 for the lining.

8 With wrong sides together, place the completed lining into the completed bag, aligning the seams and the center fronts. Pin the bag to the lining around the upper edge and baste ⅛" from the edge.

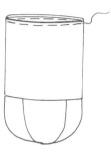

9 With wrong sides together, lightly press the binding strip in half lengthwise. Fold the outer edges in to meet the center crease and press it in half again.

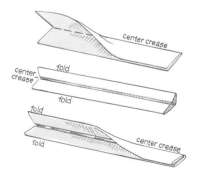

Open out one long edge of the binding. Press under one short end ½". With right sides together, place this pressed-under short end at the center back of the bag and pin.

Continue pinning the binding around the bag until you come to the origination point and overlap ½". Cut off any remaining binding. Stitch a ⅜" seam around the top of bag.

Fold the binding to the wrong side and press. Hand-stitch the lower folded edge of the binding to the bag on the wrong side using an invisible stitch.

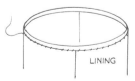

10 With the bag wrong side out, straighten the bag and the lining, aligning the seams as much as possible. Pin the bag and the lining together around the casing. Using thread to match the outer bag and beginning at one side seam, stitch along the upper casing line. Stitch around the lower casing line. Turn the bag right side out.

11 To form the drawstrings, press the bias piece in half lengthwise with wrong sides together. Fold the long edges in to meet the center crease and press again. Pin. Stitch close to the folds. Repeat for the second drawstring.

12 From the right side, pull a drawstring through the casing opening on one side of the bag using an attached safety pin. When you reach the same opening, pull the drawstring out and align the cut ends. The casing is open on the inside just to help you guide the drawstrings. These will be stitched closed at the end.

13 With a safety pin attached, pull the remaining drawstring through the opposite side seam opening, keeping the second drawstring on top of the first drawstring. When you reach the opening again, pull the drawstring out and align the cut ends.

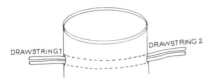

14 On each side, tie the ends of the drawstring together in a knot leaving an approximately 1" tail.

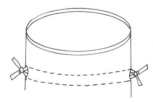

Slipstitch the side seam openings in the lining to close.

15 If necessary, stitch the bias sections together to attain the 48" length for the strap. With right sides together, pin on the diagonal and stitch a ¼"

seam. Press open the seam allowances. See Chapter 1, page 27 for additional instructions on making bias tape.

16 When required length is attained, with wrong sides together, lightly press the bias strap piece in half lengthwise. Fold the outer edges in to meet the center crease and press it in half again. Cut a narrow strip of sew-in interfacing the length of the strap. Slide it into the crease. You can use more than one piece if necessary to cover the entire length. Fold the strap over the interfacing and pin. Stitch close to the outer folds. Cut the short ends straight across and press under ½".

17 Place the pressed-under short end on the inside of the bag just below the casing, centered over the side seam. Pin and hand-stitch to secure it.

Without twisting the strap, stitch the opposite end of the strap to the opposite side of the bag in the same manner.

18 Pull the knots straight out from the bag simultaneously to cinch the bag closed. Place your hands in the upper bag and push outward to open.

19 Leave the top of the bag up or fold over the casing to reveal the contrasting lining.

MAKE YOUR OWN MAGIC

✂ Construct from cotton canvas, cotton duck, or colored denim yardage and add self fabric loops to the inside on the side seams. Attach purchased purse hardware to the loops and a narrow leather strap for a daytime look.

← A purple wool lends regal structure to a bag.

Dress up for evening with green raw silk. →

Use a batik print for a bohemian vibe. →

6 Suggested Fabrics *for the* Francesca Handbag

← Use neutral colors and a classic print to make a bag that you can wear daily.

Black and white polka dots are timeless. →

If you aren't confident wearing a statement fabric, here's your chance to incorporate it into a small accessory! →

"Then, when all is done, put on a smile that expresses the finest that is in you. . . . And if, to this smile, you add all the kindliness that you can command, all the happiness that you can summon, your friends and your very own folks will declare you charming."

—Mary Brooks Picken, 1924

APPENDIX

Resources

Most of the stores and companies listed here can be found nationwide as independent or chain fabric stores or online. Be sure to check your local stores first; they can be a treasure trove of both materials and expertise.

FABRIC

The key to a beautifully made garment is quality fabric. The following fabric stores have been providing their customers with fine fashion and home decor fabrics for years. If you are lucky enough to visit their stores, you can take advantage of their classes and expertise. If you are an online shopper, no worries, they will virtually help you find that perfect fabric. Of course there are many more wonderful fabric stores out there. Do a little digging in your backyard to see what is near you!

B & J Fabrics: A family-run fabric store that specializes in ladies' fashion textiles. *bandjfabrics.com*

Britex Fabrics: For over sixty years Britex has been a San Francisco landmark carrying a large selection of fine fashion fabrics. *britexfabrics.com*

Fabric Depot: Opened in 1992, this independently owned store is one of the largest fabric stores in America and offers a vast array of fabrics, notions, trims, and patterns. *fabricdepot.com*

Haberman Fabrics: Opened in 1958, Haberman Fabrics has been providing fine apparel and home decor fabrics to sewing professionals and hobbyists alike. *habermanfabrics.com*

Hancock Fabrics: A small chain of stores that offers quilting, garment, and home decor fabrics, notions, and classes. *hancockfabrics.com*

Jo Ann Fabrics: A fabric store chain that offers quilting, fashion, and home decor fabrics, notions, and classes. Sign up for the app to keep abreast of sales and coupons. Also carries a huge supply of craft materials. *joann.com*

M & J Trimming: Provides a huge selection of buttons, ribbons, trims, notions, and embellishments. *mjtrim.com*

Mood: The store made famous by *Project Runway* offers a vast array of fabric and trims. *moodfabrics.com*

Pacific Fabrics: A family-owned store with roots that date back to 1917, Pacific Fabrics offers a large selection of fabric for apparel, craft, and home decor, as well as other craft notions and trim. *pacificfabrics.com*

Purl SoHo: Offers a large selection of high-end quilting cottons and apparel fabrics, as well as yarns, notions, and patterns. *purlsoho.com*

Sewing Workshop: Pattern designer, writer, and teacher Linda Lee specializes in apparel fabrics and has a great selection of knits. *sewingworkshop.com*

NOTIONS

The term notions is a large umbrella that covers everything from thread, pins, and zippers to more focused tools like bias tape makers, quilting rulers, and mini irons. Every sewist's collection of necessary items will vary so talk to a few other sewists to see what notions they use.

You should be able to find most sewing notions and tools at the fabric stores listed previously (just head to the notions department), but with the variety of brands available on the shelf, it can be hard to know which to drop in your shopping cart. I've worked with many different notions in my time, and here are a few companies who always put out a great and helpful product.

Sewing Tools

You will definitely need a pincushion, ruler, and seam ripper. But maybe you also need a pom-pom maker. Immerse yourself in cool sewing tools and don't be afraid to try something new!

Clover: Offers fun sewing tools such as pom-pom and yo-yo makers. Also check out their bias tape makers and bamboo notions. *clover-usa.com*

Prym-Dritz: This company produces a vast array of sewing notions designed to make your hobby easier. Find them at most local stores and nationwide chains. *dritz.com*

Buttons

I love buttons. I collect buttons. I think they can make or break a garment, and since there are so many amazing designs out there, you can try many different sizes and styles. Both of the following brands should be readily available at your local store. Browse their selection online to see what all they offer!

Dill Buttons: *dill-buttons.com*

JHB: *buttons.com*

Scissors

The first rule I learned from my mom, who was a seamstress: Never ever, under any condition, use fabric scissors on anything else. Never. They will dull immediately and give you a rough cut on your lovely fabric. Just remember, Mom is always right.

Fiskars: Scissors to cut everything from the sheerest fabrics to the thickest leather. *fiskars.com*

Gingher: Rotary cutters and scissors for the fashion sewist. *gingher.com*

Needles

Needles can be a tricky business. While there are all-purpose needles out there, if you are working with garment fabrics, it is important to do a little research to see what needle coordinates with your fabric. Also, another tip: Change your needle after every project! The tips will get dull and can make a mess of your machine.

It's better for everyone to just change them regularly.

Schmetz: Sewing machine needles for myriad machines and fabrics. Be sure to check out the app to see what needle works with what fabric. *schmetzneedles.com*

Thread

It seems like anyone who has sewn for a long time has a tried-and-true thread brand they love. You won't find your perfect thread right away; it's important that you try different brands and see what works best for you and your machine. Also, make sure you are using the proper thread for your project fabric!

Coats & Clark: *coatsandclark.com*

Gutermann: *gutermann.com*

Madeira: *madeirausa.com*

Sulky: *sulky.com*

General Notions

Although your local independent and chain stores should have a vast array of notions for you to choose from, you can find even more at these online stores.

Annie's Catalog (formerly Clotilde): An extensive online and mail-order resource for tools and notions to help complete your projects. *anniescatalog.com*

Nancy's Notions: A huge online and mail-order catalog selection of tools, kits, patterns, fabric, and more. *nancysnotions.com*

SEWING MACHINES

A sewing machine is a very personal attachment. When you find "the one," you find yourself naming it, taking care of it, and maybe even defending its honor at your sewing circle. The following brands are offered through independent retailers across the country. It might take a little dating before you find "the one." Find your local dealers and go practice on their floor samples. All the following brands offer machines for a range of sewists from beginner to advanced. Also, look for embroidery and quilting machines as well as sergers.

Baby Lock: *babylock.com*

Bernina: *berninausa.com*

Brother: *brother-usa.com*

Husqvarna/Viking: *husqvarnaviking.com*

Janome: *janome.com*

Pfaff: *pfaffusa.com*

Singer: *singerco.com*

FABRIC DESIGN COMPANIES

As I've said before, the main ingredient in making a spectacular one-of-a-kind garment is fabric. Here are some of my favorite independent fabric design companies—worth checking out for a wide variety of choices.

Alexander Henry: The whimsical, fun, and sometimes outrageous designs from Alexander Henry are helmed by the De Leon Design Group. This family of artists paints each design by hand, which brings a unique, artistic flavor to their wonderful prints. Fabric types include cotton, cotton lawn, home decor weight, flannel, and laminate. *ahfabrics.com*

Dear Stella: Fun, fresh fabrics with a contemporary feel. You will be inspired by the ladylike prints and gorgeous colors all in cotton weight. *dearstelladesign.com*

Free Spirit Fabric: Free Spirit Fabric is ground zero for the modern fabric movement. You will find bright colors, abundant florals, masculine geometrics, and more. Designers such as Anna Maria Horner, Joel Dewberry, Denyse Schmidt, and Parson Grey are all under the Free Spirit umbrella and release their beautiful prints in fabrics such as cotton, linen, rayon, voile, velveteen, and laminate. *freespiritfabric.com*

James Thompson: The James Thompson fabric company has been a leader in the industry since 1860. The ability to innovate and adapt has kept the company producing high-quality fabrics for both the home sewist and for designers, such as its signature buckram, which has been a millinery staple since the company opened its doors. Today, aside from producing products such as canvas, flannel, twill, burlap, muslin, osnaburg, and ticking, James Thompson is also the producer of my denim line, Crossroads Denim by Amy Barickman, which is a 54" wide soft denim available in a variety of colors and perfect for garments and accessories. *jamesthompson.com*

Marcus Brothers: Marcus Fabrics, founded in 1911, produces high-quality textiles for quilting and crafts. Aside from designing new, fun fabrics, the company is also well known for creating reproduction fabrics for quilters, keeping fabric design history alive in the modern age. You will find not only cotton from Marcus but also soft flannels. *marcusfabrics.com*

Michael Miller Fabrics: This family business was started in 1999 in a Manhattan apartment. The company grew to be renowned for its original, fun prints and capricious designs. The company also offers a wide variety of substrates, including cotton, sateen, corduroy, flannel, eyelet, fleece, knits, laminate, poly satin, and organics. *michaelmillerfabrics.com*

Moda/United Notions: Moda is a company with a seemingly endless array of gorgeous fabrics—prints and colors for every style and substrates for every project. You can find cotton, linen, laminate, leather, canvas, and wool from Moda. *unitednotions.com*

Red Rooster Fabrics: Red Rooster offers a range of both traditional and contemporary designs, beautiful textures, reproductions, and seasonal and novelty prints, all in 100% cotton. I have been designing for Red Rooster for many years now and just recently released my fifteenth fabric collection, SoHo Bandana. *redroosterfabrics.com*

Riley Blake: Founded in 2008, Riley Blake quickly became established as a fashion-forward company that provides sewists with sophisticated prints that reflect a vintage sensibility and a modern attitude. Their versatile fabrics include cotton, organics, flannel, knit, and laminate. *rileyblakedesigns.com*

Robert Kaufman: Robert Kaufman Fabrics was formed in 1942. Originally focused on producing fabrics for garment manufacturers, they launched their cotton brand in the 1980s. Today they are the home of two design houses, which explains their vast array of prints and fabrics that include microfiber, denim, chambray, jersey, rayon, twill, flannel, tencel, seersucker, knits, linen, canvas, voile, and organics. *robertkaufman.com*

Timeless Treasures: Timeless Treasures is a family-owned business that likes to get a little crazy. Novelty cotton prints (think piggies on motorcycles) are indicative of the fun, eccentric Timeless Treasures style. *ttfabrics.com*

Westminster Fibers: Westminster Fibers is the home of renowned designers such as Kaffe Fassett and Amy Butler. Bright botanicals, cheery chintzes, and reproduction prints from the Arts & Crafts movement can be found here in cottons, rayons, voiles, and laminates. *westminsterfabrics.com*

Further Reading

MARY BROOKS PICKEN AND THE WOMAN'S INSTITUTE

If you would like to learn more about Mary Brooks Picken and her work with the Woman's Institute, take a look at my book *Vintage Notions: An Inspirational Guide to Needlework, Cooking, Sewing, Fashion & Fun*, which I wrote to honor Mary and her work. The book features inspirational essays and projects for each month of the year, seasonal recipes and decorating ideas, and Mary's original Magic Patterns.

Also, visit my blog, AmyBarickman .com/blog, where I regularly share information from my ongoing research into the world and works of Mary Brooks Picken.

PERIODICALS

Magazines are some of my favorite sources of inspiration. Call me old-fashioned, but I like nothing more than curling up with my new issue and a glass of wine. Here are a few of my favorites:

Mollie Makes: British sewing and craft magazine whose projects feature embroidery, upcycling, and more. *molliemakes.com*

Sew News: A bimonthly magazine with sewing ideas, inspirations, and techniques. *sewnews.com*

Stitch: A quarterly magazine all about creating with fabric and thread. Discover project tutorials for wearables, home decor, and gifts.

Threads: A bimonthly magazine full of sewing tips and tutorials for garment sewers. *threadsmagazine.com*

BLOGS AND WEBSITES

We all know the Internet is a font of information, ideas, and inspiration. Sometimes, though, it can be a little overwhelming trying to find the good sites from among the bad ones. Here I've listed a few of my favorite sewing websites and blogs for you as a starter list.

BurdaStyle: An online community to share projects, ideas, and patterns. *burdastyle.com*

Indygo Junction: My own pattern company, Indygo Junction, hosts a blog where we review patterns and fabric, host monthly technique tutorials, share sewing tips and tricks, and discuss what's new in the sewing world. *indygojunction.com/blog*

Kollabora: Patterns, ideas, and tutorials as well as a sharing forum. *kollabora.com*

Nancy Zieman: The host of PBS's *Sewing with Nancy* offers sewing tutorials, advice, and ideas. You can purchase her books and videos as well as watch episodes of the show. *nancyzieman.com/blog*

Sew4Home: Free daily home decor, accessory, and gift patterns. *Sew4Home.com*

Sew Mama Sew: Host to sewing challenges, and offers pattern reviews and tutorials. *sewmamasew.com*

Sewing Secrets: Offers ideas for quilting and sewing as well as tutorials and contests. *coatsandclarksewingsecrets.com*

We All Sew: Projects, inspiration, and education for crafters, embroiderers, and sewists. *weallsew.com*

ORGANIZATIONS AND GUILDS

These nationwide organizations are made up of members and local chapters. Local chapters often have monthly meetings where the community can discuss projects and inspiration and educate each other. Find a chapter near you, and see what your community has to offer!

American Sewing Guild: With more than 20,000 members, the ASG is dedicated to keeping the interest in and the tradition of home sewing alive. *asg.org*

The Fashion Group International: Mary Brooks Picken, who inspired this book, was one of the founders of The Fashion Group International in 1928. Today, FGI is still going strong and is committed to being the preeminent authority on the business of fashion and design, and to help its members in their careers. *fgi.org*

ONLINE CLASSES AND WORKSHOPS

Education is important, even for hobbyists! Local stores will offer a variety of classes and workshops, but sometimes those don't fit into our busy schedules. Here are a few sites that offer classes by great teachers that you can take any time.

Craftsy: Offers online classes for a multitude of interests including sewing, quilting, embroidering, crocheting, knitting, and more. *craftsy.com*

CreativeBug: Workshops, classes, and tutorials for sewing, knitting crafts, and even craft business courses. *creativebug.com*

Indygo Junction: Pattern reviews, free projects, and technique tutorials. *indygojunction.com/how-to*

Susan Kahlje: A well-known sewing teacher, she hosts workshops on couture sewing and trips to Paris for fabric shopping. *SusanKhalje.com*

The Sewing Workshop: San Francisco's sewing and arts school offers many different class options for garment and gift sewists, taught by many of the country's most renowned sewing experts. *thesewingworkshop.com*

Common Conversions

MEASUREMENTS

1/8 inch	3-4 mm
1/4 inch	5-6 mm
3/8 inch	10 mm
1/2 inch	12 mm
5/8 inch	1.5 cm
3/4 inch	2 cm
1 inch	2.5 cm
4 1/2 inches	11.5 cm
9 inches	23 cm
12 inches	30 cm
13 1/2 inches	34.3 cm
18 inches	45 cm
22 1/2 inches	57.1 cm
24 inches	61 cm
27 inches	68.5 cm
31 1/2 inches	80 cm
36 inches	90 cm
39 inches	100 cm

FABRIC YARDAGE

1/8 yard	4 1/2 inches	11.5 cm
1/4 yard	9 inches	23 cm
1/3 yard	12 inches	23 cm
3/8 yard	13 1/2 inches	34.3 cm
1/2 yard	18 inches	45 cm
5/8 yard	22 1/2 inches	57.1 cm
2/3 yard	24 inches	61 cm
3/4 yard	27 inches	68.5 cm
7/8 yard	31 1/2 inches	80 cm
1 yard	36 inches	90 cm

FABRIC WIDTH

45 inches	115 cm
60 inches	150 cm

FRACTION TO DECIMAL

1/8	0.126
1/4	0.25
1/3	0.333
3/8	0.375
1/2	0.5
5/8	0.625
2/3	0.666
3/4	0.75
7/8	0.875

About the Author

AMY BARICKMAN is the founder/designer of pattern company Indygo Junction, author of the self-published *Vintage Notions*, and director of AmyBarickman.com. Amy founded Indygo Junction, a leader in the fashion sewing, needlework, and craft design industry, in 1990.

Her company has identified and marketed more than thirty designers and has sold more than 2 million patterns and books internationally over the last twenty years. In 2013, Amy launched her fifteenth cotton fabric collection with Red Rooster fabrics, and debuted her first fabric line for fashion and home, "Crossroads Denim."

She'd love to hear from you—contact her at info@indygojunction.com to let her know what sort of magic you're making, and follow her creative journey at Amy Barickman.com/blog.

Index